UNIX FOR MVS PROGRAMMERS

HARRY SINGH

PRENTICE HALL PTR
Upper Saddle River, New Jersey 07458

Library of Congress Cataloging-in-Publication Data

Singh, Harry
UNIX for MVS programmers / Harry Singh.
p. cm.
Includes bibliographical references and index.
ISBN 0-13-442989-3
1. UNIX (Computer file) 2. IBM MVS. I. Title.
QA76.76.063S5646 1996
005.4'3—dc20 96-19154
CIP

Production Editor: *Kerry Reardon*
Acquisitions Editor: *Michael Meehan*
Cover Designer: *The Works*
Cover Design Director: *Jerry Votta*
Manufacturing Manager: *Alexis R. Heydt*

Prentice-Hall, Inc.
A Simon & Schuster Company
Upper Saddle River, New Jersey 07458

The publisher offers discounts on this book when ordered in bulk quantities.
For more information contact:

Corporate Sales Department
Prentice Hall PTR
One Lake Street
Upper Saddle River, N.J. 07458
Phone: 800-382-3419
FAX: 201-236-7141
E-mail: corpsales@prenhall.com

Printed in the United States of America

10 9 8 7 6 5 4 3 2 1

ISBN 0-13-442989-3

Prentice-Hall International (UK) Limited, *London*
Prentice-Hall of Australia Pty. Limited, *Sydney*
Prentice-Hall Canada Inc., *Toronto*
Prentice-Hall Hispanoamericana, S.A., *Mexico*
Prentice-Hall of India Private Limited, *New Delhi*
Prentice-Hall of Japan, *Tokyo*
Simon & Schuster Asia Pte. Ltd., *Singapore*
Editora Prentice-Hall do Brasil, Ltda., *Rio de Janeiro*

Dedication

To my children Sarita, Sushila, Sanjay, and Samita, who provide the challenge
and
to my loving parents, who instilled the courage

Trademarks

Contents

Preface

INTRODUCTION

Information systems environments today consist of mainframes, workstations, and PCs, all using disparate operating systems. With the trend towards downsizing, UNIX has become a standard operating system of choice, taking advantage of new hardware technologies and architectures such as RISC and SMP. Consequently, the traditional systems programmer, especially in the prevalent MVS mainframe environment, is faced with a task of learning yet another operating system all over again. Therefore, this book is composed to facilitate the transition for such users from the MVS to the UNIX Operating System.

This book is also for a person who is faced with adopting processors that use UNIX and will likely need to learn a version of the UNIX operating system. This book is designed to mold the skills learned using the MVS system into the skills necessary for operating in the UNIX framework.

This book is to help the reader to become familiar with UNIX, its components, and usage. This is accomplished with special emphasis on the fact that the reader is knowledgeable in the MVS environment. Wherever applicable, the explanations are provided for equivalent commands and structures for both MVS and UNIX, pointing out subtle differences between the two operating systems. The explanations are further supplemented with practical examples.

THE PURPOSES SERVED

The UNIX operating system has become the standard operating system for computers in scientific, engineering, and research environments, but it isn't an easy system to master.

UNIX For MVS Programmers is a comprehensive guide to UNIX—a handbook you can use both as a manual to learn UNIX and as a ready reference for fast answers to specific UNIX questions. Clear, concise, and readable, UNIX For MVS Programmers is written for the technically oriented UNIX user who isn't already an expert. It describes "generic" UNIX—the core of programs and facilities common to nearly all UNIX systems—concentrating on System V while also discussing the major BSD UNIX variations, with familiar equivalent MVS command syntax.

UNIX for MVS Programmers covers most of UNIX in as much specific detail as the system manual. Organized functionally so that you can easily find the right tool for any task. UNIX for MVS Programmers also includes a complete summary for fast lookup by name of the commands. Abundant cross-references and a thorough index speed retrieval of information on any topic. An extensive discussion of underlying UNIX concepts, supplemented by a glossary, enables even a UNIX beginner to penetrate quickly the mysteries of UNIX terminology.

Topics Include:

- Starting and terminating a UNIX session.
- File manipulations and management.
- Standard editors—vi, ed.
- Text manipulations.
- Document preparation.
- Bourne Shell and Shell programming.
- Communicating with the world.
- Remote communications—TELNET, ftp, uucp, and others.

I've consciously aimed the book at readers who are comfortable with technical material, presenting the subject as concisely as possible rather than in the gentle steps of a tutorial book. What other authors cover in an entire volume, I cover in a section. I achieve this not by omitting details but by omitting long explanations supplemented with numerous examples that illustrate a single point. The tutorial approach may be less demanding.

THE UNIX OPERATING SYSTEM

Unlike other major operating systems, UNIX is not irrevocably tied to a particular computer architecture. Designed to be used interactively, UNIX is not bound by inherent memory constraints, handles multiple processes and users easily and naturally, and is well suited as a platform for networking and graphical environments. Commercially supported versions of UNIX are available for most commonly used computers.

But UNIX isn't easy to learn. In the early days when UNIX was still a research project, one person could understand all of it. No longer is that true. Today's UNIX user faces great obstacles to mastery: the variety of implementations; the rapid pace of change; the proliferation of related subsystems; the profusion of commands and their options; variables, and subcommands; the sheer volume of material to be assimilated; the historical accretions; and the assumption prevalent in UNIX documentation that the reader is already familiar with what is being described.

I include a chapter covering the common concepts of UNIX and a glossary. When you encounter a technical term that you haven't seen before, you can easily find out what it means. I provide abundant cross-references to help you through the thicket of dependencies among different UNIX commands and concepts. To get you oriented, I provide a discussion of how to use this book in Chapter 1.

You'll find topics covered in this book that don't make it into most UNIX books. Some examples are the archiving files with *tar*, using communications programs such as *ftp*, and the addressing conventions used for *UUCP* electronic mail. Although I hope this book is the first one you take off the shelf, I realize it may not be the last, so I provide a list of printed and electronic resources you can use for additional information or for another view of the same material.

I have attempted to explain UNIX clearly without neglecting difficult or complicated, but nevertheless essential, details. While some of these details may not seem important when you first see them, you're likely to find them indispensable as you read the manuals supplied with your system.

This text is intended as a self-administered course for a wide variety of computer professionals, who need to learn UNIX. It is well suited for the following audiences:

- MVS Programmers
- MVS users migrating to UNIX
- Systems Analysts and Programmers
- Network Systems Administrators
- Application Developers

ORGANIZATION OF THE BOOK

The book is organized in a modular fashion. If a reader has prior knowledge of certain subjects, the reader will not need to start from the beginning. Most of the book consists of command descriptions. These descriptions are not as detailed as those in your system's manual—but I present them in a way that you can understand. I've organized the book and its parts down to the level of the command descriptions, logically by function rather than alphabetically so that you can see how different commands and options relate to one another and find the right tools for a particular task. I have made it easy for you to look up commands and their options by including a summary of commands cross-referenced to the chapters where you'll find the full explanations. I also provide an index and a synopsis.

ACKNOWLEDGMENTS

This book began as an exercise to teach MVS–UNIX to field personnel who were faced with the prospect of migrating from MVS to UNIX-based operating systems. It soon grew into a project to cover more comprehensive treatment of the two operating systems and their environments.

I wish to thank our colleagues at Prentice-Hall who made this book possible: Michael E. Meehan, executive editor, who conceived the idea of the book and whose encouragement and helpful suggestions were invaluable; Dori Steinhauff, his editorial assistant, who patiently and unfailingly navigated this book past many obstacles; Brett Bartow, assistant editor, who handled the initial manuscript development; Sophie Papanikolaou, production supervisor and Kerry Reardon, whose energy, good taste, and deep knowledge of everything from the fine points of English grammar and usage to the intricacies of technical book reviews never ceased to impress me.

I thank our proofreader, for an exceptionally thorough job performed under stringent time constraints. And I especially thank our reviewers, whose comments and feedback made the book far better than it would have been otherwise.

Special thanks to Derrick Bast, who helped refine the original plan of the book. Derrick not only reviewed every section of the manuscript but he also tested all the commands described and made significant contributions to the accuracy of the text. Then there are my individual debts of gratitude to those who provided me with support and encouragement and were so patient and understanding.

Harry Singh

1

Introduction

Over the last few years, enterprises worldwide have shifted away from the "glass house" mainframe environments toward the realm of distributed computing and client/server applications. The rapidly growing performance and reliability of workstations as well as the development of system tools have made that possible. Downsizing or transporting mainframe systems totally or partially onto workstations and/or network environment has been available for some years now.

Companies worldwide are abandoning their mainframes and minicomputers in favor of open-systems desktops and servers. Enterprise computing today relies more on networked configurations of these platforms—networked not only locally, but globally as well. This transition from centralized mainframes to distributed systems is called rightsizing. For hardware rightsizing to be successful, software rightsizing is essential. Large, monolithic applications that traditionally resided on mainframes do not fit the distributed computing model. That has generated the requirement for learning operating systems that are most common to networking and the desktops, that is, UNIX.

GUIDE TO THE READER

This book is in response to the current trends in migration from a centralized glass house to open and distributed environments. Since the glass house has been dominated by application rich MVS operating system, there is a need for a simple mechanism to facilitate smooth migration from an IBM's Multiple Virtual Storage or MVS-based mainframe to a UNIX-based platform. Even with OpenEdition, MVS-based operating interface, knowledge of UNIX is essential.

This book is intended as a learning guide for those who are seasoned MVS users/programmers and are delving into the world of UNIX. This is also intended as a reference for those who have some knowledge of either or both the MVS and UNIX operating systems.

Although basic topics are emphasized, this book touches upon a series of introductory subjects and moves quickly through them. Presumably, you already know what an operating system is. This book is not a beginner's introduction to computers. This book will serve you better as a reference and a guide to facilitate transition from MVS-based systems to UNIX-based systems, including OpenEdition MVS (OS/390).

Throughout the book, you will find command by command comparisons, wherever possible, between UNIX and MVS functional equivalents. In addition, for quick reference, you will find a MVS-UNIX command summary chart at the end of most chapters and appendixes at the end of the book.

Two major forms of UNIX have been prevalent among most vendors. These are AT&T UNIX System V and the University of California at Berkeley's Berkeley Software Distribution (BSD). This book concentrates on the BSD version with some insertions from the AT&T's System V and provides an introduction to the most commonly used variants of the UNIX operating system.

I do not intend to teach you either the terminology or the commands of the MVS operating system. I assume no prior knowledge of UNIX; however, you must have a working knowledge of the MVS operating system. Under any pretense, this book is not designed to convince you whether MVS is more preferable than UNIX or vice versa. At the same time, it will become apparent to you that some functions performed, by UNIX or MVS, can be used more easily and/or efficiently than the other.

Even though you will find many similarities between the two operating systems, MVS and UNIX are two most diverse operating systems with differing design characteristics and function requirements. Therefore, there is hardly any one-to-one function correlation. We will learn how to perform a particular function in UNIX, with equivalents in MVS. Even though such descriptions are useful, I have attempted to portray some of the features that make UNIX an equally powerful medium, for those who need to develop complex applications. Since both UNIX and MVS are a conglomeration of many differing products, I have attempted to compare only the basic, most commonly used functions, such as

- Starting and stopping sessions.
- Basic operating functions.
- Files (filenames, organization, manipulation).
- The text editors (ed, vi, TSO XEDIT, ISPF).
- Printing text files.
- Command files.
- Sending and receiving mail.
- Special functions.

PREREQUISITES

As previously mentioned, this book is not a beginner's introduction to computers. It assumes that you know the fundamentals of an operating system—a supervisory program that runs on a computer at all times, taking your instructions to run other programs or to manipulate and print files and carry out these instructions while it coordinates among other users on the system.

You know what a file is, and you know that a processor which can store thousands of files needs a way to organize them. Therefore, one of the first steps in learning about an operating system is to grasp the file system and its idiosyncrasies. You also know the basic operations that we must perform with text editors and word processors: creating new files, creating text, deleting and adding text, and saving or aborting the edits made in a given session.

UNIX, in general, is a command line-driven operating system—the kind where you type commands and press "enter" or "return" to execute that command. Modern UNIX systems include mouse-driven graphical user interfaces to handle applications and files, similar to those found in DOS Windows and Macintosh environments. However, it is a more efficient way to accomplish things by typing out commands. Ideally, you should have some experience with a command line-driven operating system.

MIGRATION FROM MVS AND THE MAINFRAME

If one can ignore, for just a moment, the rigidity of a mainframe environment from the user's perspective, one would have to admit that it provides a very efficient model for data sharing and administration. These two ingredients are key in the successful implementation of a corporatewide migration solution. But, as the PC revolution has made abundantly clear, individual needs must also be met.

Unfortunately, a by-product of the PC culture was that it frustrated the growth of applications and information sharing as network support became problematic and as personal data storage became prevalent. Scheduling tools in particular were demoted from a corporate communication system to the role of a secondary personal desktop accessory. Without the ability to easily share information, the utility of scheduling tools was greatly diminished. As a result, while gaining many advantages in moving to a PC or workstation environment, users lost access to tools and capabilities they may not even have realized were available in the older mainframe world.

The growth of network-ready environments like UNIX and the proliferation of PC networks has reenabled effective group scheduling for the nonmainframe user. The trick is making the UNIX solution easy for everyone and minimizing resistance to adoption.

Mainframes

Reports of the death of mainframes are greatly exaggerated. Historically, mainframes have come to be extremely reliable processors to store huge amounts of data and process these data at very high speeds. It is true that plenty of former mainframe tasks can now be done better and cheaper on minicomputers or PCs, but many jobs remain that are more suited to mainframes. Since so many computers are connected together, the best possible system is one that distributes the applications and tasks so that each computer does what it is best suited for.

PCs (at the user level) seem to provide the best user interface, whereas the mainframe coordinates vast amounts of data that many users might be trying to use simultaneously. In addition, the mainframes provide unique strengths in reliability, data management, system management, and storage capacities. This has resulted in changing the role of the mainframes from "do it all" to act as servers.

UNIX in the IBM Environment

As the market for commercial applications of UNIX grows steadily each year, the major vendors are trying to establish themselves as leaders both in hardware and software, each with their particular variant of UNIX. IBM's presence in virtually every large enterprise guarantees it a slice of the action.

Integrating UNIX successfully into an organization where the mainframe has always dominated is a task that has proved beyond the means of most over the last few years. We need to present a carefully planned approach to exploit UNIX alongside the mainframe, building modern client/server systems where appropriate, yet avoiding the temptation to use open systems for applications that are best suited to the mainframe environment. For many users, the changing nature of business problems will mean that "traditional" mainframe applications will need to be moved to a distributed, UNIX-based platform.

MVS, long the epitome of the proprietary, established operating system standard, is being reshaped to support a distributed computing environment (DCE) and emerging open standards such as POSIX. Whether this move will make MVS accessible to UNIX users and therefore more attractive to proprietary paranoiacs, or simply serve to detract from the good name of MVS to the point of alienating diehard mainframe enthusiasts, remains to be seen.

The customer information control system (CICS) and the world of UNIX and open systems do not sit easily together. While UNIX enjoys a reputation of flexibility and price/performance, at the expense of integrity and security, CICS epitomizes the mainframe environment, seen by many as too expensive, out of date, and inflexible, but even the most ardent antimainframe hacker will envy its utter dependability in the commercial environment. The question that has been addressed recently, however, is: How do we integrate the two and enjoy the best of both worlds?

A simplistic summary of the opinions reveals that UNIX systems cost less than the mainframe, but in other respects are immature, lacking facilities (security, reliability, integrity, manageability) that mainframe users take for granted. Given that a large number of organizations have at least one UNIX application now, it seems that customers consider it worth putting up with the drawbacks of UNIX systems in exchange for the cost savings.

A significant number of sites are definitely moving off the mainframe regardless of IBM's "open" initiatives such as OpenEdition MVS (OS/390). However, a large majority are probably or definitely staying with the mainframe MVS. Some of those expect to adopt the new open features and a few more would have moved off the mainframe if the open features hadn't been available. On the other hand, a significant number of enterprises will keep the mainframe anyway and ignore the open features. In the aggregate, the definite migrators account for just a few percentage points. These sites also have markedly lower rates of growth in mainframe MIPS, so their presence or absence has relatively little influence on the total movement from MVS to UNIX.

For many users, the changing nature of business problems will mean that "traditional" mainframe applications will need to be moved or rewritten to a distributed, UNIX-based platform.

MVS VERSUS UNIX

The most basic, necessary tasks on either of these operating systems are pretty much the same. The only time that we notice drastic differences are in the granularity of the way functions are performed and the operating system priorities established.

As you know, MVS is a very powerful robust operating system running on large mainframes, excelling in batch job processing. However, UNIX has been the mainstay of the smaller processors, mostly in interactive modes. MVS does provide the interactive facilities in time sharing option (TSO) and interactive system productivity facility (ISPF), but UNIX seems to be more versatile.

The following table indicates how basic tasks are performed in the MVS and the UNIX environments.

FUNCTION	MVS ENVIRONMENT	UNIX ENVIRONMENT
1. Editing	TSO EDIT or ISPF editors	*ed, ex,* or *vi* editors
2. File manipulation	CLISTs, REXX, TSO commands	File and data manipulation commands
3. Data management	TSO, ISPF, DFSMShsm, IEHMOVE, IEBCOPY utilities	*tar, cpio, pax*
4. Text processing	ISPF/PDF or TSO/EDIT, SCRIPT/VS, Sort, Merge	*troff, nroff, awk, sed, sort, merge*
5. Programming	Compilers, LINK, JCL	*cc, f77,* shell commands
6. Job control	JCL and SDSF (system display and search facility)	*ps, jobs, kill,* etc.
7. Background jobs	TSO (submit job)	Command &, *at, batch,* etc.
8. Communicating with other users	TSO: SEND, RECEIVE, TRANSMIT, LISTBC, LOGON	*mail, mailx, talk, ftp, telnet,* or *r* or *remote* commands
9. File security	RACF, PROTECT, ALLOCATE	*chmod, chown*
10. Debugging	TSO test, inspect	*dbx* command

1. *Editing:* In MVS, you can edit the MVS files using TSO or ISPF editors, and you can edit OpenEdition hierarchical file system (HFS) files using OpenMVS File edit with ISPF or via the OEDIT editor. In UNIX, *vi* and *ed* provide a powerful editing command set.
2. *File Manipulation:* In MVS, CLIST language allows you to work efficiently with TSO/E. CLIST is essentially a command procedure that performs a task or a group of tasks. There are a number of UNIX commands that can be used to manipulate files.
3. *Data Management:* In MVS, you can use data facility system-managed storage hierarchical storage manager (DFSMShsm) to automatically back up and archive file systems. However, in MVS, there is no facility to back up individual files. You can copy archive files to an MVS data set and then to tape. You can retrieve archive files from a tape into an MVS data set and then copy them into the file.

   In UNIX, *tar, pax,* and *cpio* allow the user to read or write an archive file in the file system. There is no automatic backup.
4. *Text Processing:* SCRIPT/VS runs in the TSO foreground. TSO's interactive editing interactive system productivity facility/program development facility (ISPF/PDF or EDIT) and related facilities provide the text entry, editing, and data set management that are used with SCRIPT/VS for text processing. SCRIPT/VS provides a flexible composition for printing on terminals, impact printers, or nonimpact printers as an alternative to independent typesetting machines. When SCRIPT/VS formats a document, it takes into consideration the characteristics of the specific physical output device. SCRIPT/VS can also be used to prepare documents for processing by other programs or applications, such as formatters and photocomposers.

   In UNIX, *nroff, troff, awk, sed,* and *sort/merge* are the basic facilities for text processing.
5. *Programming:* In MVS, you can use C/370 compiler and the linkage editor to create a traditional application program as a load or executable module. In UNIX, you can also use the *cc* command to invoke a front-end program that invokes the preprocessor, compiler, assembler, and linkage editor, as appropriate.
6. *Job Control:* In MVS/TSO, you can use the system display and search facility to monitor and control a job or issue CANCEL, STATUS, and OUTPUT commands. In UNIX, you can use the *ps* command to report status about active processes or *jobs* command (in some UNIX versions) to check the status of a job and the *kill* command to terminate a job before it completes.

   In addition, in UNIX, you can use the *<EscChar-Z>* sequence to stop, or suspend, a foreground job and then enter the *bg* command to run it in the background or issue the *fg* command to restart it in the foreground.
7. *Background Jobs:* In MVS/TSO, you can write a background job in job control language (JCL) and start it with the SUBMIT command. In UNIX, you can start a background job by typing an & (with or without a space) at the end of a command line.

8. *Communicating with Other Users:* In MVS/TSO, you can communicate with other users by using
   - SEND command to send short messages to other users or the operator.
   - LISTBC command to check all current broadcast messages.
   - TRANSMIT command to transmit data sets and longer messages.
   - RECEIVE command to receive transmitted messages from other users.

   In UNIX, *mail* and *mailx* commands allow you to send and receive (exchange) messages and or files between users and systems.
9. *File Security:* In MVS, RACF provides the security protection for files. Unlike UNIX, the PROTECT command sets or changes passwords and protection modes (read or write protection) for a data set on a direct access device. For day-to-day usage, the UNIX file security system is simpler, by using the *chmod* command. The *chmod* command allows you to assign (change) permissions of a file, whereas the *chown* command allows you to change the owner or group of a file.
10. *Debugging:* In MVS/TSO, TEST and INSPECT facilities can be utilized for debugging. *dbx* is a tool for source-level debugging and execution of programs under UNIX. The machine-level facilities of *dbx* can be used on any UNIX program.

ORGANIZATION OF THIS TEXT

Broadly speaking, this book is organized into four major parts: basics, data manipulation, programming and utilities, and communications. For a quick review of the covered subjects, a summary is provided at the conclusion of each chapter.

Basics: Part 1 lays the foundation for UNIX and its comparative perspectives with MVS, starting with a discussion of the objectives and the UNIX evolution, leading to similarities and differences of the two operating systems. The Chapters 2 through 4 in this part discuss the history of UNIX and MVS, ending with the commands to logon and starting a session.

Data Manipulation: The primary purpose of a computer is to manipulate data/files. The operating systems provide techniques and facilities to operate upon the data that are usable by the programmers and other recipients. A detailed discussion of the commonly used commands with examples is provided along with comparison of UNIX with MVS/TSO and MVS/ISPF facilities. Chapters 5 through 10 deal with file manipulations, data management, and editing functions.

Programming and Utilities: Part 3 carries the commands discussed in previous chapters, forward, by adding advanced features provided by "shells" and "utilities." Chapters 11 through 13 cover document preparation, printing, and other programming features.

Communications: Part 4 (chapters 14 and 15) builds upon the commands and concepts described in previous chapters to help users to communicate with each other, send/receive files from one system to another, and schedule jobs in the background or foreground.

The book is concluded with comprehensive appendixes, bibliography, and an index as follows:

- Appendix 1: Command summaries for MVS and their equivalents in UNIX, for quick review of some of the major commands utilized in data manipulations.
- Appendix 2: Command summaries of UNIX editors compared those with MVS/ISPF and MVS/TSO editors.
- Appendix 3: A comprehensive summary of file management commands for MVS and UNIX.
- Appendix 4: A list of commonly used UNIX files.
- Bibliography and an index for references.

SUMMARY

UNIX has been around for about 30 years, and many consider it the operating system of the future. The idea appealed to a variety of researchers and enthusiasts since UNIX was designed to run on mini- and microcomputers. As the PCs and microprocessors are becoming cheaper and more powerful, the portability and multitasking capability of UNIX make it a strong candidate for an operating system of choice.

Most UNIX installations include large file servers storing gigabits of data and automated backup systems to provide a high level of data security. UNIX provides features that can change the way people use computers on their desktops. Innovative hardware architectures using reduced instruction set computers (RISC) technology, pipelining, multitasking, multiprocessing, multiuser, and vectorization are invading the turf traditionally held by large mainframes. If you are faced with the task of migration from MVS or any other operating system on the mainframe, you will likely need to learn a version of the UNIX operating system.

In spite of the inherent power, UNIX has not been widely adopted in the glass house environments. Although the underlying architecture of UNIX is easy to understand, the UNIX command line can appear hostile and forbidding to the unprepared user. This book has been designed to reduce the learning curve required to become proficient with UNIX in a rightsized MIS or a downsized workstation environment.

On the other hand, MVS is a very powerful operating system and is well suited for centrally managed environments.

2

Is UNIX Really MVS in Disguise?

UNIX is a powerful computer operating system originally developed at AT&T Bell Laboratories. It has been very popular among the scientific, engineering, and academic communities due to its multiuser and multitasking environment; flexibility and portability; electronic mail and networking capabilities; and the availability of numerous programming, text processing, and scientific utilities. It has also gained widespread acceptance in government and business. Over the years, two major forms (with several vendor's variants of each) of UNIX have evolved: AT&T UNIX System V and the University of California at Berkeley's Berkeley Software Distribution (BSD). Other prevalent versions are

SunOS 4.1.2
IBM's AIX
Apple's A/UX

SCO

NeXT's NeXTSTEP (based on Mach, based on BSD, ...)

Many many more

To assist you as you start on this journey, a few selected references are provided at the end of this chapter.

INTRODUCTION TO UNIX

The purpose of this chapter is to describe the historical development of the UNIX operating system, including introductory information about the various versions and main features.

UNIX has been implemented on a wider range of machines than any other operating system. BSD was developed at the University of California at Berkeley as an enhanced version of AT&T's UNIX. It was developed out of a need for better utilities in programming and networking. Many of these enhancements have been implemented into the latest release of AT&T's UNIX. AT&T's latest release is called System V or System 5 and BSD is on release 4.4. Because of licensing problems many vendors chose to write their own versions of UNIX. For instance, Hewlett-Packard's UNIX operating system or HP-UX and Hitachi's UNIX operating system HI-OSF/1 are based on both System V and BSD, but with their own added enhancements.

UNIX is a multiuser operating system. Many users can use the same machine simultaneously. This is directly related to multitasking since each user just has their own set of processes. The multiuser aspect allows groups of people to work easily together, sharing files and utilities.

UNIX networking is built into the operating system. A diverse and powerful set of networking tools have been developed over the lifetime of UNIX. Today some of these tools are becoming standards in non-UNIX environments.

Open Systems: Problems and Pitfalls

Open systems appear to provide some significant advantages over IBM proprietary standards, but many of their claimed benefits may be illusory. The allure of open systems is based on claims of the lower costs and improved interoperability of open systems compared with proprietary mainframes.

A common flaw in migrating from proprietary to open systems is to underestimate the relative cost of systems management in the UNIX environment. The cost of management in the traditional mainframe environment is kept down by a mature base of software products, tools, and experienced personnel—the open-systems environment is, by comparison, the domain of a few highly paid professionals, who are needed to maintain and administer the system because of the lack of user-friendly, packaged management solutions.

Application Development Under UNIX

Since the development of UNIX applications at large, traditionally mainframe-based sites are often considered something of a "black art," there are many considerations that are easily overlooked. Having grown up alongside UNIX over the last 20 years, **C** has finally begun to have an impact on commercial computing. It is, however, a highly complex language, with the advantages of flexibility countered by the difficulty in maintaining C-written code.

Although UNIX is almost 30 years old, it has, in many respects, suffered from something of a misspent youth, languishing in the academic domain instead of gaining in stature in the real world of commerce, as would be expected of its contemporaries, such as MVS. The result is that necessary levels of security, integrity, and manageability were not built in, leaving the job to be done later in life.

Description of UNIX

When you use UNIX, several layers of interaction are occurring between the computer hardware and you. The first layer is the *kernel*, which runs on the actual machine hardware and manages all interactions with the hardware (Figure 2.1). All applications and

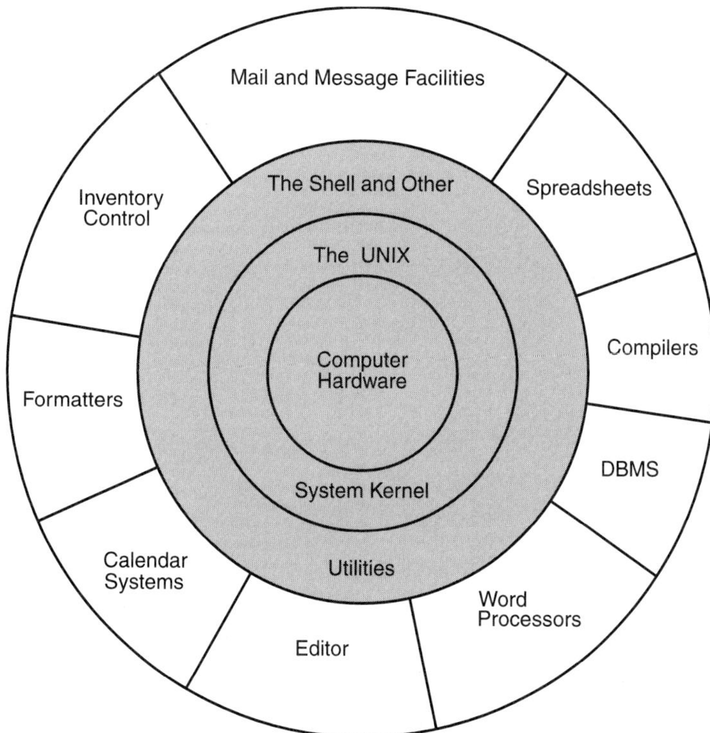

FIGURE 2.1 UNIX Layers.

commands in UNIX interact with the kernel, rather than the hardware directly, and they make up the second layer. On top of the applications and commands is the command-interpreter program; the shell, which manages the interaction between you, your applications, and the available UNIX commands.

Most UNIX commands are separate programs, distinct from the kernel. A final layer, which may or may not be present on your system, is a *windowing system* such as X. The windowing system usually interacts with the shell, but it can also interact directly with applications. The final "layer" is you, the user. You will interact with the entire operating system through just the shell, or through a combination of the shell and the window system. Figure 2.1 provides a visual representation of the layers of UNIX.

You need to be familiar with *six basic elements* of UNIX. They are commands, files, directories, your environment, processes, and jobs.

- *Commands* are the instructions you give the system to tell it what to do.
- *Files* are collections of data that have been given filenames. A file is analogous to a container in which you can store documents, raw data, or programs (it can contain only one kind of data at a time). A single file might contain the text of a research project, statistical data, or an equation processing formula. Files are stored in directories.
- A *directory* is similar to a file cabinet drawer that contains many files. A directory can also contain other directories. Every directory has a name, like files.
- *Your environment* is a collection of items that describe or modify how your computing session will be carried out. It contains things such as where the commands are located and which printer to send your output to.
- A command or application running on the computer is called a *process*.
- The sequence of instructions given to the computer from the time you initiate a particular task until it ends it is called a *job.* A job may have one or more processes in it.

We will explore each of these elements in a little greater detail later on, but first you need to learn about UNIX and how to get on to your system.

UNIX was developed to provide an efficient computing environment. UNIX is capable of multitasking (many programs running asynchronously), multiuser (many users simultaneously), hierarchical file system (directories or ordinary files), and machine independence (small kernel and number of utility). Simply, it does more than one task at once for more than one user and runs on many different machines. UNIX is a collection of useful tools and programs that includes many building blocks for building your own programs.

UNIX is not an acronym but rather a name given to the operating system by the developer. The name UNIX is a pun on MULTICS, an early multiuser interactive operating system. MULTICS was so named because it supported multiusers, and was a very

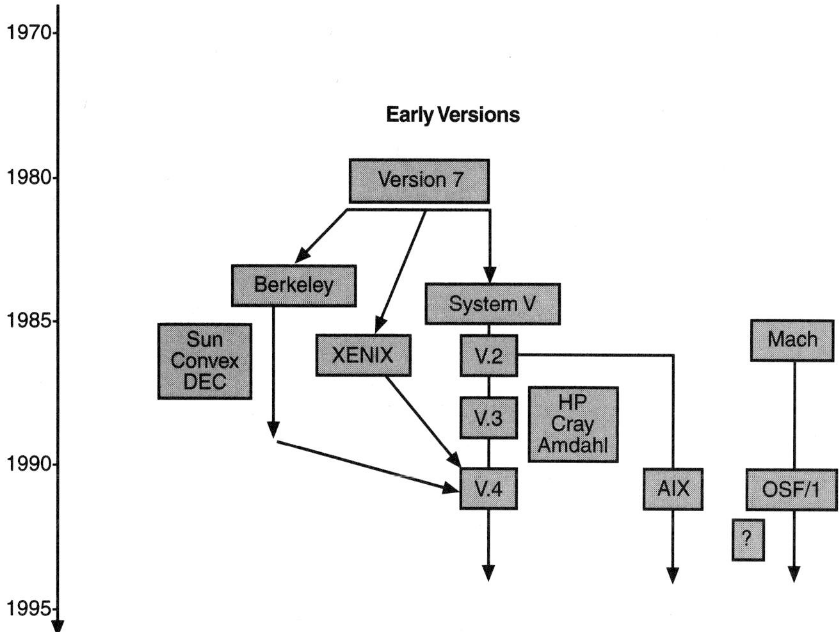

FIGURE 2.2 Evolution of UNIX.

big system. UNIX was so named because it was, by comparison, a very small operating system.

EVOLUTION OF UNIX

To understand the concepts of the operating system, it is useful to have an appreciation of the development of UNIX (Figure 2.2).

Initial Development

Development of UNIX started in 1969. At first, it was not a proposed project of Bell Laboratories, but grew out of a need of their development group. Bell Labs pulled out of the MULTICS project as it was too limiting for the Labs' purposes. So in 1969, the Computer Science Research Group at Bell Labs began the search for a replacement environment.

It was Ken Thompson, a member of the Bell Labs' development group, who actually started the development of what is now known as UNIX. Using a Digital Equipment Corporations PDP-7, Thompson developed an operating system that he felt would be more usable by program developers. He wanted a small, efficient system that would provide a set of facilities which could be built upon to achieve any desired effect.

First Version of UNIX

The first version of UNIX was written in assembler language, which made it machine dependent. However, to help make the software more portable, Thompson also developed a high-level language called B, based on another language called BCPL.

Development of C

In early 1970, Dennis Ritchie made several modifications to Thompson's B language and called this new language C. One of the changes was to add a system of types. He subsequently converted most of the UNIX operating system to C, making UNIX a highly portable operating system. In fact, in 1972, UNIX was transported to other DEC systems throughout Bell Laboratories.

Initial Distribution

Having redesigned the operating system, Bell Labs and its parent company, Western Electric, soon became interested, and word rapidly spread about the capabilities of the system.

In 1973, Bell Labs agreed to distribute UNIX to any organization that agreed not to use the system for commercial purposes. This was because of the antitrust laws, which meant that they were not allowed to sell software. It was, therefore, distributed free of charge to educational establishments throughout America. Today, the majority of major universities in the United States and abroad use UNIX, which is one of the primary reasons for not only its popularity, but also its commercial success.

Commercial Availability

In 1979, Bell Laboratories released the seventh edition of UNIX, and with this release, a major change in the use of the UNIX system was noticed.

Bell Laboratories announced a major cost reduction for UNIX object license, with several manufacturers and developers being attracted to the commercial use of the system. Early implementations of UNIX included VENIX from Venturcom, UNIPLUS from Unisoft, and XENIX from Microsoft.

Continuing Improvements—UNIX System V

In January 1983, AT&T announced the availability of UNIX System V for commercial users. This marked the beginning of a more aggressive approach by AT&T in the development of a market for UNIX-based systems. System V includes a number of features and performance enhancements that make the UNIX system better suited to the commercial world. In particular, AT&T announced software support for System V; previous versions of UNIX from AT&T had been licensed "as is," with no support available.

UNIX became a generic operating system of choice during the 1980s. Work continued to improve the system. A new file system allowing for larger files was written, and the shell was modernized to provide better support for the many programs written in this language.

Growth Factors

The rise of UNIX in the early 1980s has almost entirely to do with economics and hardware—and the two are inextricably linked. It has almost nothing to do with "open systems" or any of the ex post facto justifications or explanations that have circulated.

Quite simply, beginning with Sun Microsystems' first workstations, UNIX was the software that ran on the best low-cost available hardware. For a given price, you could get much more performance than was possible before. The proprietary vendors (DEC, etc.) got behind the performance curve, and stayed behind it. Pretty soon (by 1985, if not 1986), there was absolutely no reason to buy DEC hardware, except to run VAX/VMS—and, if VAX/VMS was making you suffer subpar performance, that reason wore pretty thin. UNIX, in whatever flavor, became the leader because you could buy faster hardware, at cheaper prices. You could put a workstation on everyone's desk and still have spent less than a mainframe would have cost.

But why did all those aggressive little start-up vendors go after UNIX? Well, in fact, they didn't: Apollo is a notable exception. But most start-ups relied on UNIX ports. Why? This doesn't have anything to do with any intrinsic virtue in UNIX—rather, it's purely economic. For a relatively small piece of change ($20K or so) you could buy a complete working operating system, with source. That's nothing compared to the expense and time of developing an operating system from scratch. To make it concrete, Multiflow Computer had its first complete (hardware) board set sometime around August 1986. By October, there was a machine you could *rlogin* to. By November, UNIX was running stably. By January, there was a product on the market. Of course, before any hardware existed, the software people were working busily with instruction set simulators and the like. But that kind of quick development just would not have been possible if Multiflow had to develop a proprietary operating system (OS). Nor could Multiflow conceivably have had the money to develop a proprietary OS.

The story was repeated again and again: Sun, Convex, Multiflow, SGI, Pyramid, Stardent, and so on. NeXT is at the end of this list. In short, by 1985 if you were going to have "modern" computers, you were going to have a computer that ran UNIX. Small start-ups built better hardware than the mainstream vendors, like DEC and IBM, and the small start-ups couldn't afford the time or the money to develop a proprietary operating system. Soon, the companies with proprietary operating systems even started moving to UNIX, with DEC and IBM being the big exceptions.

Education was another factor in UNIX's growth. Ultimately, this is also an economic factor. Schools were turning out loads of very competent computer users (and systems programmers) who already knew UNIX. You could therefore "buy" a ready made programming staff. You didn't have to train them on the intricacies of some unknown operating system. It takes a long time to become a guru; with UNIX, you could buy them ready made. A friend of mine at IBM said "You may not believe it, but IBM really is committed to UNIX. They've realized that they can't hire people out of school who know anything about their mainframe system. They can't even hire system administrators." For IBM, this was the writing on the wall.

A third factor was evolution. UNIX provided an evolutionary path—the UNIX of 1996 is significantly different from the UNIX of 1978, with sophisticated networking, many utilities and tools, a windowing system, and new shells. However, that evolutionary path worked because Berkeley (primarily), AT&T, and Open Software Foundation put a lot of effort into integrating new developments into the basic system. Most other operating systems have remained more or less the same from their invention until their obsolescence; they've added incremental improvements, but haven't been able to transcend their origins. And, again, this is an economic factor.

Users want new features; vendors want to sell new features; developing new features in house is expensive. Again, Multiflow provides an interesting example: its machine was probably the first stand-alone computer to have a network interface before it had working serial ports! That couldn't have happened without the BSD networking code.

I haven't mentioned "open systems" or anything like that because, frankly, "open systems" as a concept was invented sometime around 1988—after the fact. The fact is, running UNIX was a decided disadvantage until sometime around 1988. You could guarantee that any interesting third-party application software wasn't ported to UNIX; you could also guarantee that the vendors of these software packages were not happy about having to port to dozens of slightly different UNIX platforms.

Given that people really buy computers to run applications, the world wasn't all that rosy. Eventually, the hardware advantage forced the software vendors to play ball—particularly in the scientific arena, where customers could exert a lot of pressure on vendors to port software to faster platforms. To some extent, though, UNIX still labors under the "application software" disadvantage (though, now, the comparison is to Windows rather than VMS or VM/CMS or MVS). The fact is that the "advantages of open systems" (whatever open systems might be, and that's another essay—open systems is itself a largely meaningless term) are real, but they were only appreciated afterwards. Corporate users realized "Gee, we have all these UNIX systems, and they're more or less alike, and more or less compatible with each other, and we can hire people straight out of school and put them to work without training them on MVS—there are some real advantages here."

Where does that lead us, then? The hardware and applications drive the market; users are going to buy the best hardware at the lowest price on which they can run their important applications. In reality, there is not any inherent loyalty to UNIX, much less to "openness," or to anything aside from getting more done for less cost. What we have been aiming at is to figure out what the historical factors are that allowed UNIX to succeed, and see if we can use them to figure where the market is now, and what's happening next. Here are some observations:

Now that Berkeley and AT&T are both out of the UNIX business, it's not clear what the evolutionary path is. Who is going to integrate the new developments into a "base release" that can become a de facto standard and, as such, prevent various UNIX versions from diverging? The various UNIX industry consortia haven't accomplished much, and probably won't accomplish much in the future; commercial vendors just aren't very good at cooperation.

Finally, there's the evolutionary factor—in which, of course, education played a very important role. If UNIX is going to continue to compete, it's critical for it to retain the ability to evolve. UNIX grew because it ran on great hardware, it had a central role in universities, and it had an evolutionary path.

STATUS OF UNIX

The UNIX profile is changing radically. This is illustrated by the breakdown of users over the past few years.

In 1979

USER	% OF TOTAL
Bell Systems	55
Universities	32
Government	10
Commercial	3

In 1982

USER	% OF TOTAL
Bell Systems	24
Universities	18
Government	4
Commercial	54

As we come close to the 21st century, the UNIX system is now regarded as a standard operating system and has been implemented on many different computers ranging from micros to mainframes. Some differences exist between various versions (Figure 2.2) both in the operating system and in the commands. In spite of these differences, the UNIX operating system is highly portable and interoperable from platform to platform.

FEATURES OF UNIX

UNIX is an interactive, multiuser, multitasking system. One or more users can do one or more things each and the computer creates an illusion of doing everything at once. UNIX has hierarchical (tree-structured) file system—an "open" system (others can tell what you're doing to some extent). Other users can tell if you are logged on. Other users may have access to your files (but you can prevent normal users from accessing your files if you desire). Likewise, you can obtain some information about other users and their files.

UNIX exhibits small tools (each doing one thing well) pieced together to do big things. UNIX commands are files and are totally movable/replaceable, designed for people who know what they're doing. At the same time UNIX is highly customizable.

UNIX has many important and powerful features. Perhaps the three that have contributed most to its success are multitasking, multiuser, and built-in networking.

Multitasking: UNIX is a multitasking operating system. UNIX can run many programs (processes) at once, and one user may have many programs running asynchronously. A user can perform more than one task at a time. This allows a user to run, for instance, a compilation in background and to edit files simultaneously. These tasks or processes can be run in the background so that the user can continue with other activities. For example, a user could be sorting a file or making a calculation in the background at the same time as he is editing a file.

Multiuser: UNIX is a multiuser operating system. UNIX can have many users using the system at one time. Many users can use the same machine simultaneously. This is directly related to multitasking since each user has their own set of processes. The multiuser aspect allows groups of people to work easily together, sharing files and utilities.

Networking: UNIX networking is built into the operating system. A diverse and powerful set of networking tools have developed over the lifetime of UNIX. Today, some of these tools are becoming standards even in the non-UNIX environments.

Other operating system features are

Machine Independence: The UNIX operating system consists of a relatively small memory resident kernel and a number of utility programs. Approximately 95% of the system is written in C, which means that it can run, and is running, on many different systems, such as Sun, Digital, IBM PC, RS/6000, OS/390, SP/2, Hewlett-Packard, Hitachi, Amdahl, among others.

Device-Independent I/O: All devices, whether disks, terminals, printers, or interprocess I/O channels, look the same to UNIX programs, so it is possible to direct output to any device as and when required.

By comparison, under most operating systems, it is necessary to write multiple programs to output to the printer, the terminal, or the disk.

Using redirected I/O under UNIX, one program accomplishes all these tasks.

Portable Software: UNIX software written for one system is relatively transportable to any other system. This means that there is a great variety of application software available to run under UNIX.

Powerful Standard Utilities: The standard commands provided by UNIX are a well-designed set of tools that work well together.

One of the primary tools is the command interpreter (shell), which allows the user to run a series of commands and to pass the output of one command to the input of another.

Many of the standard tools are filters which read their input, apply a transformation to it, and send the result to their output.

Thus, small programs are used as basic building blocks, which are combined to make more powerful customized tools.

Flexibility: The kernel treats both commands and the shell the same way, for simplicity, so it is easy to write special commands for special purposes.

UNIX was developed primarily for use by program developers, so the environment is well suited to program development. However, the flexibility of the system makes it easy to provide other environments which are more suited to less sophisticated users of the system.

UNIX CONCEPTS

The File System

UNIX uses a hierarchical file system. The file system is a hierarchy of directories which can contain either ordinary files, or other directories. The top of the hierarchy is the root directory or just "/." Below this directory are the subdirectories such as */bin*, which is short for binary (executable) and contain many of the utility programs, and */tmp,* which stores temporary files. The file system can be made secure so that users cannot interfere with other users' files, unless the owner gives them permission.

When you log into the system you are placed in your home directory. The home directory is where your personal files and directories reside. The location of the home directory is determined by the system administrator. For instance, when the user "*scot*" starts his session, he will be placed in the */home/admin/scot* directory.

The Shell

The shell is the most commonly used utility program in UNIX. Each time you execute a command, the shell interprets the command and directs the work that needs to be done to perform the command. The shell is an interface between the user and the rest of the system. Since the shell is nothing more than a utility program, you have a choice of shells (Table 2.1).

Currently there are five major shells: Bourne, Korn, C, T, and Bash. All these support both foreground and background processes, pipes, filters, input/output redirection, and other similar standard features of UNIX.

TABLE 2.1 Shells

SHELL	DEFAULT	PROMPT	HOME START-UP FILES
Bourne shell	*sh*	$	*$HOME/.profile*
Korn shell	*ksh*	$	*$HOME/.profile*
C shell	*csh*	% %	*$HOME/.cshrc*
T shell	*tcsh*	% %	*$HOME/.tcshrc* or *$HOME/.cshrc*
Bash	*bash*	*bash$*	*$HOME/.bashrc*

The *Bourne shell* was the original shell. It is the smallest shell and lacks many of the features of the other four shells. The *Korn shell* retains the complete functionality of the Bourne shell and includes some enhancements.

The *C shell* was developed at Berkeley and is useful for **C** language programmers. The *T shell* retains the complete functionality of the *C shell* while adding many useful features, such as name completion and command line editing.

Bash or the *GNU "Bourne Again Shell"* incorporates many features of the Korn and *C shells* and follows the IEEE POSIX standard. Currently the *T shell* is the most popular because it has "the most bells and whistles"; however, *Bash* is gaining in popularity.

When a shell is started it looks for start-up files that sets it behavior. The shell looks for system start-up files, and then it looks in your home directory (*$HOME*) for personal start-up files. These home start-up files allows you customize the behavior of the shell.

If you did not ask for a specific shell, your system administrator has probably assigned you one. You can determine your shell, among other things, by using the *finger* command.

Command Line Options and Arguments

You can vary the operation of certain commands by using command options. Options are usually preceded by a minus (-) sign followed by a letter of the alphabet.

```
ls -l

total 1094
-rw-r----- 1 scot     admin       242 Mar 7 17:00 Makefile
-rwxr-xr-x 1 scot     admin     42036 Mar 7 17:00 hello
-rw-r--r-- 1 scot     admin        70 Mar 7 17:00 hello.cc
-rwxr-xr-x 1 scot     admin        48 Mar 7 17:00 hello.pl
```

The *ls* command is used to list files and directories. The *-l* options causes *ls* to give you a "long listing" of the files in a directory. If a command has more than one option, the options can be bundled together using a single minus sign. Not only can commands have options, they can also have arguments. The command arguments are usually files. However, they can also be variables with values or possibly words to be matched.

grep hello greetings.txt

The *grep* command does pattern searching. This command will display every line in the file *greetings.txt* that contains the pattern hello.

Wildcards or MetaCharacters

One of the most powerful features of the shell is the capacity to use "shorthand" notation for operating upon whole aggregates of files and directories in a single command. For instance, the characters that specify these options are called *wildcard* or *metacharacters* (Table 2.2).

We can use wildcards to search for specific files.

ls [0-9].txt*

This command will list all the files that begin with the characters 0 through 9 and end with the character string *.txt*. Wildcards can be used in any UNIX command. They are not limited to the *ls* command.

TABLE 2.2 Wildcards

*	Represents any arbitrary character string
?	Represents any single character
[ ]	Encloses a list of characters where the match is on "any single character enclosed in the bracket." The hyphen character is used inside the bracket to indicate a range of characters.

File Permissions

UNIX has a standard method of allowing access to certain files and directories. The *ls* command with the *-l* option will display file permissions. You can set the permission of the file to allow access by certain classes of users. These three classes are the *user*, the *user group*, and *other.*

The *user* is the person who created the file. A *group* is a combination of users that can be used to restrict access. For instance, all faculty members could be in a group that allows them to see privileged information. The last class is *other*, which is anyone with a username on your system.

These classes of users can have different combinations of *read, write, execute* (for a file) or *search* (for a directory) permissions. All together each file has nine permissions: three for owner, three for the owner's group, and three for others.

The *chmod* command is used to change the permissions of a file or directory as shown in Table 2.3.

TABLE 2.3 Permissions Examples

PERMISSION	MEANING
rw-r--r--	File is read/write for user and read only for both the users group and other users.
rwx------	File is read/write/execute for the user only.
r-xr-xr-x	File is read/execute for user, group, and other.
dr-xr-x---	Directory is read/search for the user and his group.

Redirecting Input/Output

Usually you are inputting from the keyboard and the output is going to the screen. However, you can redirect the input and output with the less than (<) and greater than (>) symbols, respectively.

mailx scot < memo

The *mailx* command is one way to send electronic mail. This command will send the file memo to user *scot.*

ls > listfile

This command will place a listing of all the file and directories into a file called *listfile.* If *listfile* already existed, previous contents of the file will be deleted. If you do not want to lose the contents of the file you could append to the end of the file by using two greater than symbols (>>).

We have discussed the standard input and standard output. However, UNIX provides another output stream called *standard error.* The standard error is used to output any error messages that should not appear in the standard output; it is usually used for debugging purposes.

ls nofile >> listfile
nofile not found

Here we have tried to list a file that does not exist. Notice that the error message is not placed in the file *listfile*, however the *listfile* is created.

ls nofile >> listfile

The >> tells the shell to send the standard output and the standard error to the file *listfile*.

TABLE 2.4 Input/Output Redirection

SYMBOL	ACTION	SHELL
<	Redirect input from	All
>	Redirect output to	All
>>	Redirect output and append to	All

Connecting Commands with Pipes

All the commands you have seen have been single commands. One of the most powerful features of UNIX is the ability to connect these commands together to form a sequence of operations. The tool to accomplish this is called a *pipe*, which is denoted by a vertical bar "|." With a *pipe* the standard output from one command can be the standard input to another command.

ls -l | wc -l
29

The *wc* command with the *-l* option gives you a count of lines. This command will *pipe* the output of our *ls -l* command to the *wc* (word count) command, giving us the total number of files and directories in our current directory.

Pipes are not limited to two commands; by using filters, you can have pipes of unlimited length.

Filters

A *filter* is a command that takes its input from standard input and sends its output to standard output. Most commands in UNIX are filters, taking some input performing an action and sending it to standard output. Filters are often used in pipes to change the data as they travel through the pipe. Some commands, such as *grep* and *sort,* are good examples of programs that can be used as filters, whereas the *ls* command can not be a filter since it does not accept standard input. Actually *ls* can only be used as the first command in a *pipe.* The *lp* command cannot be used as a filter since it can only send to the printer and not to standard output. In fact, *lp* can be used only as the last command in a *pipe.*

Process Management

Another feature of UNIX is its multitasking ability. UNIX is able to multitask through the use of processes. A process is simply a program in execution. A typical UNIX machine has anywhere from 10 to 150 processes running concurrently. Each process must share the one central processor. The system gives the illusion of simultaneously performing many tasks by switching the CPU, very rapidly, from one process to the next.

Each time you execute a command, an independent process is created to perform the command. Every command that has been executed has been a process; even the shell is a process. The system does not use the command name to keep track of the process; instead, it knows a process by its process identification number (PID). To see what processes you currently have running on the system, use the *ps* command.

ps

PID	TTY	TIME COMMAND
10315	ttyp5	0:00 *ps*
1548	ttyp5	0:00 *tcsh*

We can see there are two processes running. The *ps* command, which we just used to view the processes, and *tcsh.*

SUMMARY

UNIX

- Communicates with you via the shell (the shell is programmable).
- Works on more than one job at a time.
- Communicates with other users.
- Edits files with screen-, line-, and stream-oriented editors.
- Delays execution of jobs.
- Stores files in a hierarchical file system.
- Permits jobs (processes) to communicate with one another in different ways.
- Is designed around tool building philosophy.
- Includes several hundred utilities.
- Supports many users concurrently.
- Supports many tasks.
- Communicates with you via the shell.
- Has a hierarchical file system.
- Has security for private and shared files.
- Has device-independent input and out.
- Has interprocess communication.
- Has few restrictions.
- Assumes you know what you are doing and are responsible.
- The environment (libraries and flexible powerful utilities) is consistent.
- Is simple to build and maintain tools.
- Is file driven.
- Has many utilities that simplify the programmer's chores.

- Has libraries (system calls and functions) for many purposes.
- Is comprehensible and configurable.
- Shares common databases.
- Shares expensive peripherals.
- Features interaction.
- Balances the workload.
- Enables problem-solving network communications.
- Provides security.

REFERENCES

ARICK, MARTIN. *UNIX C Shell: Desk Reference*, QED Technical Publishing, Boston, 1992.

AT&T. *UNIX System V Release 4 BSD/XENIX Compatibility Guide,* Prentice Hall, Englewood Cliffs, N.J., 1990.

BOSLER, KURT. *MVS TSO ISPF: A Guide for Users and Developers,* McGraw-Hill, New York, 1993.

BOURNE, S. R. *The UNIX System,* Addison-Wesley, Reading, Mass., 1983.

FENG, LYNDA. *System Files and Devices Reference: UNIX SVR4.2,* Prentice Hall, Englewood Cliffs, N.J., 1992.

GARDNER, JAMES. *Learning UNIX,* SAMS, Indianapolis, Ind., 1991.

INTERNATIONAL BUSINESS MACHINES. *OS/VS2 TSO Command Language Reference VS2 Release 3.7,* IBM, Poughkeepsie, N.Y., 1994. GC28-0646.

INTERNATIONAL BUSINESS MACHINES. *Interactive System Productivity Facility (ISPF) Getting Started,* IBM, Poughkeepsie, N.Y., 1994. SC34-4440.

INTERNATIONAL BUSINESS MACHINES. *Interactive System Productivity Facility (ISPF) Edit and Edit Macros,* IBM, Poughkeepsie, N.Y., 1994. SC34-4446.

INTERNATIONAL BUSINESS MACHINES. *Introducing OpenEdition MVS,* IBM, Poughkeepsie, N.Y., 1993. GC23-3010.

INTERNATIONAL BUSINESS MACHINES. *MVS/ESA OpenEdition MVS Command Reference,* IBM, Poughkeepsie, N.Y., 1994. SC23-3014.

LOWE, DOUG. *MVS/TSO Concepts, Commands, JCL, and CLISTS,* IBM, Poughkeepsie, N.Y., 1984.

TOPHAM, DOUGLAS W. *A System V Guide to UNIX and XENIX*, Springer-Verlag, New York, 1992.

WOODCOCK, JOANNE, HALVORSON, MICHAEL, and ROBERT ACKERMAN. *Running UNIX: An Introduction to SCO UNIX System V/386 and XENIX Operating Systems*, Microsoft Press, Richmond, Wash., 1990.

3

Rightsizing/Downsizing to UNIX

INTRODUCTION

The current corporate computing environment is a patchwork of different hardware and software technologies. The largest homogeneous group is represented by mainframe application users. This group provides an especially fertile environment for moving to a networked corporate scheduling solution. Moving this large group, intact, to such a solution will preempt further splintering.

The explosive growth of data traffic volumes is endemic across all industry groups. One source of this growth is the increase in mips (millions of instructions per second) at the desktop as PC prices become extremely competitive. A common industry rule of thumb suggests that workstations and PCs are capable of generating 1 megabyte of data for every 2 mips of processing power. And PCs are rapidly increasing in processing power.

Companies must address this growth in processing power and data volume through increased network bandwidth within and between their local area networks.

The objectives of this chapter are to explore the reasons why UNIX is gaining in importance, various facets of MVS environments, and evolution of MVS operating system.

DOWNSIZING AND DISTRIBUTED APPLICATIONS

Companies that are downsizing from mainframes to more cost-effective solutions are in a unique position to leapfrog from outdated to leading edge environments by utilizing client/server architectures and implementing networked computing technologies such as UNIX. These companies already have in place both the technical and social environments necessary to take advantage of the benefits of a networked computing strategy and to ensure optimal performance of that strategy.

As many companies have discovered, downsizing can prove to be more painful and expensive than anticipated. Rather than take on the enormous task of implementing everything-but-the-kitchen-sink solutions, a company should prioritize its data sharing requirements and evaluate the switching costs. In many cases, it may not make sense to switch all applications. However, there are some applications like group scheduling and e-mail where efficient information sharing is essential and the costs of moving to networked solutions can be effectively managed.

Heterogeneity

In todays' corporate computing environment, heterogeneity is already a reality. Mainframes, midrange systems, workstations, personal computers, and microprocessors all are unique, use unique applications and operating systems. Emerging technologies, re-engineering, and economics are further complicating the landscape.

As most MIS managers can attest, getting all users to agree on and adopt any single application is as easy as herding cats. In addition, until recently, adopting a single application meant limiting choices in operating and hardware environments. Such an undertaking would be considered heretical in light of the open-systems ideal. Fortunately, emerging network computing technologies in the area of group scheduling offer a promising solution for MIS managers and end users alike.

The emerging technologies address the needs of the individual as well as the group with a minimum of compromise. Using distributed client/server technology with TCP/IP links, an organization can maintain a main scheduling database server that accesses native clients on each user's device.

To further reduce resistance to this solution, database APIs enable the rugged individualists to interface their favorite scheduling tool with the main scheduling database server. This ability is especially important for palmtop and laptop users. And, after all is said and done, the PC users can continue using whatever individual applications are near and dear to their hearts.

The newer generation of group scheduling applications attempts to bring some of the advantages of mainframe environments to the networked world. They are network savvy, provide modern GUIs, as well as not so modern character interfaces, and allow for instantaneous sharing of scheduling information, be it in the same building, in the same city, or around the world. These new scheduling applications also provide a variety of "front ends" to allow users the ability to access information from any platform or operating environment. Once a solution is in place, all users can enjoy what mainframe users have long taken for granted: effortless communication and scheduling with coworkers and an end to costly telephone and e-mail tag.

Open Standards

Although thousands of PC users still connect to character-based UNIX applications with terminal emulation software and access print and file services with proprietary protocols, the new generation of PC-UNIX products is built on open standards integrating TCP/IP, NFS, and PC X Windows software. These open standard solutions are rapidly gaining widespread acceptance as key interoperability technologies for networking PCs to UNIX-based computer systems.

Emerging in the early 1980s, Ethernet and the TCP/IP protocol suite represented major technological advances in the evolution of PC-UNIX connectivity. Ethernet significantly increased the bandwidth, speed, and functionality of networks from snail-like 2,400–9,600 bps serial lines to a warp speed of 10 Mbps. The TCP/IP protocol is as standard for networking UNIX systems, and has rapidly become a de facto standard for PC-UNIX integration.

Although a variety of other options exist for connecting PCs to UNIX hosts, the TCP/IP protocol suite is scalable, provides transparent internetwork connectivity (interoperability), and integrates Sun Microsystems' Network File System (NFS) as a common element.

The Windows Sockets' Application Programming Interface (WinSock API) is recognized as an open standard specification for the development of Microsoft Windows and Windows NT TCP/IP applications. The objective of WinSock is to provide a single API for application developers and a standard interface that all TCP/IP suppliers can support. A major advantage of WinSock is that applications (X Windows display servers, terminal emulators, SQL Interfaces, etc.) that are compliant with the API will be able to run over any WinSock compliant TCP/IP.

Perhaps one of the most important software products built upon the Ethernet-TCP/IP platform is Sun Microsystems' Network File Server, which has become a de facto standard for PC-UNIX hosts connectivity. NFS provides file and print services and allows PCs to remotely mount UNIX file systems, so that they appear transparent to the PC user, as if they were another drive on the PC.

Switch to Open Systems

Many large enterprises are in the process of switching users from PROFS scheduling and e-mail to UNIX-based scheduling and e-mail. The organizations are using a client/server strategy in their efforts to provide services to all their users, regardless of what platform each user is on.

When PROFS scheduling and e-mail was first introduced, the initial response to PROFS scheduling was: "Why would I want to use this?" But within six months to a year, everyone had to have it. The adoption rate accelerated when key people started to use it—"You were a leper if you didn't have your own PROFS account." There are currently thousands of active users of the PROFS scheduling tool. The users are so dependent upon the information sharing aspect of their system that they have indicated they are individually unwilling to switch to a new system until all users are brought on-line. A disruption of services is unacceptable to them.

Open systems appear to provide some significant advantages over IBM proprietary standards, but many of their claimed benefits may be illusory. Here, we examine the progress of open systems to date, and consider what they really have to offer to cost-conscious mainframe installations.

Availability of PC and workstation business applications is growing rapidly. One of the biggest cost savings associated with migration from mainframes to these LAN-based applications is the ability to outsource business applications that were previously developed and supported in-house. Recent studies demonstrate what many have suspected regarding the rapid data volume growth in LAN traffic and the extremely high peak-to-average ratios associated with that traffic. Data growth places demands on bandwidth availability. Equally important, however, are the low delay demands on the network which also feed bandwidth requirements. It is essential that the low delay tolerance of LAN-based applications are supported through appropriately sized LAN interconnect solutions. LAN interconnect services that minimize latency may be the key to successful distributed computing.

The economic weight of the desktop market is currently attracting a major share of R&D spending and creative energies. This focus is accelerating the movement away from the mainframes and toward downsized LAN-based distributed applications. The one common outcome of distributing applications is increased bandwidth requirements requiring reevaluation of network designs and network service provisioning.

A common flaw in open systems and downsizing plans is to underestimate the relative cost of systems management in the UNIX environment. The cost of management in the traditional mainframe environment is kept down by a mature base of software products, tools, and experienced personnel—the open-systems environment is, by comparison, the domain of a few highly paid professionals, who are needed to maintain and administer the system because of the lack of user friendly, packaged management solutions.

The financial rewards from this growing trend can be significant. One company reportedly reduced computing costs by 70%. Companies are obviously motivated to downsize applications for cost savings. They also report that moving to a LAN-based environment improves service, shortens application development time, and enables access to newer, more productive technologies such as groupware applications. With these benefits to be gained, the trend toward distributed applications will continue and accelerate. Indeed, a recent survey of senior business managers found that a full 35% were actively pursuing downsizing, and an additional 19% were seriously considering it. Interestingly, the applications being downsized are both more complex and more mission critical than previously expected.

RIGHTSIZING

The distributed computing revolution focused on hardware rightsizing, where large mainframes were replaced by networks of powerful workstations in client/server configurations. However, large applications that ran on the mainframe were moved intact to the workstation servers. This lead to little change in the way people write and maintain applications. Programmer productivity fails to keep pace with increased complexity of applications, cost of application development keeps going up, and companies have a hard time adapting in this fast-changing, global economy.

The advent of the microprocessor allowed powerful networked workstations to achieve levels of sophistication previously known only to large minicomputers and mainframes. Corporations have been taking advantage of this revolution by replacing the expensive mainframes with such networks of client and server workstations. Similarly, departments using personal computers understood that these were not designed for cooperative work, and began to invest heavily in networked computers. This phenomenon was termed "rightsizing." UNIX operating systems affords the mix of programming and networking environments.

If one can ignore, for just a moment, the rigidity of a mainframe environment from the user's perspective, one would have to admit that it provides a very efficient model for data sharing and administration. These two ingredients are key in the successful implementation of a corporatewide group scheduling solution. But, as the PC revolution has made abundantly clear, individual needs must also be met.

Unfortunately, a by-product of the PC culture was that it frustrated the growth of workgroup applications and information sharing as network support became problematic and as personal data storage became prevalent. Scheduling tools in particular were demoted from a corporate communication system to the role of a secondary personal desktop accessory. Without the ability to easily share information, the utility of scheduling tools was greatly diminished. As a result, while gaining many advantages in moving to a PC or workstation environment, users lost access to tools and capabilities they may not even have realized were available in the older mainframe world.

The growth of network-ready environments like UNIX and the proliferation of PC networks has reenabled effective group scheduling for the nonmainframe user. The trick is making the scheduling solution available to everyone and minimizing resistance to adoption.

Distributed Object Environment: An Infrastructure for Enterprise Rightsizing

The software community has invested heavily in object-oriented techniques which bring marked improvements in productivity and reliability, due to their emphasis on reuse, as well as adaptation to change.

Some companies allow programmers to build applications by assembling components together, thereby improving programmer productivity. Developers can reuse, or purchase, existing components which adhere to standard interfaces and manipulate them with high-level tools. Most software vendors work with the standards bodies, chiefly the Object Management Group (OMG), to ensure that third-party solutions are available for vertical markets.

Hardware Rightsizing: Half of the Solution

But hardware rightsizing did not fundamentally change the way software was developed or deployed. There is a need to apply rightsizing technology to the large and complex software applications that, ultimately, run today's businesses.

In an environment where mainframes were being replaced by relatively inexpensive workstations, and networks were being reconfigured to match the realities of enterprise-level reorganizations, we saw how application components would have to be added or modified dynamically. Furthermore, the applications themselves would need customization to keep pace with the requirements imposed on enterprises by the global economy.

Our vision of the future is to allow applications to be assembled together from networked components composed of distributed objects.

Software Rightsizing

Companies worldwide are abandoning their mainframes and minicomputers in favor of open-systems desktops and servers. Enterprise computing today relies more on networked configurations of these platforms—networked not only locally, but globally as well. This transition from centralized mainframes to distributed systems is called rightsizing.

For hardware rightsizing to be successful, software rightsizing is essential. Large applications that traditionally resided on mainframes do not fit the distributed computing model.

We are now at the crossroads, where software applications are rapidly becoming too large, sophisticated, and distributed to be contained on one machine. We have reached the intersection of the two vectors shown above. Today's distributed applications must take advantage of networked, distributed hardware. With software rightsizing, the size of any one machine is no barrier if the application is also distributed.

Unfortunately, the software technology to enable distributed applications has lagged behind hardware advancements. These tools and technologies are critical to software rightsizing success.

Why Distributed Objects?

The process of moving a monolithic application from a mainframe to a distributed computing environment means "chunking" the application. Different parts of the software can then run on different computers. A portion of a spreadsheet can run locally on a workstation and transparently access both code and data residing on a variety of remote systems.

A single network management application can be spread across multiple machines over a wide area and interchange information as if it were all on one machine. A computer-intensive scientific application can be decomposed into parallel execution paths and divided among multiple processors in different machines, resulting in much faster execution.

MVS ENVIRONMENTS

MVS (Multiple Virtual Storage) is a mature yet evolving operating system for IBM's or IBM-compatible medium- to large-scale processors. The latest MVS operating systems are called the MVS/Enterprise Systems Architecture (MVS/ESA) and OpenEdition MVS or OS/390. MVS/ESA provides up to 2 gigabytes of virtual storage for each of many tasks that can be running concurrently. To minimize I/O overhead, each job can access multiple shared data spaces, each up to 2 gigabytes of virtual storage. The version of MVS that you use has no effect on any of the basic commands.

MVS operating systems are familiar to thousands of organizations for which MVS and the processors it runs on have become the repository of valuable and critical information resources. In addition to proven reliability, MVS offers the ability to guarantee data integrity, provide automatic data backup, regulate security, analyze resource usage, and provide a range of facilities unmatched in capability at even the most sophisticated network of workstation systems.

In rightsizing a network of resources and users, you can view MVS in a number of ways:

- As a very large computing and data server.
- As the controller of a data warehouse.
- As a peer in a coordinated network of large and small nodes.
- As a point from which to view and control a network of distributed resources.

You may also consider MVS as an extremely large, powerful, and flexible extension for a large number of workstation users. MVS can thus be used as a tool in an enterprise that wants both decentralized or semiautonomous system for its users and, at the same time, efficient use of resources and automated procedures for critical applications and data.

AIX

IBM has implemented AIX (Advanced Interactive Executive) on a number of platforms. These platforms include AIX for IBM RISC System/6000, AIX/RT, AIX/PS2, VM, MVS, and AIX/370. In addition to the base UNIX operating system, IBM implemented a network file system (NFS) and network computing system (NCS) comprising remote procedure calls (RPCs). The rationale for implementing AIX on System/370 environment was to support the client/server solutions where System/370 could be used as a server host in a LAN or other network environments.

MVS/ESA

MVS/ESA was introduced in 1988 along with ESA/370 mainframes. MVS/ESA was designed to take advantage of the increased power of the new hardware. MVS/ESA allows an address space access to one or more data spaces. A data space is like an address space, a virtual storage area. While an address space contains system programs and data, a data space can contain only data. In addition, each data space can provide up to 2 gigabytes of virtual storage for data.

MVS/ESA SP Version 4 extends the processing power of MVS/ESA by providing ways to connect MVS systems in a multisystem environment and in a communication network. A multisystem environment provides the ability to do more work and also enhances availability—if one processor is stopped or fails, another can continue processing the work. MVS/ESA SP Version 4 also introduced the sysplex concept (system complex), which the installation can set up to include multiple MVS systems residing on multiple processors.

OpenEdition MVS (OS/390)

OpenEdition MVS brings together the open world and the MVS worlds, such as

- The standard C language application programming interface with operating systems (POSIX.1).
- The standard shell and utilities interface (POSIX.2).
- A subset of the proposed standard for programming interface to managing threads (POSIX.4a).

OpenEdition MVS provides new MVS commands so that MVS data sets can be copied for access by POSIX applications. Users can copy an MVS data set to a hierarchical file or vice versa. Current MVS applications run as usual and the users enjoy all the services of MVS available.

OpenEdition MVS combines the personal power of the workstation, the flexibility of open systems, and the strength of MVS, to create a new information environment for the future. OpenEdition MVS provides a UNIX-like interface to the UNIX programmer and an MVS-like interface to the TSO user. Thus the users to switch back and forth between TSO interface and the OpenEdition shell interface.

It is true that UNIX-skilled users can use OpenEdition shell interface, whereas the MVS-skilled users can interact via TSO commands and menus. Since the MVS system programmers and application programmers will have access to both sets of interfaces to choose from, it is extremely important that they understand both the UNIX and MVS systems and commands.

The Personal Power of the Workstation

Because the workstation is becoming more powerful, users are becoming more demanding. Increasingly, information systems are user driven. Even where some central management is essential to an enterprise, its value must be demonstrated to users.

The workstation user is increasingly self-sufficient. A growing number of application packages are available on OS/2, UNIX, and other platforms. User interfaces are becoming easier to use and at the same time more sophisticated. An increasing amount of information is becoming accessible through CD-ROM technology and telephony. Yet many workstation users find the need to work together with other users, to share and be part of a network of resources. Linked today with LAN servers and groupware, tomorrow's users will need access to even more information and applications. The workstation user will expect this network of services to be managed elsewhere, freeing the user to be more creative and productive.

The Flexibility of Open Systems

One of the original characteristics of the UNIX world was its spirit of freeware and the sharing of ideas. Gradually, users and manufacturers began to standardize these ideas so that everyone could have a common foundation to build on—a world of products adhering to a set of common or open interfaces.

In the world of open systems, an enterprise using systems that conform to the standard interfaces can exchange or reuse applications, data, and skills on the conforming operating system of any manufacturer.

This world of open systems promises the freedom to design a network of resources best suited to present needs—in terms of capability, performance, and cost—with assurance that the current investment in applications and data will be portable to the new configurations of the future.

A New Information Environment for the Future

OpenEdition MVS takes advantage of the power of the workstation, the flexibility of UNIX systems, and the strengths of MVS to a new environment. Offering new, open interfaces for applications and interactive users, OpenEdition MVS (OS/390) supports and fosters a super environment of larger operating systems or servers and of distributed systems and workstations that share common interfaces.

With OpenEdition MVS, your enterprise has the industrial strength long associated with MVS while gaining access to applications and data in multivendor systems. Your enterprise can create client/server applications primarily developed at workstation systems. At the same time, many new application solutions will become available, developed by vendors, application integrators, and possibly by users at the workstations within your enterprise.

Applications you create or buy that conform to the Portable Operating System Interface (POSIX) 1003.1 standard for C programs (called, for short, the POSIX.1 standard) or, beginning with MVS 5.2.2, that conform with the single UNIX specification (XPG 4.2) can be moved with relative ease among conforming computer systems.

With OpenEdition MVS, your existing investment in MVS applications and data is protected and even enhanced. Meanwhile, new applications will have access to existing data.

Using OpenEdition MVS

Users can switch back and forth between MVS's TSO/E interface and the OpenEdition shell interface. UNIX-skilled users can interact with MVS using a familiar set of standard commands and utilities.

MVS-skilled users can interact with MVS using familiar TSO/E commands and interactive menus to create and manage hierarchical file system files and to copy data back and forth between MVS data sets and files.

Application programmers can code using a standard C language interface and, after making appropriate design decisions, also take advantage of proprietary MVS programming interfaces.

Now your enterprise can use the recognized capabilities of MVS as a powerful platform within an open and expanding environment of computing resources. Starting with MVS 5.1, this new environment includes OpenEdition DCE.

The OpenEdition Shell

The OpenEdition shell is modeled after the UNIX System V shell with some of the features found in the Korn shell. The OpenEdition shell conforms to the POSIX standard 1003.2. The OpenEdition shell is the command processor that you can use to

- Invoke shell commands or utilities that request services from the system, as depicted in Figure 3.1.
- Write shell scripts using the shell programming language.
- Run shell scripts and C language programs interactively (in the foreground), in the background, or in batch.

Interoperability

The OpenEdition provides strong interoperability with MVS and the OpenEdition shell. Interoperability ability allows you to

- Switch between MVS/TSO and OpenEdition shell.
- Move and copy data between MVS data sets and the OpenEdition hierarchical file system.
- Use TSO/E commands or shell commands, or the ISPF shell. For example, you can create directory by using TSO/E MKDIR command, or the OpenMVS ISPF shell, or the UNIX shell *mkdir* command.
- Issue TSO/E commands from the shell command line.
- Edit OpenEdition hierarchical files from the shell command line.
- Write MVS JCL that includes shell commands.

TSO and ISPF

For interactive usage of the MVS facilities, IBM supports two separate products: TSO and SPF. TSO (Time Sharing Option) is a command-driven software product which typical-

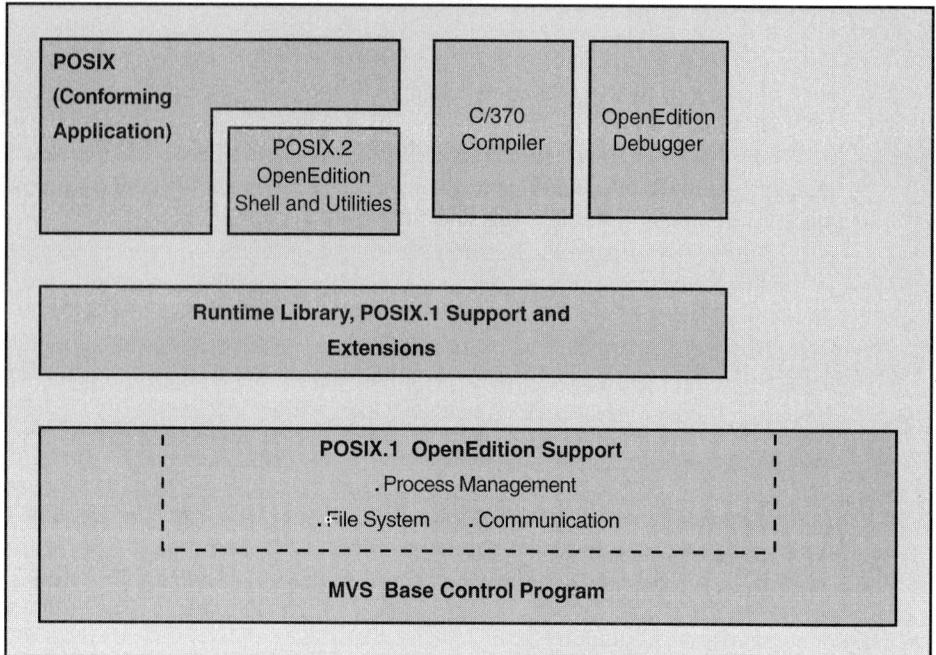

FIGURE 3.1 MVS and OpenEdition shell.

ly employs one-word or one-line commands, while SPF (System Productivity Facility) is a newer, full-screen, menu-driven product which both simplifies and extends the capabilities of TSO.

TSO allows you and a number of other users to use the facilities of the system concurrently and in a conversational manner. You can communicate with the system by typing requests for work (commands) on a terminal. The TSO reference manual(s) describe(s) what each command can do and how to enter a command at your terminal.

ISPF allows you to perform almost all of TSO's functions by using menus and panels—and can often simplify your work on the system by making it unnecessary to remember or key in longer TSO commands. Most experienced TSO/SPF users, however, use a combination of the capabilities of TSO and SPF, choosing to use one product or the other depending on which one happens to be simpler or faster or clearer for the particular application.

History of MVS

MVS descended from the forefather of modern operating systems—the OS. IBM introduced OS, short for "operating system," in 1964 when IBM announced the 360 series of computers. In subsequent years, as IBM introduced additional versions of the OS, it allowed more users the ability to simultaneously run more programs and to let each of these programs use more memory.

IBM called the successive versions MFT (Multiprogramming with Fixed number of Tasks), MVT (Multiprogramming with a Variable number of Tasks, SVS (Single Virtual Storage), MVS/XA Multiple Virtual Storage/Extended Architecture, and MVS/ESA (MVS Extended System Architecture).

MVS grew with the proliferation of users working at interactive terminals needing larger memory and independent virtual storage. MVS/XA increased the number of virtual addresses available to keep track of bytes by increasing the size of the field that holds these addresses, making it a 31-bit addressing scheme. This extended addressing from 16 megabytes in MVS to 2 gigabytes in MVS/XA systems.

MVS/ESA extended the same concept even further by allowing an address space access to one or more data spaces—a virtual three-dimensional system. In addition to the 2 gigabytes a job has available to it for holding instructions and data in an address space, each job can also have access to many data spaces. Thus you can think of data spaces as expanding virtual storage horizontally rather than vertically as in MVS/XA.

Evolution of the MVS Operating System

An operating system is a collection of programs that manage the internal workings of a computer system. A good operating system keeps hardware resources as busy as possible, ensuring that the maximum amount of work is processed, and that each unit of work is processed efficiently. Although an operating system cannot increase the speed of a computer, it can maximize its use, thereby making the computer seem faster. MVS can process large amounts of work efficiently because it keeps track of storage in a way that makes its storage capacity seem greater than it is.

Early operating systems could not meet the demand to process work more quickly because they did not make full use of the processor. In these operating systems, requests for work, called "jobs," entered the system one at a time. The operating system processed each job as a unit and did not start the next job until the one ahead of it had completed. This arrangement could work only if a job could execute continuously. But often a job had to wait, most frequently for information to be read in from or written out to an external media or device such as a tape drive, disk drive, or a printer. Input and output (I/O) still takes a long time as compared to the electronic speed of the processors. Therefore, during an I/O operation, the processor remained idle. The solution was multiprogramming. MVS makes multiprogramming possible by capturing and saving all the relevant information about the interrupted program before allowing another program to execute.

Soon, the processing speed of computers increased so much that, even with multiprogramming, the processor could execute more programs in a given period of time than it could hold in its own storage. Potential processing power remained unused because there was not enough storage.

With the proliferation of users working at terminals (interactive users), installations outgrew early virtual storage systems. By providing a separate virtual storage table for each address space in the system, each address space could have access to the full range of virtual addresses, that is, each address space having access to 16 megabytes of virtual storage.

MVS STRENGTHS

Today, a remarkably large number of business enterprises worldwide depend on the strength of one particular operating system for the critical information processing of bank account balances, product orders, personnel records, payroll checks, progress reports, insurance claims, operating plans, and other information. While making plans to move applications and data to the optimum location in a network, the large, growing business depends more than ever on the dynamic strength of the third building block in our new information environment: MVS.

Today's MVS offers large-scale, high-performance transaction, interactive, and batch computing on a scale unmatched by smaller and less sophisticated operating systems. Moreover, MVS offers tools for managing, analyzing, controlling, and optimizing applications and data and, through its SystemView architecture, a single view of a network and a way to manage it. Among the strengths of MVS are

- The efficient sharing of system resources, including access to high-speed, large-volume storage devices and high-speed printers. (The typical MVS system handles many billions of bytes of storage with millions of requests for data access per day.)
- Sophisticated data backup and archival facilities.
- Thousands of application solutions from IBM and other vendors.
- The ability to handle a large number of interactive users.
- Extensive security and auditing features. The ability to take advantage of IBM's System/390 processors and architecture, including the ESCON architecture.
- Recoverability and system integrity features.
- An outstanding record of reliability and service.
- An extension of the MVS operating system to OpenEdition with POSIX.

SUMMARY

Enterprises are downsizing from mainframes to more cost-effective solutions by utilizing client/server architectures and implementing networked computing technologies such as UNIX. As many companies have discovered, downsizing can prove to be more painful and expensive than anticipated. The growth of network-ready environments like UNIX and the proliferation of PC networks has reenabled effective group scheduling for the nonmainframe user.

MVS operating systems are familiar to thousands of organizations for which MVS and the processors it runs on have become the repository of valuable and critical information resources. MVS is a mature operating system. The latest MVS operating systems, MVS/ESA and OS/390, provide up to 2 gigabytes of virtual storage for each of many tasks that can be running concurrently.

In the following chapters, we will study UNIX and MVS operating systems components and functions in more detail and outline similarities and fundamental differences between the two environments.

4

Getting Started

INTRODUCTION

This chapter is only a brief introduction to UNIX. It is intended to introduce you to the UNIX operating system and does not include information on how to use all of its capabilities. It will provide you with a basic understanding of the UNIX operating system, its file and directory structure, basic UNIX commands, and how to get on-line help.

ENTERING THE UNIX SYSTEM

As in MVS TSO or SPF, each UNIX user also has a *login* name on the system. Your *login* name is your unique identifier to the system. In addition to the *login* name you are assigned a *password*. Passwords should not be trivial (e.g., your names) and should preferably contain letters and digits.

Case Sensitivity

UNIX is a case-sensitive operating system. It treats lowercase characters differently than uppercase characters. For example, the files *readme, Readme, and README* would be treated as three different files. Most command names and files are entirely in lowercase. Therefore, you should generally plan to type in lowercase for most commands, command line arguments, and option letters.

On the other hand, MVS/TSO or SPF are not case sensitive.

Getting the Login Prompt

Before you can start using the system, you must *log in* to it. The method that you use to *log in* varies depending on the type of device that you are using to *log in*. The *login* procedures in both MVS TSO and UNIX systems are similar. Since UNIX is case sensitive, always use caution when selecting or entering login IDs, *usually lowercase.*

When you are assigned your account information, you are also given a *userid* and a password. This combination of information allows you to access your account. Type your userid using lowercase letters; then press the RETURN or ENTER key. If you make a typing mistake, you can correct it by pressing the DELETE key once for each character you wish to erase. However, you must make your corrections before you press the RETURN key.

No matter what type of machine you are working on you should now have received a prompt to *login:*. Enter your *userid* and press RETURN. Now you will be prompted to enter your *password:*. Notice that when you do this, the characters you type are not printed back on the screen. This is a security feature to prevent others from seeing your password. If you have done these two things correctly, you will be logged on shortly. If not, you will be prompted for a *userid* again.

Entering Your Userid and Password

If you are using a TTY-type terminal (a TTY is line-at-a-time oriented as opposed to page oriented) and the screen is blank, you only need to press RETURN and a login prompt should appear on the screen. Since most TSO implementations are custom, the UNIX screen as compared to the TSO screen is much simpler.

If you are using a workstation, you may see a dark screen with a brief message similar to this:

FUNCTION	MVS/TSO	UNIX
Format	**LOGON** user-identity [/password[/newpassword]] [mail/nomail] [notices/nonotices] [reconnect] [options]	**Login:** **Password:** NOTICE: The system will be down from 14:00 to 17:00 today. Remember, Status meeting this Weds at 9:30 AM.

FUNCTION	MVS/TSO	UNIX
Example	**ENTER USERID** (also known as **logonid**): Enter your TSO USERID and default DESTination and press ENTER.	XYZ **login:** Enter your login ID. XYZ could be userID.
Example	**ENTER PASSWORD:** Enter your password and press ENTER.	**Password:** Enter your password.

Almost every login prompt includes the workstation name before the word "**login**."

If the display features a box in the center of the screen, then you are using a workstation that is configured to run a *windowing system*, the X Window system. These machines are called X terminals.

If the screen is entirely black, then a screen-saving program is running automatically to protect the monitor from damage. Moving the mouse or pressing the RETURN key should "wake it up."

After you have entered your *userid*, the system will prompt you for your *password* (by displaying the word "password"). Enter your *password* and press the RETURN key.

If you receive a message similar to "Login failed, please try again," you may have typed your *userid* or *password* incorrectly. Try again, making sure to type in your userid and password correctly. When you have successfully logged on, the system will pause for a moment, and then display a few lines telling you when and from which machine you last logged on and any messages from the system administrator.

Your new account is provided with a set of command procedures which are executed each time you log in. You can change part of your UNIX environment by changing these setup files (accounts are normally set up to produce a default environment).

The system will then display the command prompt. The prompt signals that the system is ready for you to enter your next command. The name of the workstation followed by a percent sign (% for C shell or $ for Bourne shell) forms the command prompt (e.g., XYZ%). Once you finish typing a command, you must always press RETURN to execute it.

Changing Passwords

Once you have successfully logged in, it is time to change your *password.* You should change your password at reasonably frequent intervals for security reasons. Use the UNIX *passwd* command to change your password.

In TSO, new passwords can also be assigned while in a logon screen.

In UNIX, however, you can change your password at any time. You should change it the first time that you log in, and we recommend that you change it on a regular basis. At the command prompt, type the command *passwd.* You will be prompted to enter your old password and be asked twice to enter your new password. Neither your old nor new password will appear on the screen as you type. To be accepted, your password must meet the following conditions:

- It should be at least seven to eight characters long.
- It must not match anything in your UNIX account information, such as your login name or an item from your account information data entry.
- It must not be found in the system's spelling dictionary unless a character other than the first is capitalized. It must not have three or more consecutively repeated characters or words in the dictionary contained within it.

BAD passwords are

- Any single English word (without case variances).
- Name or number that is part of your public records.

GOOD password hints are

- Nonsense words (ex: "smedooly").
- Mix cases (ex: "surPriZe").
- Use symbol characters (ex: "10_blast").
- Combine simple words (ex: "bugfarce").
- Use anagrams (ex: "iwtghn" from "I want to go home now.").
- Take care of your password.
- Remember it (if you do not, you will need the system administrator or "root" user to reset it).

For example, changing your password from *Kat899* to *B00z0oe* will look similar to the following example, except that the keystrokes for your old and new password will not be echoed on the screen.

> *passwd*
> current password: *Kat899*
> New password (? for help): *B00z00e*
> New password (again): *B00z00e*
> Password changed for *userid*

Password changes may not take effect immediately; therefore, you can always use the old one until the new one does take effect.

Altering Terminal and Keyboard Characteristics

You may also reassign the default special key functions to different keys. If you do not like the fact that Ctrl-c terminates your program and you would rather have it be Ctrl-k (for kill), a command of the form:

FUNCTION	MVS/TSO	UNIX
Format	**PROFILE** [options] [CHAR/NOCHAR (character/BS)] [LINE/NOLINE (ATTN/character/CTLX)]	**stty** [options]
Example		**stty** *intr ^k*
	PROFILE line(&) char(!) & - line deletion character ! - character deletion character list - operand is a default if other parameters are skipped.	Ctrl-k is substituted for Ctrl-c

Place this in your *.login* directory, and it will always apply. One important reassignment that might be necessary is the DELETE key. It is sometimes necessary to assign that to the BACKSPACE key.

MVS/TSO will also allow you to interconnect to reestablish a prior terminated session to use all the same terminal profiles and characteristics. However, you must use the same TSO USERID and password of the previous session:

logon *Userid/password* **reconnect**

USING THE UNIX SYSTEM

Once you succeed in establishing a connection, you are prompted for your login-name or username. Type your login name followed by the RETURN key. For example,

login: *omar*

Notice that the login name must be typed in lowercase; most UNIX systems are case dependent. Typing mistakes can be corrected at any time before a RETURN is entered. A **Ctrl-u** key combination can be used to erase the entire line and a key marked DELETE or BACKSPACE can be used to erase a character.

After you enter your account name, the system will prompt you for a password with the line:

Password:

You then type in your password. Your password will not be echoed on the screen to ensure confidentiality. Enter a RETURN after your password. Note that the Ctrl-u and DELETE keys will work here too, but like the letters of the password itself, their actions will not be displayed (or echoed). Also note that although you can select passwords that are longer than eight characters and submit them to the prompt, the UNIX system will always ignore all characters beyond the eighth.

If an error occurs while logging in, the message

Login incorrect
login:

will appear. This means that the combination of the account name and password did not match. Make sure that you have typed your account name and password correctly and that these are the correct ones for the appropriate machine. UNIX will repeatedly ask for your account name and password.

If you change your mind and wish to terminate your session before starting it, simply type **Ctrl-z** at any of the prompts. Ctrl-z signals the end of input (or end of file) to the UNIX system.

Starting the Session

TSO

After entering your logonid and password, you will be "loggedon," recognized as a TSO user. You will be shown several lines of messages, some of which are system generated and some of which may be announcements, followed by the TSO READY prompt. The last line should simply say READY, as shown below.

READY

Whenever the READY prompt appears, TSO is ready to receive your next command. TSO allows you to spend as much time viewing a particular screen as you like. However, it also informs you when there is more for you to see. TSO does this by placing three asterisks side by side on the last line of the screen (e.g., ***). To move to the next screen—and to get rid of the three asterisks—press the ENTER key.

If you have worked with **SPF**, you are probably more familiar using "menus" to select the tasks you want to perform. Since UNIX displays more of a command-oriented screen structure, it will look quite different than you are used to in SPF, as shown below:

ISPF PRIMARY OPTION MENU

OPTION ===>

			UNIX Equivalents
0	**ISPF PARMS**	Specify terminal/user parms.	*terminal* type:
1	**BROWSE**	Display source/data output.	
2	**EDIT**	Create or change source data.	*vi* or other editor command:
3	**UTILITIES**	Perform utility functions.	*utlity* commands
4	**FOREGROUND**	Invoke language processor in foreground.	*shell* or standard commands
5	**BATCH**	Submit job for language processing.	*shell* or standard commands
6	**COMMAND**	Enter TSO command or CLIST.	single command or a shell construct
7	**DIALOG TEST**	Perform dialog testing.	
8	**LM UTILITIES**	Perform library management utility functions.	

OPTION ===>			
C	**CHANGES**	Display summary of changes for this release.	
T	**TUTORIAL**	Display information about TSO/SPF.	*man* pages
X	**EXIT**	Terminate ISPF using log and list defaults.	*logout* **or CONTROL keys**

UNIX

After cross-checking a correct account and password combination, the computer will log you in and display several pieces of information:

***Message-of-the-day*:** This includes information on the version of the system in use. It also contains extremely important and relevant announcements that concern almost every user of the system. Be sure to read the message of the day.

Terminal type: UNIX will ask you what kind of terminal you are using:

TERM = (VT100)

where VT100 is the default terminal type. If your terminal is not a VT100, enter the terminal type (it will be displayed as you type) followed by

RETURN.

If you are not on a VT100 or you do not know what type of terminal you are on, simply hit RETURN. (You should discern the terminal type before you log in again. If the terminal is not set correctly, some programs such as the editor will not function properly.) If you did not supply the correct terminal type, do not try to invoke the *vi* text editor. The **Ctrl-u** and **DELETE** keys work here the same as they do when typing your account name or password.

Eventually, a **%** or **$** prompt will appear on the bottom left-hand side of the screen indicating that you have started your computing session, as compared to READY for TSO response. The system is now ready to respond to your commands.

Special Keys and Control Characters

SPF/TSO control majority of the terminal functions via PF (program function) keys, as follows:

KEYS	DESCRIPTION
PF1	Help
PF2	Split screen into two logical screens
PF3	End (save) the current session
PF4	Return to main menu
PF5	Repeat / find

KEYS	DESCRIPTION
PF6	Repeat / change
PF7	Scroll up the screen
PF8	Scroll down the screen
PF9	Swap screens
PF10	Scroll left
PF11	Scroll right
PF12	Cancel and return to command line

UNIX controls functions differently and recognizes special keys and control-character key strokes and assigns them special functions. A special key such as the DELETE key is usually mapped to the ERASE function, which erases the most recent character that you typed on the current line. A control keystroke such as **Ctrl-c** is invoked by holding down the key labeled CONTROL and pressing the **C** key (in the same manner that you hold down the SHIFT key and press the **C** key to generate a capital C). The notation for control characters is usually **^C** or **Ctrl-c**. Some standard special keys and control characters are summarized below:

MVS/TSO	FUNCTION/DESCRIPTION	UNIX SPECIAL KEY
DEL	Acts as a rubout or erase key. Pressing DELETE once will back up and erase one character, allowing you to correct and retype mistakes.	**DELETE**
BACKSPACE	This key is sometimes used as the rubout key instead of the DELETE key. Otherwise, it is mapped as a backspace key, which generates a ^H on the display.	**BACKSPACE**
ERASE EOF	^U erases the entire command line. It is also called the line kill character.	**Ctrl-u**
	^W erases the last word on the command line.	**Ctrl-w**
	^S stops the flow of output on the display.	**Ctrl-s**
	^Q resumes the flow of output stopped by Ctrl-s.	**Ctrl-q**
PF12	^C interrupts a command or process in progress and returns to the command line. This will usually work; if it doesn't, try typing several ^C's in a row. If it still doesn't work, try typing ^\, q (for quit), exit, ^D, or ^Z.	**Ctrl-c**
PF3	^Z suspends a command or process in progress.	**Ctrl-z**
	^D generates an end-of-file character. It can be used to terminate input to a program, or to end a session with a shell.	**Ctrl-d**
	^\ quits a program and saves an image of the program in a file called core for later debugging.	**Ctrl-**

About UNIX Commands

UNIX has a wide range of commands that allow you to manipulate not only your files and data, but also your environment. This section explains the general syntax of UNIX commands to get you started. A UNIX command line consists of the name of the UNIX command followed by its arguments (options, filenames, and/or other expressions) and ends with a RETURN. Functionally, UNIX commands are similar to verbs in English. The option flags act like adverbs by modifying the action of the command, and filenames and expressions act like objects of the verb. The general syntax for a UNIX command is

command [-flag options] file/expression

The brackets around the flags and options are a shorthand way to indicate that they are often optional and need to be invoked only when you want to use that option. Also, flags need not always be specified separately, each with their own preceding dash. Many times, the flags can be listed one after the other after a single dash. Some examples later on will illustrate this concept. You should follow several rules with UNIX commands:

- Almost all commands must be typed in lowercase.
- Each word on a command line must be typed in lowercase.
- UNIX commands can only be entered at the shell prompt.
- UNIX command lines must end with a RETURN.
- UNIX options often begin with a "-" (minus sign).
- More than one option can be included with many commands.

Command Anatomy

You've probably been wondering what the relationship is between such invocations as *ls* and *ls*, *-F* and *cd*, and *cd dir_name*. It is the first word that identifies the UNIX command. The hyphen ('-') character is used to specify "options" which cause the basic command to have a slightly different effect. Words appearing after the command name and any options selected are called "arguments" and usually point UNIX to a file or directory to perform the command on. The *command name -options arguments* format is not necessary, but it is the form of most of the basic UNIX commands. Below are two annotated examples to further stress (or emphasize) the point.

EXAMPLE	COMMAND NAME	OPTIONS	ARGUMENTS
ls -F text	*ls*	*-F*	*text*
mv poem poem.bad	*mv*	*none*	*poem; poem.bad*

Selected UNIX Commands

Let us get started by becoming familiar with some simple UNIX commands and their functions. Like the *passwd* command you have already used, all UNIX commands consist of some characters typed at the prompt followed by pressing the RETURN key to tell UNIX to process the command. Most UNIX commands have lowercase names and thus must be typed in lowercase because UNIX is case sensitive (UNIX recognizes "A" and "a," "B" and "b," etc., as different symbols).

One simple command, tells you the current date and time.

date

Fri Mar 4 11:25:25 EST 1996

Another command displays the calendar for this month.

cal

March 1996

S	M	Tu	W	Th	F	S
1	2					
3	4	5	6	7	8	9
10	11	12	13	14	15	16
17	18	19	20	21	22	23
24	25	26	27	28	29	30
31						

***ls* and *cat* commands:**

Let us try the *ls* command. The list you see is a list of files and directories in your sample account. (For now, don't worry about what exactly a file or a directory is.) Now let us look at the contents of one of the files. To output the contents of a text file use the *cat* command. We will examine the file called "fluff," so type *cat fluff* at the prompt.

cat fluff
Welcome to UNIX—contents of file fluff

For a little more practice, try the UNIX command *wc* on the file "fluff" (type *wc fluff*). The letters "**wc**" stand for "word count," but you should get three numbers from *wc*. The first number indicates how many lines are in the file, the second number indicates the number of words, and the third number indicates the number of characters in the file.

wc fluff
1 (# of lines)
3 (# of words)
15 (# of characters)

You have now learned four simple UNIX commands. Do you remember what each one does? Review them:

passwd	Change your password.
ls	List contents of the current directory.
cat filename	Output the contents of file, filename to the screen.
wc filename	Show the number of lines, words, and characters in the file.

***Setup* and *Status* Commands:**

MVS/TSO COMMAND	FUNCTION	UNIX COMMAND
LOGOFF	End your UNIX session.	*logout*
LOGON	Change password by prompting for old and new passwords.	*passwd*
PROFILE	Set terminal options.	*stty*
&SYSDATE, &SYSSDATE	Display or set the date.	*date*
STATUS	Display information about users.	*finger*
	Display information about processes.	*ps*
PROFILE	Display or change current environment.	*env*
	C shell command to *set* shell variables.	*set*
	C shell command to define command abbreviations.	*alias*
	C shell command to display recent commands.	*history*

Getting On-Line Help with Commands

The standard on-line help facility available with UNIX is electronic reference manuals, known as the *man pages*, and you access them with the *man* command.

man command-name

The man pages provide an in-depth description of command-name, with an explanation of its options, examples, and further references. The information is an electronic duplicate of the paper reference manual pages. Use the man command for explicit information about how to use a particular command. Use the *-k* option to search for a keyword among the one-line descriptions in the help files.

man -k keyword

You can read about the *man* command itself using man. Type *man* at the prompt. You can see the command summary by typing

man man

In addition, other applications that reside on your system may have *man* pages. These pages can often be called up in the same manner as the operating system man pages.

The *man* command displays a command syntax plus a detailed description of the commands including its options and arguments. Also, man displays examples of command usage and provides other information such as files used, related commands, diagnostics, and possible problems.

MVS/TSO	UNIX
help help	*man cal*
help *command-name*	*cal NAME* *cal - print calendar*
SYNOPSIS	*SYNOPSIS*
help *command-name* [[[function] [syntax] [operands]] [all]]	*cal [[month] year]*
Obtain information about the command, function, syntax, operands.	*DESCRIPTION*
help listc	*man stty*

cal prints/displays a calendar for the specified *year*. If a month is also specified, a calendar for just that month is printed. If neither is specified, a calendar for the present month is printed. The year can be between 1 and 9999. The month is a decimal number between 1 and 12.

Examples

The command

> *--More--*

Will give you information on using the *cal* command. If the whole page cannot fit on your screen you will see a *--More--* at the bottom of the page. If you want to see more of the file press the **<SPACEBAR>.** If you are finished viewing and you want to quit the man pages use Ctrl-c.

Commonly Used Commands

cp (copy)

This command stands for copy and is used for copying one file to another. Type the command

> *cp .profile temp2*

This copies the file *.profile* to another called *temp2*. If *temp2* had already existed, its previous contents would've been erased. Files can also be copied to another directory. The command

** /usr/tmp*

would copy all the files in the current directory to the directory */usr/tmp*.

rm (remove)

The *rm* utility is used for erasing files and directories:

rm temp2

This removes the file *temp2*. Once a file is removed, it cannot be restored. To cover situations where mistakes might occur, a switch *-i* appended to this command will request a yes or no response before deleting the file. Type the command

rm -i temp1

Note that switches are written before the filenames. Answer *Y* to the prompt so that *temp1* is removed.

head

This is used to view the first few lines of a file. It accepts a switch specifying the number of lines to view. The command

head -2 temp

would list the first 2 lines of the file *temp* on the console. What is the command to view the first 10 lines of the file *.profile*?

tail

This is used to view the last few lines of a file. It accepts a switch specifying the number of lines to view. The command

tail -2 temp

would list the last 2 lines of the file *temp* on the console. What is the command to view the last 10 lines of the file *.profile*?

lp (line printer)

This command is used to obtain a hard-copy printout of a file. Only type this command if a printer is attached to the computer system.

lp temp

wc (word count)

This utility displays a count of the number of characters, words, and lines in a file. Type the command

wc temp

This prints out a list of the number of lines, words, and characters, respectively. The switches for this utility are

-l	Print line count.
-c	Print character count.
-w	Print word count.

pr (print)

The print utility prints the file to *stdout* (standard output). The switches it accepts are

-ln	Set page length in lines to *n*.
-wn	Set line length in characters to *n*.
-n	Number the output lines.
-t	Do not print page header or trailer.
-digit	Number of columns to use.
+digit	Start at page number.

Type the command

pr -2 -n temp

This prints the file *temp* to *stdout* (standard output), using two columns per line, numbering each line.

who

This command displays a list of the users of the system. Using the *-u* switch displays a list of those users currently logged into the UNIX server. Type the command

who -u

hello

This command sends interactive messages between users. Identify a user from the list printed by the previous *who* command. When a user receives a message, they should respond. The interactive exchange is canceled by using the **Ctrl-d** keys. When this occurs, the message "end of message" appears on the other terminal, and control is returned to the shell.

mesg (message)

This command permits or denies messages invoked using *write*. The switches it uses are *-y* and *-n*.

news

The *news* command keeps the user informed of current events.

grep

The *grep* command searches a file for a pattern. The following command

grep 'change' temp

searches the file *temp* in the current directory for the text string 'change.'

Using the * wildcard specifies all files, and using the switch *-n* will display on which line the text string is found. What is the command to search the file .profile for the text string *'TERM'* (case sensitive).

time

This command times how long it takes to execute a given command. Type the command,

time ls -la

The command responds with the elapsed time during the command, the time spent in the system, and the time spent in execution of the command.

cal (calendar)

This command prints a calendar to the screen.

man (manual)

This command locates and prints the reference page for a specified item. Type the command,

man df

The : represents a prompt. Pressing ENTER will continue the display. To quit from the *man*, type *q*. The *man* command can also accept the following names as switches.

ADM	System administration
C	Commands
M	Miscellaneous
F	File formats

HW	Hardware dependent
S	Subroutines and libraries
CP	Programming commands
DOS	DOS subroutines and libraries
LOCAL	Local utilities for your system

An example command which calls up the reference section on "Miscellaneous features" is (this may not apply to all UNIX systems).

man M

passwd (password)

All users in UNIX are assigned passwords. Currently, there is a password assigned to the user. This is changed using the *passwd* utility. The user would type the command

passwd

The utility asks for the new password (twice, to make sure you didn't misspell it). The user types in the new password, but notice that it will not be displayed on the screen when typed (for security reasons). The new password would then be in effect. If the user were to log in again, the system would ask for this password to be typed before allowing access.

mv (move)

The *mv* command is used for moving or renaming files. Type the command

mv temp temp2

This renames the file *temp* to *temp2*. As an example (do not type this), the command

mv temp2 /usr/tmp

would move the file *temp2* into the directory */usr/tmp* (it would no longer appear in your home directory).

Directory Management Commands

UNIX systems support hierarchical directory structures. Some of the commands used for directory maintenance are

pwd	Print current working directory.
cd	Change directory.

mkdir	Make a subdirectory.
rmdir	Remove a subdirectory.

pwd (print working directory)

This command prints the current working directory on the console screen. In UNIX, the hard disk area is divided into directories, much as a book is subdivided into chapters and paragraphs. The directories form a hierarchical level, which simplifies the organization of the files on the system. The topmost directory in UNIX is called *root* and consists of a number of subdirectories grouped according to function.

bin	system binary executables.
boot	file for UNIX boot code.
dev	filenames for system devices, terminals, disks, etc.
dos	file for code that boots DOS from a DOS partition.
etc	system administration files and tools, system scripts (also tcp/ip information files).
lib	library routines.
lost+found	unreferenced files are placed here by *fsck*.
mnt	empty directory used for mounting temporary file systems.
shlib	shared libraries.
tcb	trusted computing base directory, keeps trusted computing information, passwords, and audit trails.
tmp	scratch pad directory for temporary files. Users must have read/write access.
u	user files if a *u* file system is requested during installation.
unix	unix kernel.
usr	application- and system-specific information.

As you can see from the previous directory tree, there are lots of subdirectories underneath *root*.

When you use the *ls* command to list the file contents of a directory, those entries that are directories are preceded with a "**d**" character. The sample screen below shows this.

```
ls -la
total 19 files
drwxr-sr-x    3   b_brown    512   Nov 24 12:05   .
drwxr-sr-x   46   root      1024   Nov 23 16:46   ..
-rw-r--r--    1   b_brown   2501   Mar 3 1992     .profile
drwxr-s---    2   b_brown    512   Nov 24 12:05   data files
-rw-r----     1   b_brown      0   Nov 24 12:05   dirlist
-rw-r-----    1   b_brown     24   Nov 5 08:59    tmp
```

Note that data files is a subdirectory. There are two other subdirectory entries in the listing.

.	the current directory
..	the parent directory (upwards toward /)

cd (change directory)

This command is used to change the current directory. For each of the following commands, enter the current working directory after the command is executed.

cd .	....
cd ..	....
cd /	....
cd $HOME	....

mkdir (make directory)

This command makes a subdirectory under the current directory. Enter the command you would use to create a subdirectory called *junk.*

rmdir (remove directory)

This command removes (deletes) a subdirectory under the current directory. Enter the command you would use to delete a subdirectory called *junk.*

ERROR CORRECTION

Provided the return key has not been pressed, it is possible to correct typing mistakes. This can be done by erasing a single character or deleting a complete line.

Erasing Characters

The *erase* character is used to correct single-character mistakes. This is usually the BACKSPACE key (**Ctrl-h**) or the hash (#), such as

$ dar#y#te	Wed Mar 13 16:45:34 EST 1996
$ date	Wed Mar 13 16:45:34 EST 1996

Erasing Complete Lines

The *kill* character is used to delete complete lines. This is usually either a control character (**Ctrl-u**) or the at (@) character. The system will respond to the kill character by starting a new line, for example,

$ daatte@
date Wed Mar 13 16:45:34 EST 1996

ABORTING PROGRAM EXECUTION

If a program gets stuck in a loop, or produces too much output, the program can be interrupted by using another control character, which is usually the DELETE (**DEL**) key.

There are also characters that stop new characters from appearing on the display. **Ctrl-s** is usually used to stop the flow of data and **Ctrl-q** is used to start it.

EXITING THE UNIX SYSTEM

When you are finished with your session, you must exit. If you had a single shell, you would exit using the exit or logout command. As in TSO (**logoff**), the standard method for logging out of UNIX is to press **Ctrl-d** or type the command *logout*, as shown below:

FUNCTION	MVS/TSO	UNIX
Format	**logoff** [DISCONNECT/HOLD]	*logout*

Workstations and TTY Terminals

To end a work session, you must explicitly log out of a UNIX session. To do this, type *logout* at the command prompt. Once you have logged out, the system will either display the *login* prompt again or begin executing a screen saver program. You should never turn a workstation off. Turning off a terminal does not necessarily log you out.

X Terminals

To log out of the X Window system from an X terminal, move the cursor into the console window (it is labeled "console"), type the command *exit,* and press RETURN. If you try to use the *logout* command in the console window, you will receive the message, "Not in login shell." If you used the *startx* command to start the X session, following the instructions in the previous paragraph will end the X session but will not log you off. The X windows and background will vanish, and you will be returned to a text-only display. Type either the command *logout* or the command *exit* to log out.

SUMMARY (SIMPLE COMMAND REVIEW)

Now, you should be able to start and end a UNIX session, set your terminal characteristics, use special keys and control characters, learn command structures and the use of some basic commands, learn to manipulate directories and print your files, and learn how to get help.

You will become familiar with the UNIX commands for such simple operations as logging in, copying, moving, removing and viewing files, and changing directories. Below is a chart with some of the commands we will learn in later sections:

MVS/TSO COMMAND	DESCRIPTION	UNIX COMMAND
	Prints calendar on the screen.	*cal*
ALLOCATE or LIST	Outputs the contents of file, filename to the screen.	*cat filename*
ALLOCATE	Changes to the user's home directory.	*cd*
FREE, ALLOCATE	Changes working directory to *dir_name.*	*cd dir_name*
ALLOCATE, PROTECT	Changes the permissions on a file or directory, permission(s) filename(s).	*chmod class(es) {+,-,=}*
COPY	Makes a copy of source and name it *dest.*	*cp source dest*
&SYSSDATE, &SYSDATE	Prints date and time.	*date*
LISTDS	Tells what kind of file filename is.	*file filename*
	Tells who is logged on to the local machine.	*finger*
	Gives some information about user userid.	*finger -m userid*
RECEIVE	Checks for newly received mail.	*from*
FIND	Searches for a pattern.	*grep*
EDIT	Views first few lines of as file.	*head*
SEND	Sends interactive messages between users, prints words matching word in the system dictionary.	*hello* *look word*
LISTCAT, LISTDS, LISTALC	Lists contents of the current directory.	*ls*
LISTCAT, LISTDS	Identifies files, directories, and programs in the current directory.	*ls -F*
LISTALC	Lists the contents of directory *dir_name.*	*ls dir_name*
RECEIVE	Reads mail that was sent to you.	*mail*
TRANSMIT	Sends electronic mail to *userid.*	*mail userid*
HELP	Consults the manual page for command	*man command*
	permit/deny messages using *write.*	*mesg*
ALLOCATE	Makes a new directory called *dir_name.*	*mkdir dir_name*
<ENTER>	Like *cat* with a pause to read screenfuls of texts (Use RETURN for next line and SPACE for next screenful.)	*more*
RENAME	Moves (renames) source to *dest.*	*mv source dest*
LISTBC	Keeps users informed of current events.	*news*
LOGON	Changes your password.	*passwd*
DSPRINT, OUTPUT PRINTDS	Prints or displays standard output.	*pr*
LISTCAT	Prints working directory.	*pwd*
RENAME	Removes (erases) the file *file.*	*rm file*
DELETE, FREE	Removes the directory *dir_name.*	*rmdir dir_name*

MVS/TSO COMMAND	DESCRIPTION	UNIX COMMAND
PROFILE	Sets or modifies terminal characteristics.	*stty*
EDIT	Views last few lines of a file.	*tail*
TIME	Time to execute a command.	*time*
STATUS	Gives information about programs running on the local machine. Displays a count of lines, words, characters; shows the number of lines, words, and characters in file; displays the list of users on the system.	*w* *wc* *wc filename* *who*
&SYSUID	Gives your *userid.*	*whoami*

5

UNIX File System

INTRODUCTION

The UNIX operating system is a tool for managing information, which is stored in files. This chapter describes the UNIX utility programs that allow you to manage your files. Periodically, during your interactions with the UNIX system, you have to remove old information, make room for new information, adjust the file access privileges, and occasionally acquire files from other users. In this chapter, you will be introduced to details of commonly used files and directories, commands to manipulate them, and some features of file system security.

A file is a collection of letters, numbers, and special characters: it may be a program, a database, a dissertation, a reading list, or a simple letter. Most operating systems, including UNIX and MVS systems, contain programs to display information about files, to create ordinary files, to move ordinary files from one location to another, to rename files, to make copies of files, and to remove files. You need to perform these functions as necessary on your collection of files.

A file system is the organizational framework for the files and is a logical method for organizing and storing large amounts of information in a way which makes it easy to manage. The file is the smallest unit in which information is stored. On many computer systems, files are organized by lumping them together into one big heap.

Unfortunately, a simple file system is inappropriate for a multiuser computer system with large disks that can store several hundred thousand files. For convenience, the UNIX files are housed in directories, and you can create directories as needed. The key idea of the UNIX file system is that it is hierarchical, like a family tree. Directories can contain both files and directories.

In a multiuser operating system, all files are owned by someone, and it is necessary to have a privilege system so that owners can protect their files from unwanted access by others. To protect privacy and data from misuse, each file has an access permission that governs as to who and how you can access those files. In a multiuser, multiprocessor system, access modes are a necessary nuisance of shared computer systems.

One of the novel features of the UNIX system is the association of the I/O hardware of the computer with special files. Access to I/O hardware itself mimics access to ordinary disk files. Each I/O device (printer, disk, plotter, tape, terminal, etc.) is associated with at least one special file. A program can access a special file, as if it were a disk file, to access the I/O hardware.

The UNIX file system has several important features. To you, the user, it appears as though there is only one type of file in UNIX—the file which is used to hold your information.

STRUCTURE OF THE UNIX FILE SYSTEM

The UNIX file system is more than a big bunch of files; files are collected in directories, and directories are arranged in a logical hierarchy. The hierarchy makes it easier to organize and arrange your collection of files. Although the file system is often described as an inverted tree, the best analogy for the system is that of an organization chart. Figure 5.1 shows part of a typical UNIX file system structure.

File Types or Formats

Many different files are known to UNIX, although UNIX itself does not require its files to obey any particular naming restrictions according to these types. To examine file types, use the *file* command. It will tell you whether a file is a program, a command procedure, a text file, a binary file, a source file for some particular programming language, or the like.

The *file* command gives you detailed information about the specific type of a file. In the section on the *ls* command, we saw that the *ls -F* command will tell you general information about a file.

Let us get specific information about the mosaic.ps file, that is located in our postscript directory. For example:

file postscript/mosaic.ps
mosaic.ps: postscript file -version 2.0

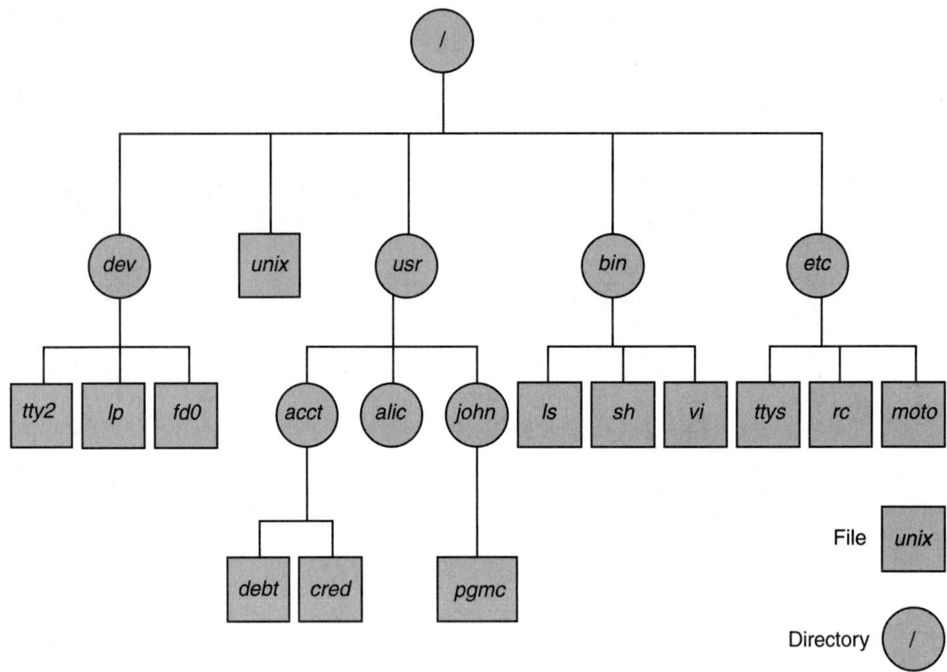

FIGURE 5.1 UNIX file system.

file test.doc
test.doc: English text

file .login
.login: ascii text

file myshar
myshar: shell commands

For every UNIX application and display device, there are different file types or formats for input and/or output. It is not always easy to tell the type of a file. UNIX recognizes four types of files:

- Ordinary files (also known as disk files)
- Directories
- Special files
- Pipes (first-in, first-out, or FIFO, files)

Ordinary Files (Also Known as Disk Files)

An ordinary file is used to store information. An ordinary file might contain a program that you can execute, the text of a document, the record of a company, or any other type of information that can be stored in a computer. Ordinary files are a vital part of a computer system, because they allow information to be stored permanently. Without long-term information storage, the information processing of computers would not be very useful.

There are two types of ordinary files: text files and binary files. *Text files* contain only ASCII (American Standard Code for Information Interchange) characters, whereas binary files may contain all 256 possible values for each byte. The source file for a computer program consists of a series of characters with lines delimited by the newline character. One example of an ordinary text file is the message-of-the day file (*'/etc/motd'*) that is printed each time you log on to your system. You can display the message-of-the day file by using the UNIX utility *cat* command:

cat /etc/motd
"The system will be down ..."

Files that contain codes that are not part of the ASCII character set are called *binary files*. Since *binary files* use full range of possible values for the bytes in the file, binary files are a slightly more efficient way to store information. A binary file cannot be typed directly on your terminal because most of the 256 possible values for each byte are not printable characters. However, you can inspect the contents of a binary file by using the octal dump (*od*) program. *od* takes the values in a file and converts them into printable characters. A binary (object) program consists of the sequence of words to be loaded into memory when the program executes.

Files that you create belong to you—you are said to "own" them—and you can set access permissions to control which other users can have access to them. Files are always contained within a directory. Virtually every command that you enter references ordinary files. Four commands are especially important for controlling your collection of ordinary files: *mv* (move), *cp* (copy), *ln* (link), and *rm* (remove).

A subclass of the ordinary file is the *hidden file*. The names of hidden files always begin with a period (.), and each file has a special function. Hidden files are so named because using *ls* command without options will not list them. You must use the command *ls -a* (list all files) to see them. The justification for having hidden files is that if you do not see them, you are less likely to damage them. The following table summarizes common hidden files and their functions.

FILENAME	FUNCTION
.cshrc	Defines environment to the **C** shell.
.exrc	Defines editing environment to the *ex* editor.
.forward	Defines a forwarding address for electronic mail.

FILENAME	FUNCTION
.history	Saves history list.
.hushlogin	Disables some *login* messages.
.login	Defines environment at login time, regardless of shell.
.logout	Defines environment at logout time.
.mailrc	Defines environment for the *mail* program.
.netrc	Defines parameters to *ftp* (file transfer program).
.profile	Defines environment to the Bourne shell.
.rhosts	Defines private remote hosts.

Directory Files

Directory is a sort of library that contains a collection of files, such as programs, tables, and data files. The UNIX operating system maintains the directory system. Executing programs can read directory files, add an entry to the list of files in a directory by asking the system to create a file, or remove an entry from a directory by asking the system to delete a file. The file structure, illustrated in Figure 5.1, resembles an inverted tree with a single root node. Called *root*, this node is referred to as "/." The operating system uses the directories */dev*, */users*, */etc*, */bin*, and */usr* as the basic set. Typically, these directories contain

DIRECTORY	DESCRIPTION
/	This is the root directory. It is always at the top of the hierarchical file system. The */root* directory contains files related directly to the kernel.
/dev	This is the devices directory and contains information about the special files that are used to interface to hardware devices, such as terminals, printers, and disks.
/bin	This contains the most commonly used utility programs or commands. Other commands are normally located in */usr/bin* and */etc*, although any directory can contain commands.
/lib	The */lib* directory is a library of binary code fragments used by the C programmers that can be incorporated into longer programs.
/etc	The */etc* directory contains any files, programs, and tables required for booting and halting the system, as well as the *password* table, which is used to record data on users. This directory also may include "the message of the day," system start-up procedures, and the file containing terminal characteristics. This directory is under exclusive control of the systems administrator and no user data should be allowed in the */etc* directory. In fact, no files in this directory should have write permission for anyone but the systems administrator.
/tmp	This directory contains temporary files which will be automatically deleted at a later stage.
/unix	This is the directory file containing the heart of the UNIX operating system, called the *kernel*.

DIRECTORY	DESCRIPTION
/usr	The */usr* directory is the primary directory for commands, program files, and user data. Typically, a file system, for example, */users,* is mounted under the */usr* directory. Users can create further levels of directories under it to logically catalog their own groups of files, by project, username, or type of file (e.g., executable, data, source, etc.).

The following is a general-purpose directory that contains a number of subdirectories which are for general use:

/usr/bin	Utility programs
/usr/tmp	Temporary files
/usr/dict	Word lists
/usr/games	Games
/usr/include	C include files
/usr/mail	Mailboxes
/usr/lib	Object libraries
/usr/man	Programmers manual

Originally, all the home directories for users were kept under this directory, but on many present-day systems, these home directories may be kept on a different disk that is normally defined directly under the root directory.

Each user has a special directory called home directory. When you log onto the system, you are placed in your home directory. During the course of the session, you are free to move from one directory to another using the *cd* command:

cd /bin
pwd
/bin

The argument *cd* specifies the directory you want to move to. The directory you are in is called the current directory or the working directory, and its name can be printed by the *pwd* (print working directory) command. The default destination directory for *cd* is your home directory, so you can easily return to your home directory.

Directory Structure

To manage the complexity of proliferating files, UNIX makes use of the notion of directories. Directories are organizational units that allow the user to group files or store them in bundles (like file cabinets). To use UNIX effectively it is important to understand UNIX's concept of files and directories.

The notion of nesting files in directories and directories, in turn, in other directories is referred to as *hierarchical file organization.* In this type of structure, there is usually one directory known as the *root* directory. With the exception of the root directory, every file and every other directory in the UNIX file system is "contained" in some other directory. The relationship between a file (or a directory) and the directory in which it is contained is often likened to a child/parent relationship.

The UNIX system is similar to the DOS system in that its disk space has a *root* directory. Unlike the DOS system, however, a UNIX compute server has only a single *root* directory known as the *root* of the file system (the DOS system has a root directory for every disk or disk partition).

The Current Working Directory

At any point you are working in a particular directory, called the *current working directory* (or *CWD*). The system keeps track of your current working directory at all times, and it assumes that every file you refer to is in that directory, unless you explicitly tell it otherwise by supplying a full file path. You can change your CWD with the *cd* command.

The Home Directory

When you first log in, you land in a special directory known as your *home directory*. In this home directory of your account, you are allowed to create files and delete them; it is the first CWD of your login session. Your home directory is determined when your account is created. You can switch back to your home directory with the *cd* command without any supplied arguments.

Paths

To the UNIX system, every file or directory is uniquely identified by the sequence of subdirectories that contain it, starting from the root of the file system. This name is known as an *absolute path*. To find out the absolute path of your home directory, issue the *print-working-directory* command:

pwd

If you are user *omar* and you issue the *pwd* command, then the command's output might look like this:

/home/cscwgrp/omar

The "/" character separates a directory from its parent directory. Reading right to left, the result of the output of *pwd* is interpreted as follows:

The current working directory is called *omar*, and it is contained in the directory (i.e., it is a subdirectory) called *cscwgrp*, which is in turn contained in the directory *home*, which is finally a subdirectory of the root directory known simply as "/". The *pwd* command helps you determine in which directory you are located at any particular point of your session. The *pwd* command can be issued at any time from a given shell.

Since absolute filenames can be very long due to directory nesting, UNIX provides a second method of naming files, relative to your current working directory (the CWD). Such filenames are known as relative pathnames. When you supply filenames (or paths) that do not start with the slash (/) to a UNIX command, it is assumed that the files are located in the CWD (or that the paths are followed, starting at the CWD). Most of the time, you will refer to files with their relative names or paths.

Special Files

Special files are a part of the UNIX file system and are read and written like user data files. One type of special files are "*device*" files. Reading from or writing to a device is accomplished by reading from or writing to the special file for that device. Even main memory is accessible through a special file. Other devices that can be accessed through the use of special files include disk drives, tape drives, printers, plotters, communication lines, and so on.

The feature that separates special files from other files is that special files reside in the directory */dev*. Links may be made to these files from other directories. While standard protection mechanisms are available to all special files, the kernel provides additional protection to special files for memory and the active disk. Special files do not use file system space, and like directories, they are marked as being block or character devices.

Pipes

Pipes are a special implementation of the UNIX file system. Internally called first-in-first-out (FIFO) files, pipes can be read or written only sequentially. The only other difference from ordinary files is that FIFO files (*pipes*) use only the direct blocks to minimize performance impact, and do not use any level of indirect block addresses.

Pipes, in a way, are special files that allow a particular type of multiprocess activity to be synchronized by the kernel, in which the output of one command becomes the input to the next command without creating any intermediate file. UNIX synchronizes two or more processes using these files, termed as a *pipeline*.

who | sort | lpr

In the above example, a vertical bar separates the UNIX commands forming the pipeline. The first output by the **who** command is the usernames where the *sort* command sorts the usernames alphabetically. The *lpr* command accepts the sorted output from the *sort* command and prints a listing of the usernames, without requiring an intermediate file.

Pipes or ordinary pipes or unnamed pipes are normally used to provide communication between two processes when an array of bytes needs to be communicated. An unnamed pipe has no directory entry and is not accessible to other processes. A command of the type

ls | pr

prints a directory listing by providing a link between the output of the *ls* command and the input of the *pr* command.

A named pipe is a special file of the type FIFO that is opened using the normal open-system call. There is one significant difference between named pipes and ordinary files. Since either a read or a write can be in process at any given time, the kernel keeps track of the reads and writes and ensures that a read does not wait on an empty pipe, nor a write on a full pipe. The processes sleep in such cases and a wakeup is issued when the required event takes place.

MVS facilitates a similar concept via concatenation, but is not as elaborate as UNIX pipes.

ABOUT UNIX FILES

Now that you understand file structure, let's discuss the objects manipulated by most commands: files. UNIX has a treelike file and directory structure where you can address any file or directory with its absolute path name starting at the file system root (denoted by **/**) or with a name relative to your current position in the file tree.

Files Defined

We've been somewhat vague up till now about exactly what a file is in UNIX. The word "file" simply refers to some information stored in a way that it can be accessed by using its name (or a path to it). Actually almost everything you do in UNIX involves using files. Below is a short explanation of the various types of files used in UNIX, followed by some information about UNIX filenames:

- Text (ASCII): human-readable
- Data writing: electronic mail
- "Source code": for programs
- Binary: machine-readable compiled and executable programs
- Directories: hierarchy of files
- Conceptual/logical files: the operating system uses for special purposes
- Input/output: device drivers and related files

Filenames in UNIX

A filename is a sequence of 14 or fewer characters. Upper- and lowercase characters are significant and different in UNIX, so filenames must be typed in exactly as shown. As a general rule, it is best to restrict the characters to letters of the alphabet (a–z), digits (0–9), the underscore (**_**), and the period (**.**). This is because the shell assigns special meaning to some characters.

As we said before, all files have a filename, and UNIX imposes few restrictions on filenames. This makes it easy for you to name your files so that you can easily recognize their contents. You will find it useful to adopt names and classes of names that indicate how important each file is and what connection it has with other files. For example, temporary files used to test commands and options could all begin with a "**t**."

A filename can be

- Up to 256 characters long, consisting of any alphanumeric character on the keyboard except the "/."
- In general, you should keep your filenames relatively short (to reduce typing effort) and use normal lowercase characters such as letters, numbers, periods, and underscores. For instance, if your program calculates employee paychecks, you might call it *payroll*, or if your file is a research paper on Frank Lloyd Wright, you might call it *wright*. Do not include blanks in your filenames, as they will make it very difficult for you to work with the file. If you do wish to separate letters in a filename, use the underscore "_" character (as in weight_paper) or the hyphen "-" character. Remember that UNIX is case sensitive, which means it recognizes the difference between uppercase and lowercase letters. For instance, Weight and weight would refer to two different files.
- When you place a single period in the middle of a filename, the part after the period is commonly referred to as an extension or suffix and usually indicates what type of information is stored in the file. You may use any extension desired; a text file might have the extension *.txt* or *.text*, a note may have the extension *.note*, and so forth. UNIX does not require extensions. They are intended to help identify similar types of files. Since some UNIX programs (especially compilers) look for certain standard extensions, it is common practice to use the following conventions: *.h* for header files, *.c* for C source files, *.f* for FORTRAN, *.p* for Pascal, and *.s* for assembler source files. So the file *wright.txt* indicates a text file, whereas the file *payroll.c* indicates a C program called "payroll."

Some UNIX files begin with a period, for example, *.cshrc* or *.login*. Files that begin with a period will not appear in a normal directory listing and are usually UNIX environment and application setup files.

A large grouping of files and directories is referred to as a file system. File systems are related to the disk size and structure, and to the internal structure of UNIX. What you should remember is that users' files and directories are usually on a different file system than the system's files and directories. If the number of users is large, the user files and directories may be on more than one file system.

In summary, filenames in UNIX have the following attributes.

- Up to 256 characters in length.
- Case sensitive ("blob'', "BlOb'', and "bloB'' are all different names).
- All characters legal (except '/'), but many are difficult.
- Recommended characters.
- Letters (a–z and A–Z).
- Numerals (0–9).

- Period, underscore, hyphen.
- Not recommended are spaces and ? > < * & ! ' " ; : ( ) [ ] { } ~ $ / \ ^

Wildcard Character Substitution

Using wildcard characters that allow you to copy, list, move, and remove items with similar names is a great help in manipulating files and directories. There are three operators you can use to indicate several files at the same time.

- The symbol * will match zero or more characters in the name.
- The symbol ? will match any single character in that position in the filename.
- Characters enclosed in brackets [*and*] will match any one of the given characters in the given position in the name. A consecutive sequence of characters can be designated by [*char char*].

For example,

- *?ab2* would match a name that starts with any single character and ends with *ab2*. *?ab?* would match all names that begin and end with any character and have *ab* in between.
- *ab** would match all names that start with *ab*, including *ab* itself.
- *a*b* would match all names that start with *a* and end with *b*.
- *s[aqz]* would match *sa*, *sq*, and *sz*.
- *s[2-7]* would match *s2*, *s3*, *s4*, *s5*, *s6,* and *s7*.

These *wildcard* symbols help in dealing with groups of files, but you should remember that the command *rm* * would erase all files in your current directory (although by default, you would be prompted to okay each deletion). The wildcard * should be used carefully.

Table 5.1 depicts some of the typical usage examples of *wildcard* symbols both in MVS and UNIX.

Naming Conventions

Filenames in UNIX are sequences of arbitrary characters. Although UNIX will allow filenames composed of any characters, some characters can make it difficult for you to refer to the file in most contexts. For example, if you were to name a file *papers/report1*, then UNIX would look in the directory *papers* for a file named *report1*, since the "/" character indicates a directory. In particular, try to avoid using any nonprinting characters in filenames, including space and tab characters.

TABLE 5.1

WILDCARD USAGE IN MVS	DESCRIPTION	WILDCARD USAGE IN UNIX	DESCRIPTION
The asterisk (*)	The asterisk can be used to represent any single qualifier in a data set name.	**The asterisk (*)**	Matches any string of characters including the null string.
listcat entries (osc.data)	The *listcat* command can use the *entries* operand to list information about a single data set. It is not as flexible in MVS as in UNIX.		The asterisk at the end of a filename has the same significance in UNIX as in MVS. It can represent zero or more characters at that position in the filename or file type. In UNIX, the asterisk is much more versatile than in MVS, because it does not have to go at the end of the expression you type.
listcat entries (osc.)*	Substituting an asterisk for one of the qualifiers means "perform this command on any data set that matches the other qualifiers, with anything in the asterisk position."	*ls *hat*	Lists all the filenames that end with the letter "hat."
listcat entries (.data)*	To list all the data sets having *data* as their last qualifier is *not* allowed in MVS. You cannot make the asterisk the first part of the data set name.	*ls *hat**	Lists out all the filenames with letters "hat" anywhere in them.
listcat entries ('samuser..data')*	By using the fully qualified name (i.e., enclose data set name in apostrophes), it will list all the data sets having *data* as their last qualifier.	*ls rpt*95*	Lists all the filenames that begin with the letters *rpt* and end with the digits *95*. regardless of how many characters are between them.
Not supported		**The question mark (?)**	It represents a single character—no more, no less. Several question marks can be used to represent a number of characters.
		ls ???95rpt.txt	Lists all the filenames with exactly three characters before the characters *95rpt.txt*.

TABLE 5.1 *(cont.)*

WILDCARD USAGE IN MVS	DESCRIPTION	WILDCARD USAGE IN UNIX	DESCRIPTION
Not supported		**[...] or {...}**	Matches any one of the enclosed characters. For example, *[a-z]* matches any lower case character, [cC] matches either upper- or lowercase c.
		name[xyz]	All files in the current directory, *namex, namey,* or *namez.*
		name[a-z4]	All files in the current directory, *namea* through *namez* and *name4.*
		name.{o,f}	All files *name.o* and *name.f* in the current directory (*C shell* only).

Exercise: Change to your home directory and make a copy of the file called *fluff.* Name the copy *fuuff.* Now try *ls f?uff.* The **?** wildcard allows any **single** character to match where the *?* was placed. The * operator allows any **string** of characters to match. Try *ls f**. Do you understand these two operators now? Using a wildcard, copy all the files beginning with the letter "f" into your *text* directory in one UNIX command.

The UNIX system, as such, does not impose any naming conventions on files. No file extensions are used by the UNIX operating system. Although certain programs (notably compilers) expect their input files to have certain endings (such as *.c* or *.f*), which is also true for MVS files. The following is a list of the common suffixes to indicate *specific file types.*

.f Indicates a FORTRAN source file.

.c Indicates a C source file.

.o Indicates an object file produced by the compiler.

There are, however, certain naming conventions followed by many programs in UNIX as well as MVS, associated with various compilers and other tools available on the system. These conventions are imposed by the programs that access these files, and not by the operating systems themselves. The convention is usually specified by one of the following:

- Adding a suffix to the filename. The suffix is after a single letter and is separated from the rest of the filename by a period.
- Using default names for output files.

Examples

SUFFIX IN MVS	DESCRIPTION	SUFFIX IN UNIX	DESCRIPTION
		.c	C language source
.COBOL	COBOL source	*.cob*	COBOL language source
.FORT	FORTRAN source	*.f*	FORTRAN source
.ASM	Assembler source	*.s*	Assembler source
.TEXT	Text file	*.txt*	Text file
.REXX	REXX source file	*.y*	Compiler compiler source
.BASIC	BASIC source file	*.bas*	Basic program source
.PASCAL	Pascal source file		
		.sh	Shell program
.TMP	Temporary file		
.TEXT	Simple text		
.CNTL	Control statements		
.CLIST	Control lists		
.PROCLIB	Procedure library		
.ISPFPROF	ISPF profiles		
.SYM	Symbolic COBOL debug		
.LIST	List from COBOL debug		
.PLI	PL/I source		
		.l	Lexical analyzer generator
		.a	Library archive
.LOAD	Executable load module	*.o*	Semicompiled object
.OBJ	Object module		
		.h	Header file
		.dbs	Database directory
		.idx	Index file
.DATA	Data statements	*.dat*	Data file

In MVS (TSO), if you try to do something to a data set and leave off the last qualifier, TSO displays the final qualifiers for data sets that begin with whatever you entered. For example, if you have data sets named OSC.MEMO.SENT and OSC.MEMO.RECEIVED and you enter the command

delete osc.memo

TSO responds with:

Qualifiers for data set *osc.memo are: sent received*

You must choose either of the two. However, in UNIX, the system is not that forgiving and responds: *file not found.* Therefore, you must always specify qualifier with a UNIX file if there are more than one such files.

File Organization

UNIX

The file organization in UNIX is hierarchical, in tree-structured directories, which means that the disk is divided into sections called directories. A directory can be divided into subsections called subdirectories, which can be further subdivided. The terms directory and subdirectory are used almost interchangeably, since every directory—except the root—is a subdirectory of another.

To understand the UNIX directory structure, just think of "root" as a tree trunk that branches into several main branches. These main branches then divide into smaller and smaller branches. In a typical UNIX system, one of the main branches usually holds most of the programs that come with the operating system. We call this the */bin* directory. Another main branch could hold the application software, called the */usr* directory. For example, the "access" database could be held in directory */access.* This subdivision's full name would be */usr/access* because it is the subdirectory of */usr* directory and the full name of a directory includes its pathname, or the name describing the path up the tree along the various branches it took to get there. The subdirectory */access* may have many subdirectories holding many individual files.

Figure 5.2 shows a sample UNIX directory tree structure. A level of indentation represents a level of the subdirectory structure. Notice how a slash character separates each component of the pathname. The pathname of the root, or main trunk of a tree, is just a slash by itself. We create a complete pathname by various subdirectories traversed to get to the subdirectory in question, separating each with a slash. No two directories can have the same name. Although, you may see multiple directories named "bin" in Figure 5.2, their pathnames are completely different: */bin*, */usr/bin*, and */usr/access/bin.*

At any given time, one of these directories is your *current* or *default* directory. This is true for many UNIX commands. For example, if you enter a command to erase a file but do not specify the directory, the UNIX system assumes it to be in the current directory. Each user is assigned his or her own subdirectory, usually known as home directory. The system administrator assigns subdirectories to users to keep their personal files.

```
/
        bin
        usr
                tmp
                bin
                access
                        source
                        demo
                        sql
        usr2            bin
                samuser
                        mail
                        personal
                janeuser
                        mail
                        payroll
```

FIGURE 5.2 Directory structure.

MVS

MVS keeps track of data sets in lists of their names and locations, called *catalogs*. The system's master catalog stores a list of the names and locations of your catalog by your ID. You may list the contents of your catalog by using the command LISTCAT. The particular storage device (disk) that holds a particular data set is termed as volume serial number (VOLSER). If your data set is cataloged (registered), the catalog entry automatically keeps track of the VOLSER related to your data set; otherwise, the MVS system will prompt you for the VOLSER if you entered the data set on the screen.

In MVS, a related term used is VTOC, the volume table of contents, a special data set that serves as the table of contents for a particular storage device. As with the VOLSER, users sometimes use VTOC to access their data more directly.

ABOUT MVS FILES

Files in MVS are known as *data sets*. Although it is common to use the term "**data set**" for a file, keep in mind that the terms are not completely interchangeable. The word "file" has a specific meaning in MVS. For example, when you use the ALLOCATE command to indicate a data set that a particular program will use, the word "FILE" is a synonym for DDNAME (data definition name in a JCL statement). In fact, the program uses the DDNAME to refer to the data set. If you wanted to save an output report in a data set instead of displaying on the screen or printing on the printer, it will expect to have a reference to DDNAME of RPTOUT allocated to a desired data set known as *dsname* for data set name, for example, *user.report.text*.

In MVS/TSO, a file is made up of a collection of one or more records. A record is composed of one or more fields. A field is composed of one or more characters. Table 5.2 depicts each of these terms.

Types of Data Sets

MVS defines three types of data sets: sequential, partitioned, and VSAM. *VSAM data sets* are used to store data for database applications and are not a pertinent comparison to UNIX files. Initially, you should know the difference between two types of data sets: sequential data sets and partitioned data sets.

A *sequential data set* is like a regular UNIX file. A sequential data set contains records stored one after the other. A partitioned data set contains one or more sequential

TABLE 5.2 A Data Set (i.e., a File).

RECORD	FIELD 1	FIELD 2	FIELD 3
record 1	BOB	7665656	ENGINEERING
record 2	TOM	7676756	FORESTRY
record 3	FAYE	7673421	LAW

TABLE 5.3 A Sequential Data Set and a Partitioned Data Set.

record1	record2	record3	record4	sequential data set
DIR	file1	file2	file3	partitioned data set
	member1	member2	member3	

files, all in one data set but separated (i.e., partitioned) from each other. In a partitioned data set, each individual file is referred to as a "member" of the data set. Table 5.3 presents simple sketches of both a sequential data set and a partitioned data set. Note that the partitioned data set also includes a "directory" to identify and locate each data set member.

A *partitioned data set (PDS)* is like a group of files under one name. Each of the files, termed as a "member" of the PDS, is basically the same as a sequential data set. In fact, when executing COPY command, we will notice how easily you can copy a member of a partitioned data set into a sequential data set or take an existing sequential data set and make it a member of an existing partitioned data set.

Because a partitioned data set is a collection of "files" or "sequential data sets," it is tempting to compare it to a directory or folder in UNIX. In practice, however, MVS programmers may not use partitioned data sets this way at all. Like a folder in UNIX, a single PDS usually holds a group of files that all serve the same purpose within their respective contexts and all have the same characteristics—record length, maximum size, and so on. Therefore, the partitioned data set is like grouping together a collection of files with the same file type or extension in UNIX. For example, a PDS could hold C program *source files* or another one could hold just *data files*.

Data Set Naming and Characteristics

All data sets have names. Each data set name is composed of two or more parts or "qualifiers" separated by periods. For example, the data set name SYS3.MESSAGE.SEMINARS has three qualifiers and the data set name CSLSU.DATA has two. Each qualifier

- Must begin with an alphabetic character or national character ($,#,@), with the first letter of the first qualifier being an alphabetic character.
- Normally contain only alphanumeric characters (A–Z,0–9).
- Cannot be longer than eight characters (a drastic change from UNIX filenames).

The first qualifier is referred to as the "high-level" qualifier. When referring to your personal data sets (i.e., a data set whose first qualifier is your logonid), the high-level qualifier need not be stated. If the high-level qualifier is omitted, MVS(TSO) automatically assumes that your logonid is the data set's high-level qualifier. But how does MVS(TSO) know if you have omitted the first qualifier?

If a data set name is given without being enclosed in apostrophes, MVS(TSO) assumes that it is one of your personal data sets and places your logonid at the front of the data set name. Data set names are said to be "fully qualified" if they are referred to by all their qualifiers.

Example

Suppose a person's logonid is SAMUSER and one of the data sets is named PROGRAM.FORT. If that data set is included in an MVS(TSO) command, it could be written as either PROGRAM.FORT or as 'SAMUSER.PROGRAM.FORT'. The fully qualified data set name is 'SAMUSER.PROGRAM.FORT'.

Partitioned data set MEMBERs also have names that follow the same rules as those given for individual qualifiers—one to eight alphanumeric characters beginning with an alphabetic character. Since members are parts of partitioned data sets, they must be referred to slightly differently than data sets themselves. Member names are enclosed in parentheses and placed after the name of the data set. For example, if NUMBER1 is a member of the partitioned data set SAMUSER.PROGRAM.FORT, it would be referred to as either PROGRAM.FORT(NUMBER1) or 'SAMUSER.PROGRAM.FORT(NUMBER1)'.

Another pair of important data set related terms are "cataloged" and "uncataloged." A data set is said to be cataloged if its name and location are listed in the system's master catalog. If its name and location are not listed in the master catalog, but it nevertheless resides on one of the system's disk packs, the data set is said to be uncataloged. The default on MVS(TSO) is that all data sets are cataloged. There is no such concept in UNIX.

There are two MVS concepts regarding data sets which can be especially troubling for the new UNIX user, but which must be understood before you can work successfully with UNIX. They might even be called "The Two Commandments of MVS."

- *Commandment 1*: Thou shall *allocate* a data set before using it. Before you can use a data set to store data or a program, you must first reserve sufficient space on a disk for that data set. The process is referred to as "allocation." That is, you must "allocate a data set." After you have allocated a data set, you may then begin to work with that data set. A later chapter explains the allocation process in detail.
- *Commandment 2*: Thou shalt *compress* partitioned data sets regularly. To compress a data set is to discard all old versions of data set members, to keep only the most recent version of all data set members, and to recoup the space used by the old versions. You cannot overcompress or squash data, no matter how many times you compress the data set. Note: Keeping old versions of members of a data set serves no useful purpose, since you cannot access these old members. They simply take up valuable space in your partitioned data set and the disk.

Example

Suppose that a 100-line program is stored in a member of a partitioned data set. Suppose, further, that the program is run, found to have errors, edited to get rid of those errors, and stored again. TSO keeps both copies of the program (i.e., the member)—the new edited version and the original version. Next suppose that the newest version of the program is run and it also is found to contain errors. Again the program is corrected and saved. At this point, the partitioned data set contains three similar versions of the same program (approximately 300 lines of code), only one of which can be accessed (the most recent).

The obvious problem in the above example is that each new version of the member requires an approximately equal portion of disk space—which has a limit. MVS does not automatically discard previous versions and then free the disk space for reuse. Rather, MVS waits indefinitely for you to tell it to get rid of the old member versions (by issuing a command to compress the data set). If no such command is given, the data set continues to fill up with outdated versions until eventually your allocated data set space is completely full. On the other hand, in UNIX, if you modify a file and then save it, it overlays the old version.

Sequential Data Sets: A sequential data set name is composed of several pieces called *qualifiers*. A period separates each qualifier. For uniqueness, for any data sets you create, MVS adds your user ID as the first (called high-level) qualifier. For example, for a data set name MEMO.TEXT for user ID SAMUSER, the fully qualified data set name in MVS would be named SAMUSER.MEMO.TEXT.

Some MVS programmers call this high-level qualifier the data set's "prefix." It is not always the user ID of the person who created it. In fact, it could be the name of the application that uses it or something else assigned by the system. The data sets you create, however, almost always have your user ID as the high-level qualifier. If you wish to create a different high-level qualifier, you may specify a fully qualified name when specifying a data set name, in a single quote, as follows:

'NEWUSER.MEMO.TEXT'

A fully qualified data set name can have as many parts (like extensions in UNIX) as you want, as long as the total number of characters, including the periods that separate the qualifiers, does not exceed 44. In addition, no qualifier is more than eight (8) characters. Although your data set name could have over a dozen qualifiers, three is the most common.

The low-level qualifier (or the lowest extension) is usually called the "type." This not only applies to three-part data sets, but also to data set names with two or more parts. The last part, the part that identifies what kind of data set it is, is always considered the low-level identifier. For example, a COBOL source program data set will be named as USER.PROGRAM.COBOL.

Partitioned Data Sets: The rules for naming partitioned data sets in MVS are the same as for sequential data sets. Since a PDS is actually a collection of data sets, we also need a way to address a particular member of the PDS. A member name is used in parentheses right after the PDS name. For example, if SAMUSER keeps his COBOL programs as members of a partitioned data sets called SAMUSER.PROGRAM.COBOL, the member MEMBER will acquire a full name: SAMUSER.PROGRAM.COBOL(MEMBER).

Members of partitioned data sets follow the same rules as qualifier names: they can be up to eight (8) characters in length. The limit of 44 characters on a data set name does not include the characters of a member name. Therefore, a PDS with a 44-character name can still have members with 8-character names.

Data Set Name Qualifiers: Qualifiers can contain letters and numbers, and must begin with a letter. Only other allowable special characters are @, $, and #. The case of the alphabetical characters does not matter in MVS, since lowercase letters are always converted to uppercase.

SUMMARY

This chapter has covered the following topics:

1. The general structure of a UNIX/MVS file system, including descriptions of the general use of some of the main directories.
2. Naming conventions for files and directories.
3. Descriptions of the current, parent, and home directories.
4. Relative and absolute pathnames.
5. The use of wildcards.
6. Special files for handling hardware devices.
7. File systems are the most fundamental features of an operating system. Therefore, it is important that you understand the UNIX/MVS file structure and naming differences.

6

Manipulating Your Files

INTRODUCTION

The UNIX operating system is a tool for managing information that is stored in files. This section describes the UNIX and MVS utility programs that allow you to manage your files. All these programs perform very simple functions. Periodically, during your interactions with the system, you have to remove old information, make room for new information, adjust the file access privileges for certain files, and occasionally acquire files from other users.

The unit of information in UNIX is the ordinary file. Both UNIX and MVS operating systems contain programs to display information about files, to create ordinary files, to move ordinary files from one location to another, to rename files, to make copies of files, and to remove files. In addition, it is necessary to have a privilege system so that owners can protect their files from unwanted access by others. Therefore, both UNIX and MVS have programs to control the access rights of files and to change the ownership of files.

In MVS, for interactive operations, you can use either ISPF or TSO. However, TSO affords more flexibility in file manipulations than ISPF.

FILES, DIRECTORIES, AND RELATED COMMANDS

There are ten basic commands for manipulating files that every UNIX user should know.

MVS COMMAND	DESCRIPTION	UNIX EQUIVALENT	DESCRIPTION
ALLOCATE	Creates data sets.	***cat***	Creates a file with redirection.
LIST	Displays the contents of data sets.	***cat***	Displays the contents of files.
LISTCAT	Lists the data sets in a catalog.	***ls***	Lists filenames.
LISTDS **LISTALC**	Lists the members in a partitioned data set.		
LISTB	Lists user and temporary data sets; lists broadcasts from system operator.		
COPY	Copies data sets and data set members.	***cp***	Copies files.
RENAME	Renames data sets and data set members.	***mv***	Renames and moves files.
DELETE	Deletes data sets and data set members.	***rm***	Deletes files.
DSPRINT, **PRINTDS**	Prints contents of data sets and data set members.	***lpr*** ***pr***	Prints files to a line printer. Titles and paginates files.
ALLOCATE **PROTECT**	Creates and provides access to data sets; grants and/or revokes access to data sets.	***chmod***	Grants and revokes access to files.
ALLOCATE	Creates and provides access to data sets.	***mkdir***	Creates subdirectories.

MVS COMMAND	DESCRIPTION	UNIX EQUIVALENT	DESCRIPTION
DELETE	Deletes data sets and data set members.	***rmdir***	Removes subdirectories.
FREE	Frees an allocated data set with or without DELETE option to delete the data set or its member.		

The following table is provided to help you understand some of the subtle differences in the usage of some of these commands.

MVS COMMANDS	USAGE	UNIX COMMANDS	USAGE
COPY sch.text sch.text.backup	Copies data set "sch.text" to data set "sch.text.backup." If sch.text.backup exists, it is overlaid; otherwise it is created.	***cp*** *source dest*	Copies filename "source" and name it "dest."
COPY memo.text (april) april.text	Copies a member "april" of a PDS "memo.text" to a sequential data set "april.text." Similarly a sequential data set may be copied to a member of a PDS.		
RENAME source.text dest.text	Renames sequential data set "source.text" to "dest.text."	***mv*** *source dest*	Moves (renames) "source" to "dest."
RENAME memo.text(april) memo.text(may)	Renames member "april" of a PDS memo.text to a new name "may."		
DELETE dest.text	Deletes the sequential data set "dest.text."	***rm*** *dest*	Removes (erases) the file "dest."

Exercise

In your home directory is a file called *fluff*. Make a copy of this file called *fred*. Then rename *fred* to *joe*. At this point check the contents of *joe*. Is it the same as *fluff*? It should be. Now erase the file *joe*.

CREATING FILES

Many files are created using a text editor. A text editor is a program that allows you to enter and save text. You can also use a text editor to manipulate saved text through corrections, deletions, or insertions. The main text editors on information systems managed networks are *vi*, *GNU Emacs*, *Pico*, and *aXe*. (Note: **vi** is included with every UNIX system, but GNU Emacs is commonly installed separately by system managers. aXe is available only if you are using the X Window system.). You should learn how to use at least one of these tools.

You can create a file without a text editor by using the *cat* command (short for concatenate) and the ">" (redirect output) symbol. To create a UNIX file using the *cat* command, type

cat > new-filename

where *new-filename* is the name you wish to give the file. The command *cat* generally reads in a file and displays it to standard output. When there is no filename directly following the command, *cat* treats standard input as a file. The **">"** symbol will redirect the output from *cat* into the new filename you specify.

cat will keep reading and writing each line you type until it encounters an end-of-file character. By typing **Ctrl-d** on a line by itself, you generate an end-of-file character. It will stop when it sees this character. Try it, using this example as a guide: *cat* > *practice*. When you reach the end of each line, press the RETURN key. You can only correct mistakes on the line you are currently typing. Use the DELETE key to move the cursor back to the mistake and then retype the rest of the line correctly. You cannot correct errors on previous lines. When you have completed the last line, press RETURN and type **Ctrl-d**.

FUNCTION	MVS	UNIX
Format	**allocate** DA {dsname} {tracks/cyl/blocks} + {space (pri sec)} {dsorg (ps/po)} {old/shr/mod} {Creates an existing or new sequential or partitioned data set.} **create** dsname [tracks(primary[,secondary])] + [dir(count)] {Stores a source program or data in a data set.}	***cat*** *[file(s)] > file2* {Concatenates or redirects output from one file to file2.}
Example 2	**allocate** DA(osc.cobol) tracks space(10 5) dsorg(ps) + {Creates a new sequential data set with 10 primary and 5 secondary tracks on a disk.}	***cat*** *chapt1 chapt2 chapt3 > book* {Concatenates three files into one, using output redirection.}
Example 3	**allocate** DA(memo.cobol) tracks space(4 2) catalog {If the data set 'memo.cobol' is not cataloged, the command will add to the user's catalog. However, if it were already cataloged to another catalog it must be freed with **free** command.}	***cat*** *chapt1 chapt2 chapt3 > book* {Concatenates three files into one, using output redirection.}

FUNCTION	MVS	UNIX
Example 4	**allocate** DA(inv.cobol) block(7200) space(10 5) dir(10) + dsorg(po) {Creates a new partitioned data set with 10 primary and 5 secondary blocks with room for 10 members.}	***cat*** > *msgforyu* {Creates a file msgforyu and reads input until EOF.} Such as: *Jerry from HDS called* *New machine arrives on Monday. He will call tomorrow.* *^D*
Example 5	**allocate** DA(hds.text) tracks space(15 10) dsorg(ps) + recfm(f,b) lrecl(80) block(1760) {Creates a new sequential fixed length blocked data set, with 10 primary and 5 secondary blocks of 1760 bytes each, and record length of 80 bytes.}	***cat*** *sched* | *more* {Pipes the output of the ***cat*** command to be used as input for the more command, which will display one screen at a time.}

MVS provides considerable more flexibility than UNIX in allocating and creating data sets. There are two kinds of allocations:

- Allocation of an existing data set readies for use by a particular program. Some of the many possible reasons for allocating an existing data set are
  - Reserving data sets that will be used by a particular application.
  - Informing the system where to find things like CLISTs (command procedures), error lists, or start-up procedures.
  - Redirecting output from a program to a specific destination (printer or file or user).
  - Unlike UNIX operating system, when creating a new data set, the MVS system needs to know much more about it than just its name. It must know whether the new data set is sequential or partitioned, how much space to be reserved, the length of its lines, and several other details that few users completely understand. This involves high degree of customization possible with MVS: allocating data sets with the best possible settings, thus the associated complexity.
  - If you want to model your new data set after an existing one in most of its details, you may use the operand '**LIKE**.' By using an operand like '**DIR**,' you may reserve six additional directory blocks to allow more room for new members of the PDS:

    allocate data set(osc2.cobol) **like** ('samuser.proj1.cobol')

  - If you do not model a new data set after an existing one, a new data set requires you to at least specify the following: (1) its name, (2) space desired, and (3) organization, whether it is sequential or partitioned.
- Commands **LISTDS** and **LISTALC** will also allow an MVS user to find the status of the allocated data sets. To some extent, commands like *ls* and *cat* allow the

user to check attributes of UNIX files, but there is no one-to-one correlation with MVS commands.

In MVS, when you log off, the system automatically unallocates any allocated data sets. MVS also provides the facility to unallocate data sets during your session. However, UNIX system has no such concept.

DISPLAYING FILES

Now that you have created a file, you can display it one of several ways. You could use the *cat* command. Just type *cat* followed by the name of the file that you want to see.

cat practice

Options

Sometimes the files you want to view are very long. When using the *cat* command, the text will scroll by very quickly. You can control the flow of text by using **Ctrl-s** and **Ctrl-q**. **Ctrl-s** stops the flow of text, and **Ctrl-q** restarts it. If you use **Ctrl-s**, stopping the flow of text, and so on, you must remember to type **Ctrl-q** or the system will not respond. Other options that work with *cat* command are

n	Displays the file with line numbers.	*f*	Truncates long lines.
s	Removes multiple blank lines.	*is*	Skips **i** lines.
c	Refreshes screen one line at a time instead of scrolling.	*q* or *Q*	Terminates file display.
i	Scrolls **i** lines.	*i/expr*	Searches for the *i*th occurrence of the expression.
t	Returns to top of file.	*:f*	Displays the current filename and line number.
if	Skips *i* screens and print.	.	Repeats the previous command.

more is a program that displays only one screen or page of information at a time. It waits for you to tell it to continue. Type *more* followed by a filename. *more* offers some of the functions of a line editor when used in read mode.

more practice

The computer will display one screen of text and then wait for you to press the space bar before it displays the next page of text, until you reach the end of the file. Pressing the "?" character will show help for more.

Displaying Files with Page at a Time

The major difference between the *cat* and *more* commands is that *cat* automatically scrolls through a file from beginning to end, making it harder for the user to read, whereas *more* pauses between each page/screen. The *more* command indicates the percentage of the file already displayed and prompts the user to hit space bar for a new screen or carriage return to advance one line at a time.

Combined, these commands (*cat* and *more*) provide a greater functionality for displaying files on the screen than the MVS command **LIST**. However, the MVS list command is lot more versatile by allowing you to list contents of an input file into another output file or the screen or printer.

The *cat* command is a multipurpose command and is UNIX's most versatile text manipulation programs. In addition to displaying text files on the screen, it is also used to combine or "concatenate" files. *cat* is an abbreviation of the word "concatenate," even though it is used far more often to put the contents of a text file on the screen.

One of UNIX's greatest strengths is its ability to make several programs work together, all by issuing one command. Combining the *cat* command with the *more* command is extremely useful. When you display files with the *cat* command, the files longer than 24 lines scroll up and off the screen until the end of the file, right in front of your eyes. The *more* command remedies this problem. It takes what you send it and gives it back to you a screenful at a time and allows you to control the paging interactively.

Any command that sends text to the screen can also send it to *more*, by using piping (|) functions.

FUNCTION	MVS	UNIX
Format	**LIST** data-set-name [member] [/password] print({*/dsname}) {Displays contents of a sequential or a member of a partitioned data set, with \ or without a password, either to a data set or a printer.}	***cat*** *[option(s)] file(s)* {Displays contents of a file.} ***cat*** *[file(s)] | more* {Pipes the output of the cat command to use as input to *more* command.} *more [option(s)] file(s)* {Displays a file a page at a time.}
Example 1	**LIST** oscfile.text {Displays contents of oscfile.text.} Oct. 5 11:30 meet Kirk for discussion 12:30 meet Dave for lunch 16:00 get first draft ready	***cat*** */etc/motd* {Types contents of file on the terminal.} *System will be down all weekend for maintenance.*
Example 2	**LIST** oscfile.text printer(*) {Displays contents of oscfile.text on printer.} Oct. 5 11:30 meet Kirk for discussion 12:30 meet Dave for lunch 16:00 get first draft ready	***cat*** *oscfile.data* {Displays contents of file.} *Oct. 5* *11:30 meet Kirk for discussion* *12:30 meet Dave for lunch* *16:00 get first draft ready*
Example 3	**LIST** myfile.text printer(output) {Displays contents of myfile.text to an output file.} 'Keep it a secret'	***cat*** *practice / more* {One screen at a time output of *cat* command file practice is piped as input for the *more* command.}

FUNCTION	MVS	UNIX
Example 4		***cat*** *-n user1/practice* {Displays file *practice* with line numbers.}
Example 5		**cat** -s {Displays file *practice* after removing multiple blank lines.}
Example 6		**more** -11../practice {Displays file *practice,* located one directory above the current directory.}
Example 7		**more** + 5 practice {Displays file *practice,* beginning at line 5.}
Example 8		**more** -f practice {Displays file *practice,* but truncates long lines.}

The LIST command in MVS is used to display the contents of a data set. Like the COPY command, LIST is technically a utility and not part of TSO. The LIST command is a good example of how you can treat a partitioned data set's individual members like sequential data sets. On the other hand, if you try to list a partitioned data set without specifying a member name, MVS looks for a member named TEMPNAME (default name) in that PDS and lists it if found; otherwise, an error message is displayed.

LISTING FILES

The *ls* command will list the files in the current directory that do not begin with a period and to list information about files. You can use two kinds of parameters after the *ls* command:

- A directory name, which shows that you want to list the files in a directory other than the current one.
- A file specification, which shows that you only want to list files whose names follow a certain pattern.

Each argument to the *ls* command is either the name of an ordinary or special file, the name of a directory, or an option list. The options are used to control the ordering of the list of files and the information that is printed for each file. For each ordinary or special file argument, the requested information is listed. For each directory argument, the requested information is listed for all the files in the directory.

Command

Below is a list of options and arguments that are frequently used with *ls*:

ls - [options] [arguments]

You can use many different options or combinations of options after the *ls* command. However, *-l*, *-t*, *-a*, and *-d* are the most frequently used options.

ls	Lists only the filenames in the current directory.
ls -a	Lists all the contents of the current directory, including files with initial periods, which are not usually listed.
ls -A	Same as -a, except that '.' and '..' are not listed.
ls -l	Lists the contents of the current directory in long format, including file permissions, size, and date information.
ls -L	If the argument is a symbolic link, lists the file or directory the link references rather than the link itself.
ls -d	Lists only the requested information for each directory in the argument list.
ls -c	Uses time of last edit or change for sorting or printing.
ls -C	Forces multicolumn output, with entries sorted down the columns and is usually a default.
ls -f	Forces each argument to be interpreted as a directory and lists the name found in each slot. This option turns off *-l*, *-t*, *-s*, and *-r* and turns on *-a*.
ls -F	Marks directories with a trailing slash ('/'), executable files with a trailing asterisk ('*').
ls -g	For *ls*, shows the group ownership of the file in a long output.
ls -i	Prints the i-node number, for each file, in the first column of the report (an i-node is an entry in a data table that the system uses to define the characteristics of a single file). If two names reference the same file, then both names will be associated with the same i-node number.
ls -q	Displays nongraphic characters in filenames as the character '?'.
ls -r	Reverses the order of sort to get the reverse alphabetic ordering.
ls -R	Recursively lists subdirectories encountered.
ls -s	Lists contents and file sizes in kilobytes of the current directory.
ls -t	Sorts the list of files according to each file's modification date.
ls -u	Uses the time of last access, instead of the last modification, for sorting.
ls -x	Lists several filenames across the screen on each line of output.
ls -1	Forces one entry per line output format.

You can use two kinds of arguments after the *ls* command:

FILENAME	A LIST OF FILES
.c	Any file with "c" suffix
*book**	Filename "book" with any suffix
directoryname	A list of one or more directories
ls -l test	Lists contents of directory "test" in long format
ls /bin	Lists contents of directory "bin"
ls -a	Lists contents of "current" directory

If you type *ls* followed by a directory name, *ls /bin*, you will see several screenfuls of filenames from the */bin* directory. If you type *ls* followed by a filename, it only lists that file's name.

If you have many files, your directory list might be longer than one screen. You can use the programs *more* with the "|" (vertical bar or pipe) symbol to pipe the directory list generated as output by the *ls* command into the *more* program. *more* will display the output from *ls* one page at a time.

ls | more

In MVS, when there is not enough room for all its output on a single page, more output appears by simply hitting ENTER on the keyboard.

Descriptions

For each filename that is a directory, *ls* lists the contents of the directory; for each filename that is a file, *ls* repeats its name and any other information requested. By default, the output is sorted alphabetically. When no argument is given, the current directory is listed. When several arguments are given, the arguments are first sorted appropriately, but file arguments are processed before directories and their contents. The following conditions define the sort order for an alphabetical listing:

- Filenames beginning with a period
- Numbers
- Uppercase letters
- Lowercase letters

Permissions

The mode listed under the "-l" option contains 10 characters, where the first character in a UNIX file description indicates the type of file. File types described by this character include

d Directory file
b Block-type special file

c	Character-type special file
l	Symbolic link
p	FIFO (pipe) special file
s	A socket
-	A plain file

The next nine characters are interpreted as three sets of three bits each. The first set refers to owner permissions, the next refers to permissions to others in the same usergroup, and the last refers to all others. Within each set, the three characters indicate permissions to read, to write, or to execute the file as a program. For a directory, execute permission is interpreted to mean permission to search the directory. The permissions are indicated as follows:

r	The file is readable.
w	The file is writable.
x	The file is executable.
-	The indicated permission is not granted.

The group execute permission is given as *s* if the file has *set-group-id* bit set; likewise, the owner-execute permission character is given as *s* if the file has the *set-user-id* bit set. Refer to discussion on *chmod* command for further details.

FUNCTION	MVS		UNIX
Format	**LIST** **LISTCAT** **LISTDS** **LISTALC** **LISTB**	data set name [operand] (data set name) data set name [member] [data set{(member)} [history] [status] [notices/nonotices] [mail/nomail]	***ls*** *-[options] [arguments]*
Example 1	**LIST**	osc.text {Lists contents of a dataset.} 00010 May 21 00020 10 AM meet Joe in cafeteria 00030 1 PM meeting with Mary 00040 3:30 PM meet Frank on training READY	***ls*** {Lists contents of current directory.} *osc.txt prog1.f tmp*
	LISTCAT	{Lists data set names in the catalog.} --IN CATALOG: OSCCAT SAMUSER.OSC.CLIST SAMUSER.OSC.ASM SAMUSER.OSC.COBOL SAMUSER.OSC.DATA SAMUSER.OSC.FOCUS READY	

FUNCTION	MVS	UNIX
Example 2	**LISTCAT** entries (osc.cobol) NONVSAM ---- AMUSER.OSC.COBOL --IN CAT ---- SYS1.OSCCTLG READY **LISTCAT** level (osc.cobol) --IN CATALOG: OSCCAT SAMUSER.INV.CLIST SAMUSER.BNCH.OBJ SAMUSER.OSC.COBOL SAMUSER.TEST.DATA SAMUSER.INV.CNTL READY	***ls*** */bin* {Lists contents of directory */bin.*} *add* *ar* . . *cat* . *who* *write*
Example 3		***ls*** *-a* {Lists all entries, including hidden files.} *.login osc.txt prog1.f tmp* *.login is a hidden file.*
Example 4	**LISTDS** autoexec.bat SAMUSER.AUTOEXEC.BAT --RECFM-LRECL-BLKSIZE-DSORG VB 84 6233 PS --VOLUMES-- OSCUSR **LISTDS** osc.cobol mem SAMUSER.OSC.COBOL --RECFM-LRECL-BLKSIZE-DSORG FB 80 23200 PO --VOLUMES-- OSCUSR --MEMBERS-- START BNCHMK ANALYS	***ls*** *-l* {Lists all entries in long format.} *-rw-rw-r-- 1 samuser field 310 May 11 1995 osc.txt* *drw-rw-r-- 1 samuser field 512 Nov 16 1994 mail* *-rwxrwxrwx 1 samuser field 31 Dec 4 1994 osc.awk* *-rw-r--r-- 1 samuser field 310 Feb 24 1995 prog1.f*
Example 5	**LISTA** {Displays names of all users allocated and temporary data sets.} SYS1.DFQLLIB UBU1.CLIST EDUC.PROGS	***ls*** *-x /bin/c** {List several files on each line.} */bin/cat /bin/cc /bin/cmp /bin/cp* */bin/cp /bin/cpio /bin/csh /bib/crypto*
Example 6	**LISTA** osc.cobol(book) history status {Displays history and status of member "book".}	***ls*** *-R* {Recursively lists subdirectories} *osc.txt prog1.f tmp* *tmp: test*
Example 7	**LISTB** notices {Displays broadcast notices sent from the system operator.}	***ls*** *-i chap5 intro* {Lists associated i-node number.} *1341 chap5* *1341 intro*

Example 1: *ls* displays the contents of the current directory, whereas the **LIST** command displays the contents of the specified data set. The **LISTCAT** command without operands will also display the names of data sets in your user ID's catalog.

Example 2: *ls /bin* command will list several screenfuls of filenames from the */bin* directory, without stopping, until it ends with screenful of filenames similar to the ones shown below:

uulog
uuname
...
...
xsend
...
ypwhich

In MVS, if you enter **LISTCAT** command without operands, it displays the names of data sets in your user ID's catalog. The ENTRIES operand takes a data set name as an argument and lists the name of the data set and the name of the catalog that holds information about the data set. The LEVEL operand tells the **LISTCAT** command to list data set names that begin with qualifier (s) entered as parameters. You can also use the LEVEL operand to list the data set names in another user ID.

Example 3: Normally, when you use the *ls* command, those files whose names begin with a period (**.**) are omitted from the list. However, when the option *a* is used, even files whose names begin with a period are also printed as shown in this example. There is no equivalent in MVS.

Example 4: The long-list option (*ls -l*) is used to print detailed information about each listed file. Without the '*l*' option, only the filenames are typed.

In MVS, the **LISTDS** command performs similar functions by listing the attributes of the data sets and the catalogs. **LISTDS** can be used for both sequential as well as partitioned data sets.

Example 5: The *-x* option is used to list several filenames (beginning with a *c*) across the screen on each line of output. The number of filenames on each line varies from system to system. If you wanted all the files in */bin* listed, you could use the command *ls -x /bin*.

The equivalent command in MVS is LISTALC (listing allocated data sets). This command will allow you to list the names of all of the allocated data sets in your catalog.

Example 6: *ls -R* lists not only the contents of the current directory but also all files in all directories lower in the hierarchical directory tree, which in this example includes the subdirectory *tmp. ls */** also lists all files in the current directory and all files both one and two levels down in the directory hierarchy. This just shows that the *ls* command is very versatile and can be used with number of options.

In MVS, the **LISTA** command without any operands will accomplish the same as *ls -R*. But **LISTA** provides an additional function of providing status of a sequential or a member of a partitioned data set by adding the operand **STATUS**.

Example 7: You can tell that the two names are actually links to just one file by using the i-node option *-i* of the *ls* command. An i-node is an entry in a data table that the system uses to define the characteristics of a single file. If two names reference the same file, then both names will be associated with the same *i-node* number. If the names are actually linked, then the *i-node* numbers (1341) will be identical.

In MVS, if a member of a partitioned data set were created with an alias, it will have the similar function as the *i-node*.

The example shown for MVS for listing broadcast messages with **LISTB** command can be accomplished in UNIX by just issuing *ls* command for a particular file containing those messages.

COPYING FILES

The UNIX command *cp* copies one file to another. To make a copy of a file, use the *cp* (copy) command.

cp filename newfilename

where *filename* is the file you wish to copy (source) and *newfilename* (destination) is the file you are creating.

cp practice sample (Makes a copy of *practice*, to a file called *sample*.)
ls practice sample

The example created a new file called *sample* that has the same contents as practice. If *sample* already exists, the *cp* command will overwrite the previous contents. User profiles are often set up so that *cp* will prompt for confirmation before it overwrites an existing file. If your profile is not set up in this manner, use the **-i** option (*cp -i*) to get the confirmation prompt.

FUNCTION	MVS	UNIX
Format	**COPY** {input dataset[(member)] [/password]/*}+ {output dataset[(member)] [/password]/*}+ [replace/noreplace] [num/nonum]	***cp*** *[option(s)] input_file output_file* ***cp*** */pathname/sourcefile /pathname/destfile*
Example 1	**COPY** osc.text osc.text.backup {Makes a backup copy of osc.text data set.}	***cp*** *chap4 chap4.archive* {Makes a copy of file *chap4* to file *chap4.archive*. It assumes that the file is in current directory.}
Example 2	**COPY** osc.text osc.text.backup nonum {Makes a backup copy of osc.text data set, but do not copy the source line numbers.}	***cp*** *-i chap4 chap5* {Requests confirmation if the destination file *chap5* already exists.}

FUNCTION	MVS	UNIX
Example 3	**COPY** memo.text(invnt) invnt.text {Makes a copy of a member of a partitioned data set memo.text to a sequential data set invnt.text.}	***cp*** */usr1/armando/mail /usr1/preet* {Makes a copy of file *mail* in directory *usr1* to file *preet* in directory *usr1*.}
Example 4	**COPY** sales.text memo.text(sales) {Adds a copy of existing data setsales.text as a new member of the PDS memo.text.}	
Example 5	**COPY** markt.text(forcast) memo.text(forcast) {Copies an existing member of a PDS markt.text to another PDS memo.text.}	

Note: In its simplest form, copying data sets in MVS is similar to copying files in UNIX.

RENAMING FILES

To rename one of your files, use the *mv* (move) command.

mv oldfilename newfilename

where *oldfilename* is the original filename and *newfilename* is the new filename. For instance, to rename sample as *workfile type*:

mv sample workfile
ls practice workfile

This moves the contents of sample into the new file *workfile*. (Note: Moving a file into an existing file overwrites the data in the existing file.) The file *workfile* will be created if it does not exist. The file *practice* will be delected if the *workfile* already existed. Profiles are often set up so that *mv* will prompt for confirmation before doing this. If your profile is not set up in this manner, use the *-i* option (*mv -i*) to get the confirmation prompt.

Other options available with the *mv* command are

i Invokes interactive mode and prompts the user for permission to process with the move operation if the file with new name already exists.
f Negates the effect of *i* option, if an alias was set up (alias *mv 'mv -i'*).
\- Indicates that the next argument is a filename beginning with a dash.

The commands *mv* (move), *cp* (copy), and *ln* (link) allow you to move and copy files. The *cp* command makes a copy of a file. The main difference between *cp* and *mv* is that *mv* obliterates the source file, whereas after a copy operation both the source and target files exist. With *ln* command, a new name is created that references the original file. *ln* command only creates a new name, but it does not make any new copies of the data and leaves the source file alone. The new name and the old name refer to the same thing (same data).

The *mv* command moves a file from one location to another. In most cases, the *mv* operation is quite fast because it is simply renaming the file; however, sometimes the file must be copied. In general, you cannot use *mv* to rename directories. If the source file is an ordinary file and the target file is a directory file, then *mv* will move the source file into the target directory, retaining the old source filename. You can always verify the operation by using the *ls* command. The *mv* command in UNIX can also be used to move multiple source files into a directory, if the target file is a directory.

FUNCTION	MVS	UNIX
Format	**RENAME** oldname newname [alias]	***mv*** *[option(s)] source_file target_file*
Example 1	**RENAME** chap3.text chap3.save.text {Renames a sequential data set chap3.text to chap3.save.text.}	***mv*** *chap3 chap3.save Bourne* {After the operation, there will be only one file, *chap3.save,* as shown below.} *ls chap** *chap3.save*
Example 2	**RENAME** chap1.text (invnt) chap1.save(sold) {Renames member 'invnt' of the PDS to 'sold'.}	***mv*** *-i chap3 chap3.save* *overwrite chap3.save? y*
Example 3	**RENAME** chap1.text chap1.save.text {Renames an entire PDS chap1.text to chap1.save.text, without affecting the members.}	***mv*** *chap1 chap2 chap3 mydir* {The command will move all three files *chap1 chap2 chap3* into the *mydir* directory.}
Example 4	**RENAME** chap2.*.text chap2.*.save {Renames multiple data sets whose qualifiers are the same except the middle.}	***mv*** *-f chap3 chap3.save* {Negates the effect of *i* option if an alias was set up with (alias ***mv*** *'mv -i'*)}
Example 5	**RENAME alias** chap2.text(myfile) chap2.text(saveit) {This will establish an alias for a member myfile.}	***mv*** *- -wrngfile scrfile* {*mv* indicates that the next argument is a filename beginning with a dash. The command renames file *-wrngfile* to *scrfile.*}

In MVS, the **RENAME** command changes the name of a data set, including cataloged data sets and members of a partitioned data sets. This command can also be used to add an alias of a partitioned data set. To rename a password protected data set, the password must be deleted first and then reassigned after the renaming. Renaming a whole

PDS and leaving its members' names alone has the same syntax as renaming a sequential data set.

Multiple data sets can be renamed simultaneously by specifying an asterisk (*) for a data set name index. The command then renames all data sets with names that match the specified name except the part indicated by the asterisk. However, the part indicated by the asterisk must be in the same location in both the old and new names.

DELETING FILES

To delete files, use the *rm* (remove) command. For instance, to delete workfile, type

rm workfile
ls practice

The *rm* command allows you to delete ordinary files. The *rmdir* command is used to remove directories (discussed later).

To remove a file, you must have a write permission in the directory containing that file, but you need neither read nor write permission for the file itself. Removing a file actually removes only an entry from the directory. If you have the directory's write permission for a file, then *rm* may, as a precaution, ask you if you really want to remove that file. In MVS, the file itself has the protection. Therefore, security deletion must be handled with **PROTECT** command, after the data set has been deleted.

The *rm* command allows the following options:

- *i* Prompts interactively if you want to remove the file.
- *f* Forces option of *rm* will suppress the verification query.
- *r* Is used to remove a directory, all its contents, and all the files and directories in that directory's subtree. The recursive option obliterates the whole tree below the mentioned point.
- * Removes all files in the current directory.

It is important to note that *rm* can be very dangerous. Once a file has been removed you cannot get it back, except, possibly, from system backups (which may or may not contain the file). It may take the system administrators several days to recover your deleted file, so use a great deal of caution when deleting files. Profiles are often set up so that *rm* will prompt for confirmation. If your profile is not set up in this manner, use the *-i* option to get the confirmation prompt. Do not use *rm* * or *rm -r* options unless you want to clean out a directory entirely.

FUNCTION	MVS	UNIX
Format	**DELETE** (entry-name)[/password][,....]	***rm*** *[option(s)] thefile*
Example 1	**DELETE** myfile1.text {Deletes the data set myfile1.text.}	***rm*** *myfile* {Remove the filet *myfile.*}

FUNCTION	MVS	UNIX
Example 2	**DELETE** osc.text(myfile1) {Deletes member of a partitioned data set.}	***rm*** * {Removes all ordinary files in the current directory.}
Example 3	**DELETE** osc.*.text {Deletes all data sets with a first qualifier of osc, a low-level qualifier of text, and any second qualifier.}	***ls*** *-1 chap** *-rw-rw-rw- 1 kc 41088 Nov 10 10:20 chap* *-r--r--r-- 1 kc 45173 Dec 23 8:30 chap.bak* ***rm*** *chap chap.bak* ***rm:*** *override protection 444 for chap.bak? y*
Example 4	**DELETE** (apl.asm test.data memos.text) {Deletes multiple data sets with completely different names.}	***rm*** *-i chap chap.bak* ***rm:*** *remove chap? y* ***rm:*** *remove chap.bak? y*
Example 5		***rm*** *-f chap chap.bak* {Removes both files without security verifications.}
Example 6		***rm*** *-r chapdir* {Remove the directory *chapdir* and all its files, subdirectories, etc.}
Example 7		**rm -i** * {Removes every file in the current directory and complains that the file *-il* is not found, etc.}

In MVS, the **DELETE** command deletes a data set from a catalog or deletes a member of a partitioned data set. However, the catalog entry from a partitioned data set can only be deleted after all partitioned data set members have been deleted, which is equivalent to deleting files in a directory in UNIX. Members of a data set can be deleted only if the members to be deleted are specified. If aliases are to be deleted, they must be specified individually.

As with **RENAME** command, you can enter an asterisk (*) instead of one of the qualifiers to **delete** multiple data sets at once. To delete multiple data sets with completely different names, just list the names of each data set between parentheses.

PRINTING FILES

The *lp* and *lpr* commands print files on the system line printer. Systems with several line printers may offer several versions of these commands, or command line options may be used to select a specific printer. *lp* is available on System V and *lpr* is available on Berkeley systems.

It is not possible to share a printer among several users simultaneously. Instead, the printer is assigned to a single user for the duration of a print request. The main role of the *lpr* command is to synchronize requests for the line printer. If the line printer is busy when you enter the *lpr* command, your files are placed in a queue and then printed when the printer is free.

The most common use of *lpr* is to print a file or group of files:

lpr filename

or

lpr [-P printername] filename

To get a list of the printers available to your machine, type

lpstat -p

This command lists all the printers that your system knows about, by name. It also gives some status information on the printers. PostScript-capable printers often have "*ps*" as some part of their names. On some systems you can use the command *lprloc* to get a list of available printers by name, along with their type and location.

The *lpr* command normally prints a banner page before and after the file (unless suppressed), but the file contents are not changed. *lpr* does not insert blank lines at the top and bottom of pages or number pages or perform any of the other actions of the *pr* command. If you wish to paginate or title the contents of the file, you should use the *pr* command first, unless you have done so with the text editor. The print output from *lpr* can be modified with the following options:

r Prints the file on the default printer and delete the file.
h Queues the file to the printer and print without the banner page.
p Prints a heater at the top of each page.
s Prints a particular version of a file directly from the user's directory.
f Prints file using any FORTRAN carriage control characters present in column 1.

The *pr* command is used to paginate and title text files. The most common use of the *pr* command is to prepare a text file for printing on a line printer. *pr* is also used to produce several columns of output, compress files by replacing spaces with tabs, expand tabs into spaces, number the lines in a file, and perform other simple reformatting tasks. You can modify the print with the following options:

h Quotes the following text.
t Completely omits page headers and footers.
n Produces multicolumn output, *N* being the number of columns.
1 Produces a page of output in one long line.

Note: Line printers are used for text-only files. Laser printers are needed to handle graphics or PostScript files. PostScript is a page-description language developed by Adobe Systems, Inc., and was specially designed for creating graphics and typography on a printed page. The option flag **-P** printername specifies which printer to use and is optional (as indicated by the brackets). When no printer is given, the print command uses the system default printer. However, on some systems, you must always specify the printer with the **-P** flag. For more information on printing commands, use the *man* command to consult the manual pages on *lpq*, *lpr*, and *lprm*.

The following examples illustrate the differences between various UNIX commands that can be used to print the output.

PR **COMMAND**	***CAT*** **COMMAND**	***LPR*** **COMMAND**
pr */etc/motd* | *head*	***cat*** */etc/motd*	***lpr*** *motd*
Jun 24 20:40 1995	*Welcome to YOUR System V*	*Welcome to YOUR System V*
Page 1	*for personal computers.*	*for personal computers.*
Welcome to YOUR System V *for personal computers.*		

FUNCTION	MVS	UNIX
Format	**DSPRINT** dsname[(member)] [/password] printer [nonum] **PRINTDS** dataset(dsname) dest(printer-name) [nonum]	***lpr*** *[option(s)] file(s)* ***lpq*** *[option(s)] [-Printer] [job#] [user]*
Example 1	**PRINTDS** dataset(my.text) dest(printer1) {Prints data set 'my.text' to printer 'printer1'}	***lpr*** *chap1.pr chap2.pr chap3.pr* {Prints a group of files.}
Example 2	**DSPRINT** my.text printer1 {Prints data set 'my.text' to printer 'printer1'.}	***lpr*** *-Plaser -#3 chap1* {Queues three copies of file *chap1* to the printer named *laser.*}
Example 3	**DSPRINT** osc.text(myfile) dest(printer1) {Prints data set 'my.text' to printer 'printer1'.}	***lpr*** *-hPlaser chap1* {Queues file *chap1* to the printer named *laser* and print it without the banner page.}
Example 4		***lpr*** *-r chap1* {Prints file *chap1* to the default printer and delete the file.}
Example 5		***lpr*** *-p chap1* {Prints file *chap1* with header on each page.}

FUNCTION	MVS	UNIX
Example 5		***lpr*** *-f chap1* {Prints file *chap1* using FORTRAN control characters in first column.}
Example 5		***lpr*** *-s chap1* {Prints file *chap1* directly from the user's directory.}
Example 6		***lpq*** *-Plaser* {Displays information about the queue *laser.*}
Example 7		***ls*** *../plot/mail | pr -t -ll -4* *plot1 plot2 plot3 plot4* {Prints four filenames on a single line as four columns and skips all headers and footers.}

In MVS, there are several ways to print data sets. Many involve printing the results of a batch job by adding commands as part of the JCL. Interactively, the simplest way to print data sets is to use **PRINTDS** or **DSPRINT**. In their simplest form, both these commands require the same information (the name of the data set and the name of the printer). The *nonum* parameter allows suppression of numbers if the data set is numbered. The main difference between the two commands is that **DSPRINT** assumes first operand to be the data set to be printed and the second identifies the printer.

PRINTDS must include the words DATASET and DEST (destination), including the proper names in the parentheses, the DEST being the name of the printer.

MANAGING FILE PERMISSIONS

Command Structure

The *chmod* (change mode), *chown* (change owner), and *chgrp* (change group) commands are used to control the access rights to files and ownership of files. The interactive ability to fine tune the file system for flexible and protected access to files is one of the strengths of the UNIX system. All these commands are usable *only by the owner of a file* or *by the superuser*. Commands *chown* and *chgrp* will be discussed later.

The *chmod* (change mode) command is used to change the permissions of a file or directory. A file has four sets of permissions for user, group, others, and all, which can be represented by the letters *u*, *g*, *o*, and *a*, respectively.

You also know that each of these groups can have different combinations of read, write, and execute, which can be represented by *r*, *w*, and *x*, respectively. Command *chmod* provides two methods for specifying a change in file/directory protection: octal or symbolic.

Symbolic to Octal Conversions

SYMBOLIC	BINARY	OCTAL
---	000	0
--x	001	1
-w-	010	2
-wx	011	3
r--	100	4
r-x	101	5
rw-	110	6
rwx	111	7

Thus, if the setting you want is *rw-r--r--*, the octal number will be 644.

Changing Access Permissions Using the chmod Command

The *chmod* command uses the plus (+) sign to *add* permissions, a minus (-) sign to *remove* permissions, or an equal (=) to *assign* permissions. Therefore, the final syntax is the user class (u, g, o, or a) followed by the action to take (+, -, or =), followed by the permission to change (r, w, or x).

ls -l friends
-rw-r--r-- 1 scot admin 416 Mar 23 12:20 friends
chmod g+w friends {Adds write access to group members for file *friends.*}
ls -l friends
-rw-rw-r-- 1 scot admin 416 Mar 23 12:20 friends

To change the permissions of all classes of users, we could do the following:

chmod ugo+x friends {Adds execute access for everyone for file *friends.*}
ls -l friends
-rwxrwxr-x 1 scot admin 416 Mar 23 12:20 friends

Instead of specifying the three groups, we can use the *a* (all) option for all users command to turn on permissions:

chmod a-x friends {Removes execute access from everyone for file *friends.*}
ls -l friends
-rw-rw-r-- 1 scot admin 416 Mar 23 12:20 friends

The *chmod* command also supports the *-R* (recursive) option to change the permissions in a directory and all its subdirectories.

FUNCTION	MVS	UNIX
Format	**ALLOCATE** dsname [(member)] [/password] **PROTECT** dsname [add/replace/delete/list] [pwread/nopwread] [pwwrite/nowrite] [data('character-string')]	***chmod*** *mode file(s)* {The mode is either specified in octal or symbolic.}
Example 1	**PROTECT** 'samuser.myfile.data' PWWRITE {Since the data set as created under TSO logon and is still allocated, the PROTECT command cannot be used until the data set is freed.}	***chmod*** *555 myfile.dat* {This command changes the protection of the file *myfile.dat* to give the owner, group members, and others read and execute access. No one has write access.}
Example 2	**PROTECT** myfile.cobol ADD(new-password) {If the old password already exists, the existing protection is assumed, but the password is changed.}	***chmod*** *+x myfile.dat* {This command adds the execute access to all types of users (owners, group members, others).}
Example 3	**PROTECT** myfile.data ADD(new-password) {NOPWREAD and PWRITE permissions are assumed.}	***chmod*** *g+x myfile.dat* {This command adds the group execute access file *myfile.dat.*}
Example 4	**PROTECT** myfile.data ADD(new-password) PWWRITE {This command adds new password for write permissions.}	***chmod*** *go-rw myfile.dat* or *chmod o-w,g-w myfile.dat* {This command removes write permissions for the file *myfile.dat* from group members and all others.}
Example 5		***chmod*** *u+x file1* {Gives your permission to execute a file that you own.} {This command gives you execute permission for the file *file1.*}
Example 6		***chmod*** *g+r file2* {Gives members of your group permission to read a file.} {This command gives the group permission to read the file *file2.*}
Example 7		***chmod*** *a+r *.pub* {Gives read permission to everyone for a particular type of file.} {This command gives everyone permission to read all files with the extension *.pub.*}
Example 8		***chmod*** *g+wx $HOME/OSC* {Gives the group write and execute permission.} {This command gives all members of the group permission to place files in the directory OSC in your home directory. They can also list (ls) the contents of this directory.}

FUNCTION	MVS	UNIX
Example 9		***chmod*** *a=rw myfile.dat* {Gives everyone read and write permission.}
Example A		***chmod*** *o-rwx myfile.dat* {This command gives absolute protection assignment by giving the own read, write, and execute access to the file *myfile.dat* and makes the file *myfile.dat* inaccessible to others.}
Example B		***chmod*** *go+rw *.txt* {This command grants read and write permissions for all files with a qualifier *txt* by using the wildcard *.}

In MVS, RACF (beyond the scope of this text) provides the security protection for files. Unlike UNIX, the **PROTECT** command sets or changes passwords and protection modes (read or write protection) for a data set on a direct access device.

MODE PROTECTION	PROTECTION	PASSWORD	NEEDS	LIST OPERAND DISPLAY
		Read	**Write**	
PWREAD	PWREAD PWWRITE	Password required	Password required	READ and WRITE PASSWORD
NOPWREAD	NOPWREAD PWWRITE	Password *not* required	Password required	WRITE PASSWORD
PWWRITE	NOPWREAD PWWRITE	Password *not* required	Password required	
NOWRITE	PWREAD NOWRITE	Password required	Write prohibited	READ ONLY

If one of the four possible protection modes is specified, the combination of protection modes, together with the types of protection provided and displays produced by the LIST operand, are illustrated above.

NOPWREAD and NOWRITE are mutually exclusive. If this combination is specified, NOPWREAD and PWWRITE are assumed. If a password is specified but the protection mode operand is omitted, then the following rules apply:

- If a password is assigned to the data set for the first time, NOPWREAD and PWWRITE are assumed
- If a password is changed, the existing protection mode is assumed
- If the data set that was allocated by LOGON or ALLOCATE command, no protection can be applied until the data set is freed.

For day-to-day usage, the UNIX file security system is much simpler and versatile.

Changing Access Permissions Using the umask Command

The *umask* command sets the default file protection and is inverse of the *chmod* command. An octal "7" implies "no protection" in *umask.* When you first create a file it is given a set of permissions, that are determined by the *umask* (user mask) which is a built-in shell command.

```
umask
22
```

The *umask* command without any arguments will display the current values. Actually, the *umask* is 022, but leading zeros are ignored. The number is called a mask because each digit is subtracted from a system default value. The default value is usually *rw-rw-rw-* or 666 in octal notation. Because the *umask* is subtracted from the default value, you cannot turn on permissions that are already turned off in the default value.

Determining the *umask*

OCTAL VALUE	CORRESPONDING PERMISSIONS
666 (current default permissions)	*rw-rw-rw-*
600 (permissions you want)	*rw----------*
066 (umask)	

The *T shell* uses a default *umask* of 022 which will create files with *-rw-r--r--* permissions. The only arguments to *umask* is to set the *umask.*

```
umask 066
cat new
ls -l new
-rw-------   1 scot   admin      0 Mar 29 09:51 new
```

With a *umask* of 066, only the creator of the file will be able to read or write to the file; therefore, you might want to change the *umask* back to 022.

DIRECTORIES AND CATALOGS

A directory is a file that can contain other files and directories. You have already been used to changing directories with *cd* and specifying paths to other directories with operators such as **..** and **/**. In this section we'll learn about more directory operators and more about paths.

Directory Structure

UNIX directories are similar to regular files; they both have names and both contain information. Directories, however, contain other files and directories. Many of the same rules and commands that apply to files also apply to directories. All files and directories in the UNIX system are stored in a hierarchical tree structure. Envision it as an upside-down tree, as shown in Figure 6.1.

At the top of the tree is the root directory. Its directory name is simply / (a slash character). Below the root directory is a set of major subdirectories that usually include *bin*, *dev*, *etc*, *lib*, *pub*, *tmp*, and *usr*. For example, the */bin* directory is a subdirectory, or child, of / (the root directory). The root directory, in this case, is also the parent directory of the *bin* directory. Each path leading down, away from the root, ends in a file or directory. Other paths can branch out from directories, but not from files.

Many directories on a UNIX system have traditional names and traditional contents. For example, directories named *bin* contain binary files, which are the executable command and application files. A *lib* directory contains library files, which are often collections of routines that can be included in programs by a compiler. *dev* contains device files, which are the software components of terminals, printers, disks, and the like. *tmp* directories are for temporary storage, such as when a program creates a file for something and then deletes it when it is done. The *etc* directory is used for miscellaneous administrative files and commands. *pub* is for public files that anyone can use. And *usr* has traditionally been reserved for user directories, but on large systems it usually contains other *bin*, *tmp*, and *lib* directories.

Your *home* directory is the directory that you start out from when you first *log in*. It is the top-level directory of your account. Your home directory name is almost always the same as your userid.

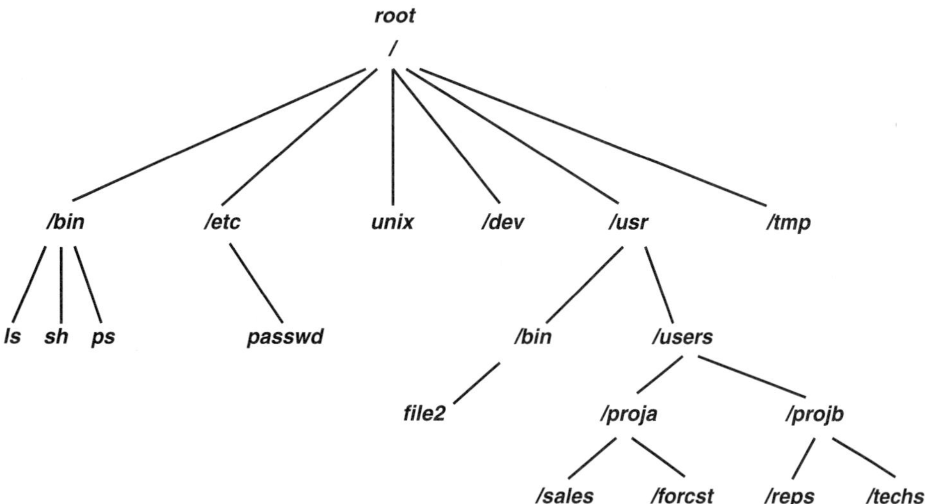

FIGURE 6.1 UNIX directory structure.

Every directory and file on the system has a path by which it is accessed, starting from the root directory. The path to the directory is called its *pathname*. You can refer to any point in the directory hierarchy in two different ways: using its full (or *absolute*) pathname or its *relative* pathname. The full pathname traces the absolute position of a file or directory back to the root directory, using slashes (/) to connect every point in the path. For example, in Figure 6.1, the full pathname of *file2* would be */usr/bin/file2*.

Relative pathnames begin with the current directory (also called the working directory, the one you are in). If */usr* were your current directory, then the relative pathname for *file2* would be *bin/file2*.

If you are using *C shell*, *T shell*, or the *Bourne-Again shell*, UNIX provides some abbreviations for a few special directories. The character "~" (tilde) refers to your home directory. The home directory of any user (including you, if you want) can be abbreviated from */parent-directories/userid* to *~userid*. Likewise, you can abbreviate */parent-directories/youruserid/file* to *~/file*. The current directory has the abbreviation **.** (period). The parent of the current working directory uses **..** (two consecutive periods) as its abbreviation.

If a directory name is the new working directory. This means that any files you now create or modify will be placed, or must reside, in the directoryname. The argument directoryname is optional; if you enter *cd* with no argument, your current directory is set to your home directory.

It is possible to move through your own *home* directory hierarchy and also through much of the UNIX system directory hierarchy with the *cd* command. To aid in directory traversal, the special names **.** and **..** are defined as follows:

. Indicates the current working directory (CWD).

.. Indicates the parent of the current working directory.

For example, to move to the parent directory of your CWD, enter the command:

cd ..

There are a number of UNIX commands which facilitate directory manipulations. Some of these functions are

- Displaying / creating pathnames
- Creating directories
- Removing / deleting directories
- Displaying / browsing directories
- Changing directories
- Moving files between directories
- Moving or relocating directories
- Copying files between directories
- Copying directories
- Renaming directories
- Listing files in a directory
- Printing working directories

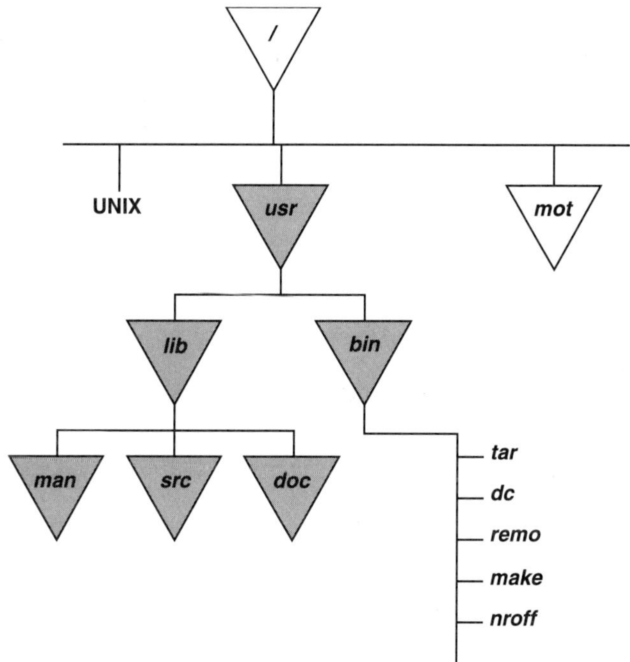

FIGURE 6.2 The current directory and its subtree.

Displaying / Creating Pathnames

The files that in the current directory are directly accessible and they can be referenced by simply entering their name. Files that are not in the current directory must be referenced using a pathname. A pathname specifies a path through the file system that leads to the desired file, as illustrated in Figure 6.2.

The most important thing to remember about paths through the file system is that they can start only in one of two places, your current directory or the root directory. Pathnames that start with the "/" (slash) character are *absolute pathnames*, specifying a path starting in the root directory. All other pathnames are *relative pathnames*, and they specify a path starting in your current directory. A few simple rules apply to all pathnames:

- If the pathname starts with a slash, then the path starts in the root directory. All other paths start in the current directory.
- A pathname is either a list of names separated by slashes or a single name. The initial names in the list (if there are any) are directories. The final name in the list is the target file, which may be a file of any type. For example,

  /usr/lib/doc

- You can ascend the file system hierarchy by specifying the name .. in a pathname. All other names in a pathname descend the hierarchy. For example,

../../lib/doc

- No spaces are allowed in a pathname.

Examples (Figure 6.3)

1. The pathname */usr1/kc* is an *absolute* pathname specifying the file *kc*. Since the pathname starts with a slash, it is an absolute pathname that starts in the root directory. Obviously the directory *usr1* is a subdirectory of the root directory (Figure 6.3). The file *lib* in the */usr* directory is also a directory; it is my *home* directory.
2. The pathname *book/dos/w31* is a *relative* pathname, because it does not start with a slash. Hence the path starts from the current directory, which is */usr1/kc*. The directory *book* is a subdirectory of the current directory, *dos* is a subdirectory of *book*, and *w31* is the target file in directory *dos*.
3. The pathname *../../sam/mbox* is harder to understand. The path starts in the current directory, which is */usr1/kc/report*. The path leads to the parent of *usr1/kc/report*,

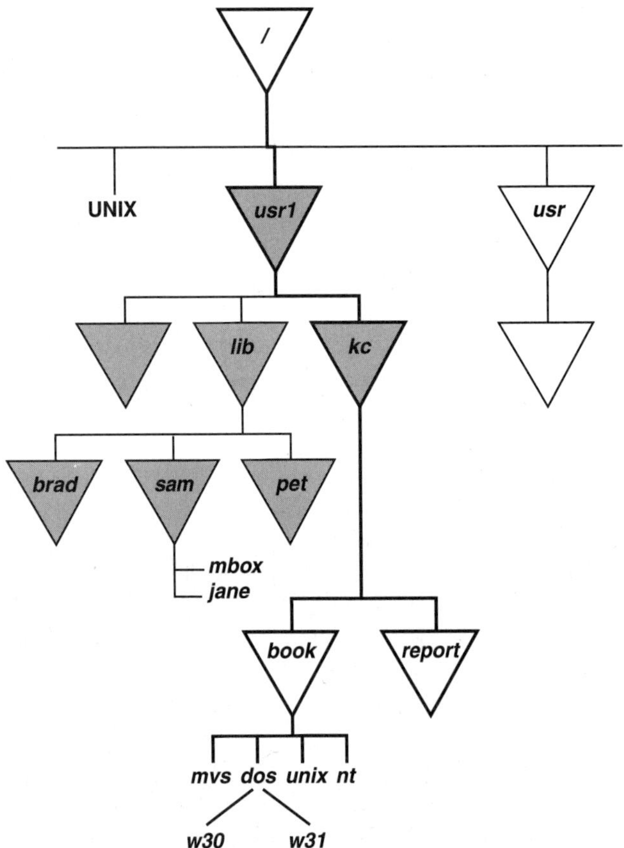

FIGURE 6.3 The pathname */usr1/kc*.

which is */usr1/kc*. The path then ascends further to */usr1* and then descends to the directory *sam*. The target file is *mbox* in the *sam* directory.

Long pathnames are very hard to use. It is usually better to *cd* (change directory) to the desired path.

Creating Directories

The *mkdir* (make directory) command is used to create directories. When the system creates a directory, it automatically inserts entries for the names **.** and **..**. The name **.** is a pseudonym for the directory, and the name **..** is a pseudonym for its parent directory. All directories contain these entries, and ordinary users are prohibited from removing these entries. A directory that contains only the entries for **.** and **..** is considered empty.

The command *mkdir* will create a directory named *mydir*, which will be a subdirectory of the current directory. If you enter the command *ls mydir*, you will discover that *mydir* does not contain any ordinary files. The command *ls -a mydir* will reveal that *mydir* contains two entries, **.** and **..**. The *i* and *d* options to *ls* can help you understand how links glue the file system together, as illustrated below:

```
ls -id . mydir/.. mydir mydir/.

1632    .
1343    mydir
1343    mydir/.
1632    mydir/..
```

You can consider directories to be filing cabinets into which you categorize your work. Just as with the filing cabinet analogy, the better you organize your work into directories, the easier it is to retrieve the file that you want. The *mkdir* (make directory) command can be used to create one or more new directories.

```
mkdir temp
ls -ld temp
drwx--x--x   2 scot   admin    24 Apr 4 13:23 temp
```

FUNCTION	MVS	UNIX
Format	**ALLOCATE** DA{dsname} {tracks/cyl/blocks} + {space (pri sec)} {dsorg (po) dir(number)} {Creates a new partitioned data set.} **ALLOCATE** DA{dsname} like(dsname) + [dir(number)]} {Creates a new partitioned data set like an existing data set but adds more directory space for additional members.}	***mkdir*** *directory_name*

FUNCTION	MVS	UNIX
	DEFMCAT (NAME(master-catalog-name) VOL(volser) + [TR/CYL/REC] [AUTH(user-security)] + [OWNER(id)] {Creates a master catalog.}	
	DEFUCAT (NAME(user-catalog-name) VOL(volser) + [TR/CYL/REC] [AUTH(user-security)] + [OWNER(id)] + [CAT(master-cat-name[/password])] {Creates a user catalog.}	
Example 1	**ALLOCATE** DA(inv.cobol) block(7200) space(10 5) + dir(10) dsorg(po) [keep/delete/**catalog**/uncatalog] {Creates a new partitioned data set with 10 primary and 5 secondary blocks with room for 10 new members.} As soon as this data set is created, it is added to the master catalog.	***mkdir*** *mydir* {Create a directory named *mydir* that will be a subdirectory of the current directory.}
Example 2	**ALLOCATE** DA{osc.cobol} like(inv.cobol) + dir(6)} {Creates a new partitioned data set like *inv.cobol* and adds 6 directory blocks for new members.}	***mkdir*** *oldmail* {Creates a subdirectory *oldmail* of the current directory.}
Example 3	**DEFMCAT** (NAME(sys1.mastcat) VOL(syslib) + [TR (10,5)] [AUTH(user-security)] + [OWNER(id)] {Creates a master catalog *sys1.mcat* on volume *syslib*; allocates 10 primary and 5 secondary tracks, with owner ID, and proper authorizations.}	***mkdir*** */bin/mickey* {Uses an absolute pathname to create a directory *mickey*.}
Example 4	**DEFUCAT** (NAME(osc.catlg) VOL(osc1) + [CYL(5,1)] [AUTH(user-security)] + [OWNER(id)] + [CAT(sys1.mcat[/bob])] {Creates a user catalog *osc.catlg* on volume *osc1*; allocates 5 primary and 1 secondary cylinders; points to *sys1.mastcat* master catalog, with owner ID and proper authorizations.}	***mkdir*** */usr/tmp/test* {Uses an absolute pathname to create a directory *test*.}
Example 5		***mkdir*** */bin/janet* **mkdir:** cannot access */bin* {You do not have write access to the */bin* directory to create a new subdirectory under it.}

There is no equivalence of a UNIX file system in MVS. The only concept of a directory hierarchy structure is allocation and definition of catalogs as illustrated in Figure 6.4.

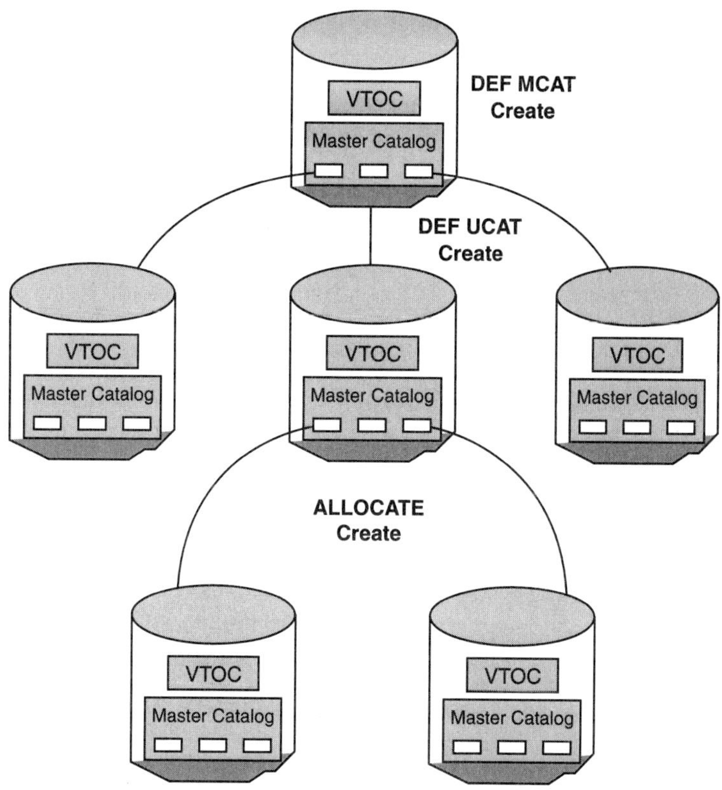

FIGURE 6.4 Overview of MVS catalog structure.

MVS supports a hierarchy of *catalogs* for a direct access device. Therefore, under the VTOC is a master catalog, which could be considered similar to the root directory. A user can also define a number of user catalogs for separation of files. A partitioned data set can be considered a simple single-level directory with members as its files. DEFMCAT and DEFUCAT are abbreviations for the *define master catalog* and *define user catalog* commands, respectively.

Removing/Deleting Directories

To remove a directory, first be sure that you are in the parent of that directory. Then use the command *rmdir* along with the directory's name. *rmdir* removes the directory only if it contains no files. You cannot remove a directory with *rmdir* unless all the files and subdirectories contained in it have been erased. Therefore, your first must remove all its contents. This prevents you from accidentally erasing important subdirectories. You could erase all the files in a directory by first going to that directory (use *cd*) and then using *rm* to remove all the files in that directory. Remember, using *rm* removes only the file. The quickest way to remove a directory and all its files and subdirectories (and their contents) is to use the *rm -r* command along with the directory's name. For example, to empty and remove your projects directory (assuming that you are in that directory), type

cd ..	Moves to that directory's parent.
rm -r projects	Removes the directory and its contents.

Directories can be deleted with the *-r* option of the *rm* command. The *-r* option recursively descends (depth-first) the file tree rooted at that directory and removes all the files (and in turn, the empty directories) it finds. Thus, the command

rm -r directoryname cite

deletes directoryname and all files and directories contained within the cite. Be very careful with this command! Another command to remove directories is the *rmdir* (remove directory) command. Unlike the *rm -r* command the **rmdir** command requires that the directory be empty.

FUNCTION	MVS	UNIX
Format	**DELETE** dsname[(member, ...)] + [user-catalog/alias/path] {Deletes a sequential data set from a catalog or a member of a partitioned data set.}	***rmdir*** *directory*
Example 1	**DELETE** osc.cobol {Deletes a sequential data set *osc.cobol* from the master catalog.}	***rmdir*** *osc* {Removes directory *osc* and its subdirectories, and files *only* if the contents are empty.}
Example 2	**DELETE** po.cobol(mem1, mem3,mem4) {Deletes members of a partitioned data set from a catalog.}	***rmdir*** */usr1/sam/janet* {Removes the directory *janet,* which is a subdirectory of */user1/sam,* provided it contains no files.}
Example 3	**DELETE** po.cobol **This partitioned data set cannot be deleted. It is not empty.**	**rmdir** janet **rmdir: janet not empty** {Checks the contents of this directory and empties them before issuing the command again.}

FUNCTION	MVS	UNIX
Format	**FREE** {dsname[(member,....)] + dsname[(member, ...)] / all} [delete/keep/catalog] {Releases allocated data sets. In addition, it deletes the data set if the **delete** option is specified.}	**rm** *-r [options(s)] directory*

FUNCTION	MVS	UNIX
Example 1	**FREE** po1.cobol(mem2, mem3) + po2.fort(fort1, fort3) delete {Deletes selected members of two data sets.}	***rm*** *- r book* {Removes the directory *book*, its subdirectories, and its files, regardless of its contents.}
Example 2	**FREE** po.cobol delete {Deletes the data set and all members of the data set.}	***rm*** *-r /usr/usr1/osc* {Removes the *osc* directory, all subdirectories of *osc*, and all files in those directories.}

In MVS, the **DELETE** command deletes a data set from a catalog or deletes a member of a partitioned data set. Like the *rmdir* command in UNIX, the catalog entry for a partitioned data set can be deleted only after all partitioned data set members have been deleted. In addition, when an entry for a data set is deleted from the catalog, the data set can be deleted at the same time. Members of a data set can be deleted only if the members to be deleted are specified. If aliases are to be specified, they must be specified individually.

If the data set is password protected, the password for the data set can be deleted with the **PROTECT** command.

The **FREE** command also deletes both sequential and partitioned data sets or their members with DELETE option.

Displaying/Browsing Directories

When you initially log in, the UNIX system places you in your home directory. The *pwd* command will display the full pathname of the current directory you are in.

pwd
/home/userid

By typing the *ls -a* command, you can see every file and directory in the current directory, regardless of whether it is your home directory. To display the contents of your home directory when it is not your current directory, enter the *ls* command followed by the full pathname of your home directory.

ls /home/userid

If you are using a shell other than the *Bourne shell*, instead of typing the full pathname for your directory, you can also use the tilde (~) symbol with the *ls* command to display the contents of your home directory.

ls~

To help you distinguish between files and directories in a listing, the *ls* command has a *-F* option that appends a distinguishing mark to the entry name showing the kind of data it contains: no mark for regular files / for directories * for executable programs.

The following example illustrates how it is possible to get a long listing of the files within a directory using the *-l* option of the *ls* command,

```
ls -l
-rwxr-xr-x 1   omar   4799 Aug 28 14:25   a.out
drwxr-xr-x 1   omar   4799 Aug 28 14:25   dirl/
-rw-r--r-- 1   omar   6541 Aug 28 14:35   prog.c
```

The first 10-character field gives the type and protection mode of the file. If the first character is a *d*, the entry is a directory (to which you may *cd* if you wish). If the character is a **-**, the entry is a plain file which may contain text, executable code, or data. The second column is the number of links, and the third column indicates the owner of the file. The fourth column is the size of the file in bytes, and the date given is that of the file's last modification. The last column is the filename itself. Many options can be used with the *ls* command.

Note that the *ls* command adds a character at the end of the filename to indicate certain features. For example, a star (*) denotes a plain file with its execute permission enabled for the user (e.g., an executable binary file), and a slash (/) denotes a directory. These characters are not part of the filename and must not be typed in when typing filenames in commands.

In MVS, the **LISTCAT** command *without* operands or with ENTRY and LEVEL operands will also display the names of data sets in your user ID's catalog. **LISTDS** *dsname mem* also can be used to list members of a partitioned data set.

Changing Directories

When given a filename, commands will usually operate on the files in the current working directory. To change directories, the *cd* command is used as follows:

```
cd directoryname
```

where *cd* is the change working directory command and *directoryname* is the new working directory. This means that any files you now create or modify will be placed, or must reside, in directoryname. The argument directoryname is optional; if you enter *cd* with no argument, your current directory is set to your home directory.

It is possible to move through your own home directory hierarchy and also through much of the UNIX system directory hierarchy with the *cd* command. To aid in directory traversal, the special names **.** and **..** are revisited as follows:

. Indicates the current working directory.

.. Indicates the parent of the current working directory.

For example, to move to the parent directory of your CWD, enter the command

```
cd ..<
```

The *cd* (change directory) command can also move the user to a different working directory. Let us change to the */usr/bin* directory.

cd /usr/bin
pwd
/usr/bin

When we changed to the */usr/bin* directory, we specified its full pathname, since it starts from the root. If we were located in the */usr* directory and we wanted to change to */usr/bin*, we could use *cd bin* instead of specifying the path from the top of the file system, this is the *relative pathname* since it is relative to your current directory.

There are special characters that are used as directory abbreviations. If we were in the *home/huron2/admin/scot* directory and we wanted to go to the parent directory or */home/huron2/admin*, we would use the command *cd ..* to change to the parent directory.

If you know the username of another user, you can change to their directory without specifying the full pathname. The *T shell* will recognize the *~username* to mean the home directory for that particular user. The ~ by itself refers to your home directory.

Directory Abbreviations

.	Current directory.
..	Next directory "up" in the hierarchy. Also called parent directory.
~	Your home directory.
~username	The username's home directory.

Note: There is no such concept in MVS. However, the data sets can be allocated or freed for use purposes.

Examples of Using the *cd* Command

To go directly to your home directory, type

cd

To move to another directory, use a relative pathname:

cd *../Secondyear*

This moves you up one level in the directory tree and then moves you into the subdirectory *Secondyear.*

To move to a directory using a full pathname:

cd */u/usr/physics/ercy04/ProjectX*

This moves you to the directory *ProjectX,* which is in the home directory of the user *ercy04.*

To get back to the parent directory of projects, you can use the special **..** directory abbreviation.

cd *..*
pwd
/home/userid

Examples of Using the *cd* Command *(cont.)*

To move down one level to a subdirectory, type *cd Firstyear* This moves you down one level from your current directory to the subdirectory *Firstyear.*	Using *pwd* will show you your new current directory. *pwd* *home/userid/projects*
To move up one level of the directory tree, type *cd ..* Every directory contains a hidden directory .. (dot dot) that is a shorthand name for this directory's parent directory. Using this shorthand name enables you to move up the directory tree very quickly without having to enter long pathnames.	To change your current directory to another directory tree, use the *cd* command. For example, to move from your home directory to your projects directory, type *cd projects* (relative pathname from home directory) or *cd ~/projects* (full pathname using ~) or, *cd /home/userid/projects* (full pathname)

If you get lost, issuing the *cd* command without any arguments will place you in your home directory. It is equivalent to *cd ~*.

Moving Files Between Directories

The *mv* command can also be used to rename a file or directory or move entire directories.

mv post posters
*ls -d p**
posters postscript
mv friends.copy friends.old
*ls f**
friends friends.old friends.pl

You can move a file into another directory using the following syntax for the *mv* command:

mv source-filename destination-directory

For example,

mv sample.txt ~/projects

moves the file *sample.txt* into the projects directory. Since the *mv* command is capable of overwriting files, it would be prudent to use the *-i* option (confirmation prompt). You can also move a file into another directory and rename it at the same time by merely specifying the new name after the directory path, as follows:

mv sample.txt ~/projects/newsample.txt

Moving or Relocating Directories

Moving entire directories from one place to another is also possible with the *-r* option to the standard file moving command *mv*.

mv -r directoryname ..

Puts directoryname, together with all its subdirectories and files, in the parent of the current working directory, preserving its subdirectory structure.

Copying Files Between Directories

The *cp* (copy) command duplicates one or more files or directories. As with the *mv* command, you can copy files to other directories:

cp sample.txt ~/projects

As with *mv*, the new file will have the same name as the old one unless you change it while copying it.

cp sample.txt ~/projects/newsample.txt
cp friends friends.copy
*ls f**
friends friends.copy friends.pl

Copying Directories

Copying entire directories from one place to another is also possible with the *-r* option to the standard file copying program *cp*. For example,

cp -r directoryname ..

puts directoryname, together with all its subdirectories and files, in the parent of the current working directory.

To copy a directory, use the command

cp -r directory1 directory2

This copies *directory1* and everything that it contains to *directory2* . The directory is created if it does not exist. If *directory2* does exist, then *directory1* is created as a subdirectory within it.

The *-r* (recursive) allows you to copy whole directories, including subdirectories.

cp -r postscript post
*ls -d p**
post postscript

Renaming Directories

Renaming a directory is done using the *mv* command.

mv oldname newname

where *oldname* and *newname* are absolute or relative pathnames of files. Note that the renaming process can cause the file to be located to another directory. For example,

mv prog ../oldprog

causes the file *prog* to be relocated to the parent directory of the current working directory and renamed *oldprog*. The following example,

mv prog.c prog.f

changes the file's name' but keeps it in the same directory.

Another way to relocate files to other directories is to specify a directory as the second argument to the *mv* command. In this case the filename is retained, but its path changes to the given directory (i.e., it has been moved to the directory). When you use wildcard characters on UNIX, you should note that some combinations might not yield the expected results. For example, if your current working directory contained the files:

ls
afile.c bfile.c cfile.c

then the command

*mv *.c *.f*

does not result in the disappearance of these files and the appearance of the files *afile.f*, *bfile.f*, and *cfile.f*. This command is expanded by the shell (before the execution of the *mv* command) as follows:

mv afile.c bfile.c cfile.c

This results in the *mv* command attempting to relocate the files *afile.c* and *bfile.c* to the directory *cfile.c*. Since no such directory exists, the command returns with a message alerting you to the proper usage.

Listing Files in a Directory

A directory is a place to put files and other directories. Directories allow you to organize your files by letting you put all like files in the same place. For instance, if you are a FORTRAN programmer, you would probably find it convenient to have all of your FORTRAN code in one directory. If you were working on several large FORTRAN projects, you could further organize your work by creating more directories, inside the FORTRAN directory, to hold each project.

The *ls* command gives you a list of files and directories but doesn't distinguish the two. If you want to know which of the items are files and which are directories, use the *ls* command with the *-F* option. Type *ls -F* now and examine the output. Compare the output of *ls* with and without the *-F* option. With *ls -F*, the / character at the end of an item signifies that that item is a directory. Items which are appended with a * character are executable programs. The rest of the items are probably "normal" text files. Remember the *ls* command and its variation *ls -F* to give you information about the files in the current directory. You will need these quite a bit as you learn and use UNIX.

The *ls* command can also be used to list the contents of subdirectories. For example, try the following command:

ls -F src

Using *ls -F* allows you to see what is inside the *src* directory. You should have noticed some directories inside the source directory. If you wanted to look a level deeper, into the *fortran* subdirectory of *src*, for example, you cannot just type *ls -F fortran*. Instead, you need to specify that *fortran* exists inside *src*. To do this, use the / character as demonstrated below:

ls -F src/fortran

Type the above command and you will see a list of files in the *src/fortran* directory. What you have done is specified a "path" to the directory you were interested in. The term "path" is used because you need to specify the directory levels, in order, from where you are to where you want to go, without skipping over any directories in between.

You've seen some of the directories "below" you, but don't assume you are at the top of the directory structure. Actually every user starts in his or her own *home directory* which is several levels deep. You can find out the name of the current directory with the *pwd* (print working directory) command. Try this command now. Again, note the use of the / character to separate the name of each directory. The very top directory is on the left signified by a / character and called the root directory. The rightmost word of the output from *pwd* identifies the current directory, which, in this case, is your home directory. Notice that your home directory has the same name as your userid.

Review Exercise

You can copy or move files from one directory to another. To do this you need to specify a path to the noncurrent directories as you did when using *ls -F* to look at the files in another directory. Move the file called *gilligan* into your *text* directory and then use ls to make sure it went where you wanted it to go.

So far we've been executing commands inside one directory, the home directory for your sample account. Now we'll try navigating through the directory structure with the UNIX *cd* (change directory) command. Change your current directory to the *text* directory with *cd* text. When you get there, try some of the commands you already know to explore this directory:

```
ls
Makefile   friends   friends.pl   hello.cc   postscript
```

Files starting with a . (dot) are hidden files. This means that *ls* won't normally display them. To display these files, we must use the *-a* (all) option. Generally, files are hidden because they are system files, there is no reason to display them under most circumstances. Most system dot files reside in your home directory.

When we issue an *ls* command, it is difficult to tell which files are directories and which are plain files. The *-F* (full) option to *ls* will append a slash (/) to files that are directories, a asterisk (*) to executable files, and an at sign (@) to hard links.

```
ls -F
Makefile   friends   friends.pl*  hello.cc   postscript/
```

This tells us that we have one executable and one directories in the current directory. One of the most common ways to list the files in a directory is with the *-l* (long) option.

```
ls -l
total 10
-rw-r--r--   1 scot   admin    242 Mar 7 17:00 Makefile
-rw-r--r--   1 scot   admin    416 Mar 23 12:20 friends
-rwxr--r--   1 scot   admin    868 Mar 15 14:24 friends.pl
-rw-r--r--   1 scot   admin     70 Mar 7 17:00 hello.cc
drwxr-xr-x   2 scot   admin   1024 Mar 24 15:43 postscript
```

The *-l* (for long) option gives information on the file permissions, number of hard links, file owner, file group, file size, time last modified, and the filename.

An argument to *ls* is the file or directory you want to list, if no argument is given ls lists the current directory. However, if you use *ls* with the directory name as the argument, you will get a listing of the files and directories located in that directory. If you wanted to see the permission of the directory use the *-d* (directory) option.

```
ls -l postscript
total 656
```

-rw-r--r-- 1 scot admin 326291 Mar 18 13:02 mosaic.ps
s -ld postscript/
drwxr-xr-x 2 scot admin 1024 Mar 24 16:17 postscript/

To get back to your home directory, you need to tell UNIX to go back up a level in the directory structure. In UNIX the directory above, you is represented by **..**, so type *cd ..* to get back to your home directory. Now type *pwd* to see that you really are there.

pwd
cat poem
more poem
wc poem

You can (and often need to) use the **..** symbol in path names. For example, trace the path in this command:

ls src/fortran/..

Review Exercise

Map out your directory structure using *ls -F*, *pwd*, and *cd*.

Below is a review of the commands we've just learned in this section and practiced including two new ones, *mkdir* and *rmdir*.

ls dir_name	Lists the contents of directory *dir_name*.
ls -F	Identifies files, directories, and programs in the current directory.
pwd	Prints working directory.
cd dir_name	Changes working directory to *dir_name*.
cd	Changes to the user's home directory.
more	Performs like *cat* with a pause to read screenfuls of text.

Use RETURN for next line and SPACE for next screenful.

mkdir dir_name	Makes a new directory called *dir_name*.
rmdir dir_name	Removes the directory *dir_name*.

Print Working Directory

The *pwd* (print working directory) command will display your current location in the file system. When you log into the system you are place in your home directory. In the following examples, we will assume that the home directory is */home/huron2/admin/scot*

pwd
/home/huron2/admin/scot

If you are using the using a shell that allows you to set the prompt, you can change the prompt to be the current location in the directory structure.

Directory Protection

The protection modes are also applied to directories, but here they take on slightly different meanings:

- Permission to read a directory means the ability to list its contents, which is very intuitive.
- Permission to write to directories refers to the ability to add or remove entries (other files and directories).

This can be done irrespective of the permissions on the files in that directory. Permission to execute a directory refers the ability to include that directory name in a pathname. Thus if a directory has the following protection mode,

drwx-----x

nobody, except its owner, can list this directory to see its contents. However, its owner can make one of the files in that directory readable by others, and once other users are informed of its name, they can copy it without restriction.

SUMMARY

This chapter has covered the following topics:

1. The general structure of a UNIX/MVS file system, including descriptions of the general use of some of the main directories.
2. Naming conventions for files and directories.
3. Descriptions of the current, parent, and home directories.
4. Relative and absolute pathnames.
5. The use of *wildcards*.
6. Various commands for manipulating files and directories.
7. UNIX file permissions.
8. Special files, for handling hardware devices.

Some of the major commands discussed are

MVS	DESCRIPTION	UNIX	DESCRIPTION
ALLOCATE	Creates data sets.	***cat***	Concatenates one or more files.
LIST	Displays the contents of data sets.		
LISTCAT	Lists the data sets in a catalog.	***ls***	Lists contents of a directory.
LISTDS **LISTALC**	Lists the members in a partitioned data set.		
LISTB	Lists user and temporary data sets. Lists broadcasts from system operator.		
RETURN	Advances carriage return to next page.	***more***	Displays information one page at a time.
FREE	Unallocates old data set(s).	***cd***	Changes directory.
ALLOCATE	Allocates new data set(s).		
COPY	Copies data sets and data set members.	***cp***	Copies file (s).
RENAME	Renames data sets and data set members.	***mv***	Renames or moves a directory.
DELETE	Deletes data sets and data set members.	***rm***	Removes or deletes files.
FREE	Unallocates old data set(s).		
ALLOCATE	Creates and provides access to data sets.	***mkdir***	Creates a new directory.
	Deletes data sets and data set members. Frees an allocated data set with or without DELETE option to delete the data set or its member.	***rmdir***	Removes directories.
FREE **ALLOCATE**	Unallocates old data set(s). Allocates new data set(s).	***chgrp***	Changes group ownership of a file.
ALLOCATE **PROTECT**	Creates and provides access to data sets. Grants and/or revokes access to data sets.	***chmod*** ***umask***	Changes permissions of a file. Sets default file permissions.
DSPRINT **PRINTDS**	Prints data sets and data set members.	***lpr***	Implements line printer spooling program.
DSPRINT **PRINTDS**	Prints data sets and data set members.	***pr***	Formats data suitable for printing.
LISTCAT	Lists the data sets in a catalog.	***pwd***	Outputs name of the current directory.

7

Advanced File Management

INTRODUCTION

In the previous sections, we discussed some simple UNIX commands and options for file management. However, there is a large number of other UNIX commands that are a bit more complex and diverse. Although they are infrequently used, they are an integral part of efficiently processing file and directory management functions in UNIX development environments.

MVS provides both in-line commands under TSO and ISPF and many utilities for file manipulations. Unfortunately, most of them work quite differently from those in UNIX. It is in the advanced file handling commands and utilities where UNIX and MVS operating systems differ considerably. IEBCOPY and IEHMOVE are the most versatile utilities to provide selective or full data set copy, data set compression/decompression, and backup/restore functions. There are other such utilities for dump/restore and file comparisons, but none closer than IEBCOPY to UNIX file commands. The basic command sets described in this section are for

1. Managing files and directories.
2. Archiving file.
3. Data sorting within files.
4. File and directory compression.
5. File and directory security attributes.
6. Pattern searching within files.
7. Linking files and directories.
8. Counting, modifying, and comparing file contents.

MORE FILE PROCESSING

UNIX has many powerful utilities that are used to describe and modify the contents of files. These commands may seem trivial when used alone, but by connecting these commands together you are able to create powerful text processing features.

Understanding UNIX Files (Revisited)

Files do not actually reside inside directories. A directory is a file that contains references to other files. The directory holds two pieces of information about each file:

- Its filename.
- An *inode number*, which acts as a pointer to where the system can find the information it needs about this file.

Filenames are only used by the system to locate a file and its corresponding *inode number*. This correspondence is called a *link*. To the system, the file is the *inode number*. Multiple filenames can be used to refer to the same file by creating a link between an *inode* and each of the filenames.

Regular Expressions in Files

Regular expressions are used in many UNIX programs to match a pattern. For example, if you wanted to find all the sentences in a file called *letters* that end in the string "goodbye," we could use the command *grep goodbye$ letters*. Matching a regular expression against a string will either succeed or fail. In the case of *grep*, we are only concerned with finding the pattern.

However, sometimes you will want to take an action depending on whether the command succeeds or fails.

.	Matches any single character, except newlines.
*	Matches any number of single characters.
^expr	Matches *expr* at the beginning of the line.
expr$	Matches *expr* at the end of the line.
expr_1, expr_2	Matches *expr_1* or *expr_2*.
[a-z]	Matches any character in the given range.
[^list]	Matches any character not listed.
\c	Interprets the character literally, not as a regular expression character.

Sometimes you will want the shell to interpret a character literally as opposed to its regular expression. You must escape the characters special meaning by preceding it with a \ (backslash). For example, the *ls* ** command would give you a listing of all the files in the current directory that begin with an asterisk.

Viewing the Contents of a File

The *cat* (concatenate) command can be used to view the contents of a file.

cat friends

Sally Johnson	*123 Ellesmere Lane*	*Athens*	*GA 12876*	*(413)345-8976*
Bob Beamon	*913 Mockingbird Lane*	*Annapolis*	*MD 17701*	*(201)962-8765*
Kim Smith	*234 Working Street*	*Hollywood*	*CA 18765*	*(678)987-9876*
Sally Miller	*510 Epping Way*	*Hobe Sound*	*FL 33455*	*(654)546-4526*
Eddy Murphy	*210 W. Hollywood*	*Los Angles*	*CA 90210*	*(876)238-9987*

On large files, you will find that the output of the command *cat* will not fit on your screen. The output will scroll across the screen, and you will not be able to view the information. The *more* command is used to display file information in screen-sized chunks. If the file is more than one screen long, the word *-More-* followed by the percentage of the file displayed is placed at the bottom of the screen. Press the SPACEBAR to see the next screen of the file or press *q* or **<Ctrl-c>** to quit. It is better to use *more* if your output is going directly to the screen and to use *cat* if your output is going to a file or pipe.

Displaying Files (od, head, tail, pr)

The UNIX command *od* (octal, decimal, hexadecimal, ASCII dump) corresponds to the LIST subcommand of TEST MVS command. The LIST (TEST) subcommand is used to display the contents of virtual storage or the contents of registers, displayed at the terminal or placed into a data set, whereas *od* is used to examine the contents of files in various formats to locate control and other nonprintable characters, especially in determining the magnetic tape formats. Examples using *od* command are the following:

FUNCTION	MVS COMMAND SYNTAX	UNIX COMMAND SYNTAX
Format	**HEX** [on VERT] [on DATA] [off]	***od*** *[option(s)] file* {Converts binary data to a displayable form in octal (-o), decimal (-d), hexadecimal (-h), or ASCII (-a).}
Example 1		***od*** *-d file* {Produces a decimal dump.}
Example 2		***od*** *-a file* {Produces an ASCII dump.}

The command *head* displays the beginning of a file, whereas *tail* displays the end. The command *pr* formats the named files on the standard output. By default, the listing is separated into pages, each headed by the page number, date and time, and the name of the file.

FUNCTION	MVS COMMAND SYNTAX	UNIX COMMAND SYNTAX
Format	**TOP** **F** [n]	***head*** *[-count] {file(s)}* {Displays first few lines of a file.}
Example 1		***head*** *-30 /usr/osc* {Lists the first 30 lines of the file *osc*.}
Example 2		***head*** **.cob >> archive* {List the first 10 lines (default) of all the files ending in *.cob* and redirects the output to archive.}
Format	**BOTTOM** **L** [n]	***tail*** *[option(s)] {file(s)}* {Displays the last part of a file.}
Example 1		***tail*** *-15cf osc* {Prints the last 15 characters of the file *osc*, followed by any lines that are appended to *osc* between the time *tail* is initiated and terminated.}
Example 2		***tail*** *-r /usr/osc | lpr* {Displays the last line first, second to last line second, and so on. It pipes the result to the printer.}
Format	**DSPRINT** data set (name) dest (name) {operands} Print data set member to a destination printer **PRINTDS** dsname prtrname {operands} Print data set to a destination printer	***pr*** *[option(s)] {file(s)}* {Formats text for a print device.}
Example 1		***pr*** *osc.dat* {Formats the file for printing using default file formatting characteristics.}

FUNCTION	MVS COMMAND SYNTAX	UNIX COMMAND SYNTAX
Example 2		***pr*** *-2 osc.dat* {Prints the file in two columns.}
Example 3		***pr*** *-m osc1.dat osc2.dat* {Prints two files side by side, for content comparison.}

MANAGING FILES AND DIRECTORIES

In the previous sections, we introduced commands for creating, deleting, and moving files between directories. Previously, we discussed UNIX commands and options for file management which a novice user might need, now we need to introduce you to some more complex commands which are essential for developing and maintaining applications and systems.

File Management

A few files will already exist in the home directory even before your first login session. To see a list of these files, use the *ls* command:

ls -a
total 11
1 ./ 1 .history 2 .openwin-menu
1 ../ 1 .login 1 dos/
1 .Xdefault 1 .logout
1 .cshrc 1 .msgsrc

ls is the *list-directory-contents* command, and *-a* is a command line option to list all files. The command *ls* without any argument will not list those filenames which begin with the . character (called *dot*). The files *.login* and *.logout* are files that tailor your environment. The . entry is in fact another name for the current working directory. The .. entry is the relative name for the parent directory of the current directory or the directory in which the current working directory is contained. The . and .. names are very useful since the exact directory to which they refer depends on the current working directory. This allows a name-independent means of specifying a directory.

Files beginning with the . *(dot)* character are hidden files since they are ignored by most UNIX commands. They are intended to perform many system chores behind the scenes for you.

Quotas

The *quota* command displays a listing of your disk storage use and limits. *Quotas* are used to limit the number of files and the amount of disk space used by each user. Disk use is measured in blocks, where 1 block equals 1024 bytes.

There a two *quota* limits, the soft limit and the hard limit. You can continue to increase your usage over the soft limit until you either reach the hard limit or the established time limit (usually a week). Once either of these events has occurred, all further attempts at file creation will fail with an error message. If you ever see the messages

DISK LIMIT REACHED -- WRITE FAILED
FILE LIMIT REACHED -- CREATE FAILED

you have exceeded your hard limit.

DISK *quotas*

	BLOCK USE				FILE USE			
Filesystem	usage	quota	limit	timeleft	files	quota	limit	timeleft
/home/huron2	1668	9000	10000	.8 wks	20	0	0	—
home directory	Current use	Soft limit	Hard limit			No quota		

If this command returns nothing, you don't have a *quota*.

img src="images/quota1.gif">

The *du* (disk use) command recursively displays the amount of disk space (in blocks) used in each directory. The *-s* (summary) will display the total blocks used by each directory and the *-a* (all) option will list filenames.

*du -s **
654 tutorial

This will summarize the disk usage starting from your home directory.

If you exceed your quota limit you can use the *tar* and *compress* commands to reduce your disk usage.

After you have compressed you files and you still need more disk space, speak with your system administrator.

Finding Files and Directories

The *find* command recursively descends a directory locating all the files that meet the criteria given on the command line. Without any options the *find* command will take no action on the files it finds, so the *-print* option is used to write the found files to standard output. The format of the *find* command and equivalent commands in UNIX are

FUNCTION	MVS COMMAND SYNTAX	UNIX COMMAND SYNTAX
Format	**LISTALC** List the allocated data set (s) **LISTDS** Determine if it is a partitioned or sequential data set and names of members if a partitioned data set **LISTCAT** Lists the names of data sets in a catalog	***find*** *pathname_list criteria action* {Pathname—specifies the pathname to be searched; criteria—true or false conditions; action—print if the condition is true.}
Example 1	**LISTDS** junk.data -- RECFM - LRECL - BUCSIZE - DSORG FB 80 23200 80 --VOLSER-- USERVL --MEMBERS-- MEM1 MEM2	***find*** */tmp -name junk -print* {Locates and prints all files in */tmp* and its subdirectories that are named *junk.*}
Example 2	**LISTALC** OSC.CUST SYSI.PROCLIB OSC.USERS OSC.CUSTOMERS ***	***find*** */ -perm 755 -exec ls "{ }" ";"* {Finds all files, starting with the root directory, on which the permission levels have been set to *755.*}
Example 3		***find*** *. -name Makefile -print* *{/home/huron2/admin/scot/tutorial/ Makefile}* {The . is a directory abbreviation for the current directory. The *-name* option specifies that only files with the given name should be found. The name option can include wildcard characters if they are quoted.}

There are many options to the *find* command, a few are listed below:

find . -name "core" -size +3 -mtime +7 -exec rm -i { } \; -print*
/home/huron2/admin/scot/core: ? (y/n) y
home/huron2/admin/scot/core

Some Options to Find

-name file	Finds files named *file.*
-size n	Finds files that contain size. *n,* exactly *n* blocks (1 block = 512 bytes) *+n,* more than *n* blocks *-n,* less than *n* blocks
-mtime n	Finds files that were modified *n,* exactly *n* days ago

Some Options to Find *(cont.)*

	+*n*, more than *n* days ago -*n*, less than *n* days ago
-exec	Executes command *cmd* on each file
-type type	Finds files that match the type *f*, ordinary file *d*, directory *b*, block device *c*, character device *p*, named pipe

Actions can be taken when files are found by using the *-exec* option. The *-exec* option uses the { } (left curly brace, right curly brace) syntax to specify the current file that *find* has found. The *exec* command ends with the \; syntax. If we did not have the print option at the end, we would not get a confirmation the file had been removed.

FILE ARCHIVING

The *tar* (tape archive) is used to either archive files to tape or to a disk. In these examples we will only be archiving to disk. In MVS, separate program products are available to perform save, restore, and archiving functions.

FUNCTION	MVS COMMAND SYNTAX	UNIX COMMAND SYNTAX
Format	**IEBCOPY** and/or **IEHMOVE** Utility {Selectively merges, moves, and copies sequential data sets and/or members of partitioned data sets.}	***tar*** *[option(s)] {file[s]}* {Saves and retrieves files within an archive.}
Example 1		***tar*** *-cv ~james* {Copies all the files of user james to the secondary storage using the ***c*** option for a new archive. The ***v*** option informs the user as each file is created.}
Example 2		***tar*** *-ruv ~james* {Illustrates the later incremental save of jame's files; ***r*** option appends new files at the end; ***u*** option directs copies only files created since the last create; ***v*** option informs the user as it copies files.}
Example 3		***tar*** *-xv* {Extracts (*x* option) the contents of the archived files and reports on each file as it is restored.}

Let's archive the tutorial files.

tar -cvf tut.tar tutorial
a tutorial/Makefile 1 blocks
a tutorial/friends 1 blocks
a tutorial/hello.cc 1 blocks
a tutorial/postscript/mosaic.ps 638 blocks
a tutorial/core symbolic link to /dev/null
a tutorial/friends.pl 2 blocks
ls tut.tar
tut.tar

Here we have created *tut.tar* as an archive of the files in our tutorial directory. The *-c* (create) option is used to create a new tape archive and write files. The *-v* (verbose) option display the names of archived files. The *-f* (file) option specifies that the next argument is the archive source or destination. If you exclude the *-f* option, *tar* will use the default (usually */dev/rmt/0m*).

Let us extract the tutorial files.

tar -xvf tut.tar
x tutorial/Makefile, 242 bytes, 1 tape blocks
x tutorial/friends, 416 bytes, 1 tape blocks
x tutorial/hello.cc, 70 bytes, 1 tape blocks
x tutorial/postscript/mosaic.ps, 326291 bytes, 638 tape blocks
x tutorial/core symbolic link to /dev/null
x tutorial/friends.pl, 864 bytes, 2 tape blocks

The *-x* (extract) option will extract the files from the tape archive. Since we have the *tut.tar* file, we can remove our tutorial directory.

Before we extracted the contents of a *tar* file, we could have used the *-t* (table) option to get a listing of the table of contents.

COMPRESSING FILES AND DIRECTORIES

The *compress* command is used to reduce the size of a file. Compressions often save as much as 30–80% of the original space, however you must *uncompress* files before they can be used. If file compression is possible the suffix *.Z* will be added to the end of the file to indicate it is compressed.

In MVS, the *copy* command will *compress* or *expand* a partitioned data set member. If specified, it will back up the data set to a separate data set before condensing. The input data set for compression must be in F or FB format. The data set for expansion is saved and input is in VBM format.

FUNCTION	MVS COMMAND SYNTAX	UNIX COMMAND SYNTAX
Format	**COPY** input-data set [(member)] [/pass-word] output-data set [(member)] [**compress**].... **compress** pds-data set	***compress*** *[option(s)] file1 file2*
Example	**COPY** osc.data(mine) save.data **compress** {Condenses the input data set member *osc.data* and save into a new data set *save.data.*}	***compress*** *-v tut.tar* *{tut.tar: Compression: 78.19% -- re-placed with tut.tar.Z}* {The "**-v**" (verbose) option is used to list the amount of compression.}
	COMPRESS osc.data {Compresses a partitioned data set.}	***ls*** *-l tut.tar.Z* *-rw-r--r-- 1 scot admin 79883 Mar 30 16:02 tut.tar.Z*
Format	**COPY** input-data set [(member)] [/pass-word] output-data set [(member)] [**expand**]....	***uncompress*** *file* {The *uncompress* command has the same syntax as compress.}
Example	**COPY** save.data osc.data(mine) **EXPAND** {Expands the saved data set *save.data* into a member of *osc.data.*}	***uncompress*** *tut.tar.Z* *ls -l tut.tar* *ls -l tut.tar* *-rw-r--r-- 1 scot admin 337920 Mar 30 16:02 tut.tar*

FILE AND DIRECTORY ATTRIBUTES

It is important to protect your UNIX files against accidental (or intentional) removal or alteration by yourself or other users. The UNIX operating system maintains information, known as attributes, for every file and directory on the system. This section describes how to inspect and change these attributes.

UNIX was designed and implemented by computer scientists working on operating systems research. Many of the fundamentals of UNIX reflect this origin in academia. A low concern for security is one of the hallmarks of UNIX operating systems. Therefore, unless you act to restrict access to your files, chances are high that other users can read them.

Create or Update Files (touch)

The *touch* command updates the access and modification times of a file by reading a character from the file and writing it back. This command can also create empty files with the same attributes. The general command format is

FUNCTION	COMMAND	SYNTAX
Format	*touch*	*[option(s)] {file(s)}*
	{**-a**	{Updates only the access times.}
	-c	{Prevents touch from creating file if it does not exist.}
	-m	{Updates only the modification times.}
	file	{Specifies the file to be updated.}
Example	*touch filea fileb*	
	{Sets the **date last modified** of both files to the current date.}	

File and Directory Permissions

All files (including directories) have an owner who can assign different types of permissions to the file for different classes of users. The *ls -l* command produces a long listing of information about a file, including file protection information.

Below is an example of the *ls -l* command output with some accompanying text to point out what various parts of the output mean. The first part of the output line deals with file permissions. This section consists of 10 characters which are each either a hyphen or a letter. For each location a hyphen means some permission is turned off and a letter means it is turned on. For the leftmost character, a *d* means this file is a directory and a hyphen means it's not.

	OWNER	SIZE	DATE	TIME	FILENAME
-rw-r--r-- 1	*crc1*	*332*	*May 21*	*15:47*	*fluff+*
-rw-r--r-- 1	*crc1*	*4027*	*May 21*	*16:27*	*fractals+*
-rw-r--r-- 1	*crc1*	*3548*	*May 21*	*16:42*	*gilligan+*

d u g o
^-^--^--^--> *four fields (directory, user, group, other)*

Every file or directory in a UNIX file system has three types of permissions (or protections) that define whether certain actions can be carried out. The permissions are

- Read (*r*): A user who has "read" permission for a file may look at its contents or make a copy of it. For a directory, read permission enables a user to find out what files are in that directory. Files with read permissions can be examined, copied, and so on.
- Write (*w*): A user who has "write" permission for a file can alter or remove the contents of that file. For a directory, the user can create and delete files in that directory. Files with write permissions can be altered, appended to, and so on.
- Execute (*x*): A user who has "execute" permission for a file can cause the contents of that file to be executed (provided that it is executable). For a directory, execute permission allows a user to change to that directory.

For each file and directory, the read, write, and execute permissions may be set separately for each of the following classes of users:

User (*u*)	The user who owns the file or directory.
Group (*g*)	Several users purposely lumped together so that they can share access to each other's files.
Others (*o*)	The remainder of the authorized users of the system.

The primary command that displays information about files and directories is *ls*. The *-l* option will display the information in a long format. You can get information about a single UNIX file by using *ls -l* filename.

Each file or subdirectory entry in a directory listing obtained with the *-l* option consists of seven fields: permission mode, link count, owner name, group name, file size in bytes, time of last modification, and the filename (the group name appears only if the *g* flag is also specified, as in *ls -lg*).

The first 10 characters make up the mode field. If the first character is a ***d***, then the item listed is a directory; if it is a -, then the item is a file; if it is an ***l***, then it is a link to another file. If a particular permission is set, the appropriate letter appears in the corresponding position; otherwise, a dash indicates that the permission is not given.

The second field in the output from *ls -l* is the number of links to the file. In most cases it is one, but other users may make links to your files, thus increasing the link count. A special warning to people using links to other people's files: your "*copies*" of their files can be counted against them by the file quota system available on certain UNIX variants. The third field gives the userid of the owner of the file. The group name follows in the fourth field (if the *-g* option is used in conjunction with *-l*). The next two fields give the size of the file (in bytes) and the date and time at which the file was last modified. The last field gives the name of the file.

ls -l myfile
-rw-r--r-- 1 owner 588 Jul 15 14:39 myfile

The chmod Command

A file's owner can change any or all of the permissions with the *chmod* (change mode) command. The *chmod* command allows you to dictate the type of access permission that you want each file to have. In the previous example, the current permissions for *myfile* are read for everybody, write for the owner, and execute by no one.

In MVS/TSO, the *protect* command allows you to establish or change permissions that must be specified to gain or grant access to your data sets. Unlike UNIX, you may assign one or more passwords to a data set. Once assigned, the password for a data set must be specified to access the data set.

The arguments supplied to *chmod* are a symbolic specification of the changes required, followed by one or more filenames. The specification consists of whose permissions are to be changed: *u* for user (owner), *g* for group, *o* for others, or some combination thereof (*a* (all) has the same effect as *ugo*), how they are to be changed (+ adds a permission, - removes a permission, and = sets the specified permissions, removing the other ones), and which permission to add or remove (*r* for read, *w* for write, and *x* for execute). For example,

FUNCTION	MVS COMMAND SYNTAX	UNIX COMMAND SYNTAX
Format	**PROTECT** data set [add/replace/delete/list (password(s))] [pwread/nopwread] [pwwrite/nowrite] [data('string')]	***chmod*** *mode filename(s)* {**pathname**—specifies the pathname to be searched; **criteria**—true or false conditions; **action**—print if the condition is true.}
Example 1	**PROTECT** sales.data pwread add (a82grifn) {Establishes a read and write access for a new data set.}	***chmod*** *a-rwx myfile* {Removes all the permissions from my-file.} *ls -l myfile* *---------- 1 owner 588 Jul 15 14:41 my-file* **Note:** *chmod a = myfile* achieves the same effect.
Example 2	**PROTECT** sales.load/ctlpass replace (my-pass) nopwread pwwrite {Changes the type of access allowed for a data set.}	***chmod*** *ugo+rw myfile* {Allows *read* and *write* permissions for all users.} *ls -l myfile* *-rw-rw-rw- 1 owner 588 Jul 15 14:42 myfile*
Example 3	**PROTECT** sales.data list (a82grifn) {Lists security information for a protected data set.}	***chmod*** *go-w myfile* {Removes write permission for your groups and other users.} *ls -l myfile* *-rw-r--r-- 1 owner 588 Jul 15 14:42 my-file*
Example 4	**PROTECT** sales.load/apple delete (a82grifn) {Deletes one of several passwords.}	***chmod*** *a=r myfile* {Allows only read permission to all users.} *ls -l myfile* *-r--r--r-- 1 owner 58 Jul 15 14:43 myfile*
Example 5		***chmod*** *755 myfile* {Changes the protection of *myfile* to give the owner read, write, and execute access; group members and the world read and execute access.} *ls -l myfile* *-rwxr-xr-x 1 owner 588 Jul 15 14:43 myfile*

Now the file is protected by allowing only read access; it cannot be written to or executed by anyone, including you. Protecting a file against writing by its owner is a safeguard against accidental overwriting, although not against accidental deletion. *chmod* will also accept a permission setting expressed as a three-digit octal number. To determine this octal number, you first write a *1* if the permission is to be set and a *0* otherwise. This produces a binary number that can be converted into octal by grouping the digits in threes and replacing each group by the corresponding octal digit according to the table below.

Symbolic to Octal Conversions

SYMBOLIC	BINARY	OCTAL
---	000	0
--x	001	1
-w-	010	2
-wx	011	3
r--	100	4
r-x	101	5
rw-	110	6
rwx	111	7

This shows that the octal equivalent of *rw-r--r--* is 644. The following example illustrates that the permissions for *myfile* have been reset to the values with which we began:

chmod 644 myfile
ls -l myfile
-rw-r--r-- 1 owner 588 Jul 15 14:44 myfile

To change the permissions back to read only, you can execute chmod as follows:

chmod 444 myfile
ls -l myfile
-r--r--r-- 1 owner 588 Jul 15 14:45 myfile

As with files, directories may also have permissions assigned. When listing directories, you may use the *-d* option to keep from descending into the directories you list. Otherwise, the contents of the directories will be displayed along with their names. Below is an example of permissions assigned to a directory:

ls -ld home
drwxrwxr-x 1 owner masc 588 Jul 15 9:45 home

The directory *home* and the files and directories under it may be read and executed by anyone, but written to only by the owner and users in the *masc group*. Assuming you are the owner of this directory, you may decide to change the permission to allow only yourself and the *masc group* to read and execute files in the home directory. You would set the permissions accordingly:

chmod o-rx home
ls -ld home
drwxrwx--- 1 owner masc 588 Jul 15 9:46 home

You may decide that only you should be able to alter the contents of the directory. You must remove the write permission for the group.

chmod 750 home
ls -ld home
drwxr-x--- 1 owner masc 588 Jul 15 9:48 home

An alternative to the previous command is *chmod g-w*.

Examples of *chmod*

chmod o-x test.1	Takes away "execute" for "other."
*chmod u+rwx test.**	Adds "r," "w," and "x" for the owner.
chmod go-rwx test.1	Takes away "r," "w," and "x" from "group" and "other."

Important: Taking away write permission prevents accidental changes, but not accidental deletion!

The umask Command

When you create a file, the system gives it a default set of permissions. These are controlled by the system administrator and will vary from installation to installation. If you would like to change the default that is in effect for you, choose your own with the *umask* command. Note that the permission specified by the *umask* setting will be applied to the file, unlike that specified in the *chmod* command, which normally only adds or deletes (few people use the = operator to *chmod*).

First, issue the command without arguments to cause the current settings to be echoed as an octal number:

umask 022

If you convert these digits to binary, you will obtain a bit pattern of 1's and 0's. A 1 indicates that the corresponding permission is to be turned off, a 0, that it is to be turned on. (Notice that the bit patterns for chmod and umask are reversed.) Hence, the mask output above is 000010010, which produces a permission setting of *rwxr-xr-x* (i.e., write permission is turned off for group and other). Suppose you decide that the default setting you prefer is rwxr-x---. This corresponds to the masking bit pattern 000010111, so the required mask is 027:

umask 27

Now, if you create a new file during this session, the permissions assigned to the file will be the 1's allowed by the mask value.

The chown, chgrp, and groups Commands

These commands allow you to change the owner and group of the file(s). To change owner or group ownerships, you must be the owner of the file and must be a member of the group being assigned to the file. The command *groups* displays group memberships. RACF in MVS allows similar functions. The format and the usage of the commands is

FUNCTION	UNIX COMMAND SYNTAX
Format	*groups [username]* {**username**—name of the user in the displayed group.}
Example	*groups james* *mktng oprns*
Format	*chgrp group file(s)* {**group**—group from which the file can be assessed; **file**—specifies the file to be changed.}
Example	*chgrp mktng osc.dat* {Changes the group ownership of the file to *mktng.*}
Format	*chown owner file(s)* {**owner**—specifies the owner of the file; **file**—specifies the file to be changed.}
Example	*chown doc filea fileb filec* {Makes *doc* the owner of these files.}
Example	*groups* *ls -lg osc.dat* *chgrp mktng osc.dat* *ls -lg osc.dat* *mkting oprns* *-rw-rw-r-- 2 system oprns 2 May 21 01:24 osc.dat* *-rw-rw-r-- 2 system mktng 2 May 21 01:24 osc.dat* {Changes the group ownership of the file *osc.dat* from *oprns* to *mktng.*}

Directory Permissions (Slightly Different Meanings)

r Reads (*ls*) the directory.

w Creates or removes files in the directory.

x Searches the directory (allows to *cd* into).

Important: To prevent accidental deletion of a file, you must remove write permission from the directory it's in.

How private are files, even when protected?

System administrator (user *root*) has *rwx* capabilities on all files at all times, but is honor-bound to use this power on "protected" files only in case of emergency or with consent of file owner. UNIX systems are fairly secure, but by no means impenetrable by outsiders. Therefore, if there's something you wish to keep completely private, you must provide extra caution to security.

Controlling Access to Your Files and Directories

Every file and directory in your account can be protected from or made accessible to other users by changing its access permissions. You can only change the permissions for files and directories that you own.

- Displaying access permissions
- Understanding access permissions
- Default access permissions
- Changing the group ownership of files
- Changing access permissions

Displaying Access Permissions

To display the access permissions of a file or directory, use the command

ls -l filename / directory /

This displays a one line summary for each file or directory. For example;

-rwxr-xr-x 1 erpl08 1995 Feb 22 15:51 my.html

This first item *-rwxr-xr-x* represents the access permissions on this file. The following items represent the number of links / to it, the username / of the person owning it, its size and the time and date it was last changed, and finally, its name.

TRANSLATING CHARACTERS IN A FILE

tr copies the standard input to the standard output with substitution or deletion of selected characters. Input characters found in *string1* are mapped into the corresponding characters of *string2*. For the substitution to work correctly, *string2* must have at least as many characters as *string1*. Excess characters in either string are ignored.

FUNCTION	UNIX COMMAND SYNTAX
Format	*tr [option(s)] string1 [string2]*
Example 1	*tr A-Z a-z <osc1> osc2* {Translates the alphabetic characters A through Z from *osc1* to their lowercase counterparts and writes output to *osc2*.}
Example 2	*tr -c A-Za-z '\012' <file1> file2* {Same as above, except that the *c* option indicates that each string of characters in *osc1* output to *osc2* with a new line.}

PATTERN SEARCHING

The *grep* (global regular expression print) command is used to search for a particular word or phrase in a file. The format of the *grep* command is

FUNCTION	MVS COMMAND SYNTAX	UNIX COMMAND SYNTAX
Format	**FIND** string [range] [options] *FIND BACKWARD 'text-string' or* *FORWARD 'text-string' or* *LINE TARGET (Stream-name)* *wirndow-name*	***grep*** *[option(s)] string filename*
Example 1	***FIND*** *backward 'link'* {Find the last time the character string 'link' was issued.}	***grep*** *-v -c 'regular' osc1* {Reports a count of the number of lines that do not contain the word *regular* in the file *osc1*.}
Example 2	***FIND*** *c'hello'* {Locates one or more occurrences of a search string.}	***grep*** *-n hello osc3* {Searches for all records in *osc3* that contain the string hello.}
Example 3	***FIND*** *forward 'edit abc.asm' test* {Find the first time you edited a data set named 'abc.asm'.}	

where *string* is the word, phrase, or regular expression you want to find and *file* is the file to be searched. Let's find all lines that contain the string *Sally* in our friend's file.

grep Sally friends

Sally Johnson	*123 Ellesmere Lane*	*Austin*	*TX 78360*	*(413)345-8976*
Sally Miller	*510 Epping Way*	*San Jose*	*CA 95120*	*(654)546-4526*

To find a pattern that is more than one word long, enclose the string within single or double quotation marks.

grep 'Sally Miller' friends

Sally Miller	*510 Epping Way*	*San Jose*	*CA 95120*	*(654)546-4526*

So far we have seen how *grep* prints all lines that contain the given character string. The *-v* (invert) option instructs *grep* to print all lines except those which match the string. This is useful when you want to remove lines from a file. Lets find all the lines in a file that do not contain the string *Sally* and place the output into the *friends.new file*.

grep -v 'Sally' > friends.new
more friends.new

Bob Beamon 913 Mockingbird Lane Annapolis MD 17701(201)962-8765
Kim Smith 234 Working Street Hollywood CA 18765 (678)987-9876
Eddy Murphy 210 W. Hollywood Los Angles CA 90210 (876)238-9987

The *grep* command can be used with regular expressions to match a pattern.

grep '26$' friends
Sally Miller 510 Epping Way San Jose CA95120 (654)546-4526

This will find all the lines that end in 26.

The *grep* command can search for a string in groups of files. When it finds a pattern that matches in more than one file, it prints the name of the file, followed by a colon (:) before the line matching the pattern. The *-i* (ignore) option to *grep* will ignore the case.

*grep -i bob **
friends: Bob Beamon 913 Mockingbird Lane Annapolis MD 17701 (201)962-8765
friends.new: Bob Beamon 913 Mockingbird Lane Annapolis MD 17701 (201)962-8765

COMPARISONS BETWEEN FILES

The *cmp* (compare) command is used to compare any two files, including executable files. The *diff* (differential file operator) command is used to display the differences between text files or directories. The order of the *diff* command is important. The format of the *cmp* command is

FUNCTION	MVS COMMAND SYNTAX	UNIX COMMAND SYNTAX
Format	**COMPARE** dataset1 dataset2	***cmp*** *[option(s)] file1 file2*
Example	**COMPARE** osc1.data osc2.data {Compares the contents of two data sets and lists any differences.}	***cmp*** *alpha beta* {Compares file *alpha* with *beta*; if they differ, it announces the byte and line number at which the difference occurred; no comment if the files are the same.}

The format of the **diff** command is:

FUNCTION	UNIX COMMAND SYNTAX
Format	*diff [option(s)] file1 file2*
Example	*diff alpha beta* {Reports each difference it finds accompanied by information describing the changes required to make the two files identical.}

diff can be used both for files and directories:

diff [options] old_file new_file
diff [options] old_dir new_dir

The *diff* command will display a listing of the editing actions that need to be performed on the old file to change it into the new file. The three ways in which *diff* indicated changes to a file are *a* (lines are added), *c* (lines are changed), and *d* (lines are deleted). Let's find the difference between the *friends* and the *friends.new* files.

```
diff friends friends.new
1d0   Sally Johnson  123 Ellesmere Lane  Athens    GA 12876 (413)345-8976
4d2   Sally Miller   510 San Ramos       San Jose  CA 95120 (654)546-4526
```

This tells us that delctions need to be made to the *friends* file to get the *friend.new* file. The *1d0* tells us that line 1 of the *friend* file has to be deleted, and the *4d2* tells us that line 4 of the *friends* file has to be deleted.

The output of *diff* can be sent to the *ed* command (another text editor) to convert the first file into the second. In fact, the using *diff* with the *-e* option will produce output suitable for input to the *ed* command.

```
diff -e friends friends.new > ed.script
(cat ed.script ; echo w) | ed friends
415
249
diff friends friends.new
```

If you eliminated the *echo w* command, *ed* would read the input from the *cat ed.script*, perform the operation, and then exit. With the *echo w* command, you are telling *ed* to write to the file *friends*. The semicolon between the *cat ed.script* and *echo w* tells the shell that these are separate commands.

MODIFYING CHARACTER STRINGS

The *sed* (stream editor) command reads lines, one by one, from an input file and applies a set of editing commands to the lines. The *sed* command is like *grep* except that it allows you to make changes to file. *sed* has no equivalent in MVS. The format of the *sed* command is

sed [options] action/string/newstring file(s)

and is shown in the following examples:

FUNCTION	UNIX COMMAND SYNTAX
Format	*sed [-n] [[-e command]...] [-f scriptfile] [file]* {**-n**—displays only the modified lines; **-e**—causes script to be taken from command line; **-f**—causes script to be taken from scriptfile; **file**—specifies the file or files that are edited, then sent to standard output.}
Example 1	*sed -n s/harry/james/p myfile* {Displays (*p*) only the files you have modified (*n*).}
Example 2	*sed -f sedfile inputfile > filea* {Processes *inputfile* according to script in *sedfile* and redirects the output to *filea*.}
Example 3	*sed -e s/mary/james/g -e /for/d myfile* {Globally changes the occurrence of *mary* to *james* on every line containing *mary*; then deletes all lines containing for.}
Example 4	*sed -n -f otherfile myfile* {Modifies *myfile* based on the edit commands contained in *otherfile* (*f* option).}

```
sed "s/(201)962-8765/(201)962-9999/" friends
Bob Beamon   913 Mockingbird Lane  Annapolis   MD 17701  (201)962-9999
Kim Smith    234 Working Street    Hollywood   CA 18765  (678)987-9876
Eddy Murphy  210 W. Hollywood      Los Angles  CA 90210  (876)238-9987
```

The *s* (substitute) option tells *sed* to substitute. We have changed the phone number. If we wanted to save these changes, we would redirect the output to a file. The *sed* command also accepts regular expressions.

```
sed '/^$/d' hello.cc
#include <iostream.h>
main( ) {
cout <<"Hello, cruel world! \n";
}
```

The *d* option tells *sed* to delete. In this case we are using a regular expression to tell *sed* to remove all blank lines from our *hello.cc* file.

SORTING DATA IN FILES

The *sort* command is used to sort the contents of a file into alphabetic or numerical order. Special utilities and ISPF *sort macro* allows sorting within a file.

	MVS COMMAND SYNTAX	UNIX COMMAND SYNTAX
Format	**TSOSORT** from-data set to-data set Fields= [(column, length, type, order), ...] **column** start column **length** number **type** type of search (character or hex..) **order A** for ascending or **D** for descending	***sort*** *[option(s)] [+posn1] [-posn2] file(s)* {Most common options are: *-o,* places output in the indicated output file; *-r,* reverses the sense of comparisons; *-b,* ignores leading blanks; *-n,* sorts by arithmetic value; and *posn1 & posn2,* restricts a sort key to one beginning at *posn1* and ending just before *posn2.* The characters at *posn1* and *posn2* are included in the sort key. Missing *posn2* indicates the end of line.}
Example 1	**TSOSORT** input.data output.data Fields=(1,4,CH,A) {Sort key is **4 ch**aracters long starting in column **1** and sort in **A**scending order.}	***sort*** *myfile* {Simplest sort using default setting and the sort key.}
Example 2		***sort*** *+1 -2 infile* {Sorts *infile* with second field as the sort key.}
Example 3		***sort*** *-r -o outfile +1.0 -1.2 infile1 infile2* {Sorts *infile1* and *outfile1* in reverse order, placing output in *outfile* and uses the first character of the second field as the sort key.}
Example 4		***sort*** *-r +1.0b -1.1b infile1 infile2* {Sorts *infile1* and *outfile1* in reverse order, using the first nonblank character of the second field as the sort key.}
Example 5		***sort*** *-t: +2n -3 /etc/passwd* {Prints the password file sorted by the numeric user ID (the third colon separated field).}

```
sort +1 friends
Bob Beamon    913 Mockingbird Lane  Annapolis   MD 17701  (201)962-8765
Eddy Murphy   210 W. Hollywood      Los Angles  CA 90210  (876)238-9987
Kim Smith     234 Working Street    Hollywood   CA 18765  (678)987-9876
```

The *+1* option tells sort to use the second field of the *sort* key rather than the beginning of the line. Fields are separated by white space; however, you can use the *-t* option to separate by any character. The *-n* options tells *sort* to sort a numeric key; otherwise, it will *sort* by the corresponding ASCII values.

Another command that is useful when you are sorting is the *uniq* command. The *uniq* command will write only one instance of each line, whereas the *sort* will print every line. Usually the output of the *sort* command is piped to the *uniq* command.

COUNTING THINGS IN A FILE

The ***wc*** (word count) command counts the number of lines, words, and characters in a file. This is especially useful for counting the number of lines of source code in a program or the number of words in a document.

wc friends
3 28 249 friends

The first number indicates the number of lines, followed by the number of words and the number of characters (including newlines). The format is as follows:

FUNCTION	UNIX COMMAND SYNTAX
Format	*wc [option(s)] {file(s)}* {*l*, number of lines in a file; *w*, number of words in a file; *c*, number of characters in a file; *file*, file to be counted}
Example	*wc filec* *1654 7680 58960 filec* {Produces list of lines, words, and characters.}

LINKING FILES AND DIRECTORIES

link is a connection between an *i-node number* and the filename(s) associated with it. Unlike a real file, a *link* has no contents; it simply acts as a pointer to something else. Therefore, links can be used instead of having multiple copies of the same file.

i-node number is a unique number associated with each filename. This number is used to look up an entry in the *i-node* table which gives information on the type, size, and location of the file and the userid of the owner of the file.

There are two types of links: *hard links* and *symbolic links* or *soft links*. *Hard links* cannot point to directories or to files in a different file system, whereas symbolic links can. If you use the *ln* command with no options, you will get a hard link. The *-s* (symbolic) option is used to get a symbolic link.

To make a link to a file in another user's home directory, type

ln ~sandra/prog.c

This makes a link between the file *prog.c* in the home directory of user *sandra* and the filename *prog.c* in the current working directory.

The Link (ln) Command

The *ln* (link) command is used to create a link to a directory or a file in the directory structure. A link is a directory entry referring to a file; the same file (together with its size, all its protection information, etc.) may have several links to it.

There are two kinds of links: hard links and symbolic links. A *hard link* to a file is indistinguishable from the original directory entry; any changes to a file are effective, independent of the name used to reference the file. Hard links may not span file systems and may not refer to directories.

A *symbolic link* (*soft link*) contains the name of the file to which it is linked. The referenced file is used when an open operation is performed on the link. Symbolic links may span file systems and may refer to directories.

The format of the *ln* command is

FUNCTION	UNIX COMMAND SYNTAX
Format	*ln [-s] filename1 [filename2]* *ln [-f] directoryname1 [directoryname2]* {*-f* causes hard link to an existing directory; *-s* cause symbolic links; *file* specifies the directory to which the file is linked; *file* specifies the file to be linked to current directory; *filenamc1* to be symbolically linked to *filename2;* *filename2* to be symbolically linked to *filename1.*}
Example 1	*ln filea fileb* {Establishes a hard link between *filea* and *fileb.* Writing to or reading from *fileb* is identical to *filea.*}
Example 2	*ln -s filea fileb* {Establishes a symbolic link between *filea* and *fileb.*}

ln [options] existing_file link_name

Let us create a *symbolic link* to the *temp* directory.

```
ln -s temp temp2
ls -ld t*
drwxr-xr-x   2 scot    admin    24 Mar 25 12:07 temp
lrwxr-xr-x   1 scot    admin     4 Mar 25 13:11 temp2 -> temp
```

A *symbolic link* to a directory is not a directory, so to remove it, you don't need the *-r* (recursive) option.

```
rm temp2
ls -ld t*
drwxr-xr-x   2 scot    admin    24 Mar 25 12:07 temp
```

A common *symbolic link* for programmers is to have a link named core that points to */dev/null*. Core files are generated when a program *core dumps* or produces debugging output. These core files take a tremendous amount of storage and are used infrequently. The */dev/null* is the UNIX equivalent of a trash can. In effect, what you are doing is telling the system to toss this file away whenever it is created.

ln -s /dev/null core
*ls -l c**
lrwxr-xr-x 1 scot admin 9 Mar 25 13:34 core -> /dev/null

Caveat: With symbolic links, you can remove the "real" file, and the symbolic link will still exist.

Linking Files to a Linkname

To *link* a file use the command,

ln filename1 linkname

Making a link to a file does not create another copy of the file; it makes a connection between the file and the linkname.

Examples of Using the ln Command

Example 1

To link files in the same directory:
ln notes circular

This creates a link circular to the file notes in the (same) current working directory.

Example 2

To make several links to a file in different directories:
ln part1.txt ../helpdata/sect1 / public/helpdoc/part1

This links *part1.txt* to *../helpdata/sect1* and */public/helpdoc/part1*.

Example 3

To use *ln* together with special pattern matching characters:
ln project/.xdh $PWD*

This links all the files with the extension *.xdh* in the subdirectory project to the current directory. The value of the environment variable *PWD* is used instead of giving the path to the current directory.

Creating Links Between Files

You can refer to one particular file by different names in different directories. The *ln* command creates a link, that "points" to the file. Note that links are simply alternative names for a single file; *ln* does not rename the file (as does *mv*) nor does it make a copy of the file (as does *cp*). It allows you to access the file from multiple directories. Since only one copy of the file actually exists, any changes that you make through one of its links will be reflected when you access it through another of its links, yet if you delete the *link*, you do not delete what it points to.

Links are useful for cross-referencing files. If you know that you will need to access a file from different directories, creating links is a better alternative to making a copy of the file for each directory (and then having to alter each one every time a change is made to the original). It is also more convenient than having to use the file's full pathname every time you need to access it. Another use for linking a file is to allow another user access to that particular file without also allowing entry into the directory that actually contains the file. The kind of link you will want to create is called a *symbolic link.* A symbolic link contains the pathname of the file you wish to create a link to. Symbolic links can tie into any file in the file structure; they are not limited to files within a file system. Symbolic links may also refer to directories as well as individual files. To create a symbolic link to a file within the same directory, type

ln -s originalFile linkName

where *originalFile* is the file that you want to link to and *linkName* is the link to that file. To create a link in a directory other than that of the original file, type

ln -s originalFile differentDirectoryName/linkName

If you create a link within the same directory as the original file, you cannot give it the same name as the original file. There is no restriction on a file's additional names outside of its own directory. Links do not change anything about a file, no matter what the link is named. If someone makes a link to one of your files, and you then delete that file, that link will no longer point to anything and may cause problems for the other user.

Problems Linking Files

1. *Message - filename: Cross-device link*

The file you are trying to make a link to is located on a different physical device. The solution is to create a symbolic link.

2. *Message - directory_name is a directory*

You are trying to make a link to a directory. Check the pathname for the file.

3. *Message - ln: filename: File already exists*

A file with the same name as the linkname already exists in the destination directory. Use a different name for the linkname.

Using Symbolic Links

You can make a *symbolic link* that points to a file that does not exist. The link becomes active when the file that it points to is created. Removing the file does not affect the *symbolic link* itself, and you can substitute another file for it to point to. Examine these examples:

Example 1

ln -s $HOME/accounts/pending current	Make a symbolic link to a nonexistent *file current.*
cat:	Accounts/pending: No such file or directory. This is what happens if you try to page it.
cp ~/accounts/may ~/accounts/pending	Now to create the file that the symbolic link points to more current XYZ Co. Accounts for May 1993.
.....	And the symbolic link works.
rm ~/accounts/pending; more current	Removing the file makes the symbolic link inactive.
cat:	Accounts/pending: No such file or directory.
cp ~/accounts/june ~/accounts/pending	More current XYZ Co. accounts for June 1993.
.....	Creating another file that the link points to makes it active once again.

Example 2

To make a symbolic link from a file in one subdirectory to a file in another subdirectory: *ln -s reports/reportA publications/ my_report*	This makes a symbolic link between the file *reportA* in the subdirectory reports and the filename *my_report* in the publications subdirectory.

Example 3

To make a symbolic link to a file in a subdirectory to your current working directory: *ln -s docs/editors/vi.ref*	This makes a symbolic link between the file *vi.ref* in the subdirectory *docs/editors/* to the filename *vi.ref* in the current working directory.

Making Links to Other User's Files

To make a link to a file belonging to another user, you need to

- Know the pathname to the file.
- Have appropriate access permissions to the file.

Only the owner can change a file's access permissions.

SUMMARY

This chapter has covered the advanced features of a UNIX/MVS file system, including descriptions of the general use of the security features. Also discussed are commands relating file descriptions, content manipulations, and archiving. The commands covered in this section are the following:

MVS	DESCRIPTIONS	UNIX	DESCRIPTIONS
ALLOCATE **CREATE**	Creates a sequential of partitioned data set.	***cat*** ***chgrp***	Concatenates one or more files. Changes group ownership of a file.
ALLOCATE **PROTECT**	Creates and changes permissions for data sets.	***chmod***	Changes permissions of a file.
DSLIST	Displays security protection information.		
- none -		***umask***	Sets default file protection.
same as ALLOCATE / PROTECT	Establishes or changes permissions that must be specified to gain or grant access to your data sets.	***chown***	Changes the owner of a file.
COMPARE	Compares the contents of two data sets and lists any differences.	***cmp*** ***diff***	Compares two files. Compares two files or directories for any differences.
COPY **COMPRESS**	Condenses partitioned data set to increase the amount of unused area.	***compress***	Compresses files and directories and reduces the size.
COPY	Expands a sequential data set to a sequential or a member of a partitioned data set.	***uncompress*** ***du***	Expands compressed files. Summarizes disk usage.
LISTCAT	List names of data sets in catalog.	***find***	Finds files (data sets).
LISTALC	List allocated data sets.		

MVS	DESCRIPTIONS	UNIX	DESCRIPTIONS
FIND		***grep***	Searches a file for a specific pattern.
		groups	Displays group memberships.
		head	Displays first few lines of a file.
		tail	Displays the last part of a file.
		ln	Makes links.
HEX		***od***	Converts data into displayable format in octal, decimal, hexadecimal, or ASCII.
DSPRINT **PRINTDS**	Prints data set to a destination printer.	***pr***	Formats text for a print device.
		quota	Displays a listing of disk storage use and limits.
		sed	Edits a stream of data.
TSOSORT	Sorts a data set from TSO.	***sort***	Sorts or merges files.
IEBCOPY or EIHMOVE utility	Selectively merges, moves, and copies sequential data sets and/or members of partitioned data sets.	***tar***	Copies fields to or from a **tar** archive.
		touch	Updates access and modification times of a file.
		tr	Translates characters.
		wc	Counts characters, words, and lines in a file.

Note: RACF under MVS provides for elaborate security features, but RACF is beyond the scope of this text.

8

The ed Editor

INTRODUCTION

This chapter introduces you to the line-based text editor, which will enable you to create, modify, and save files using *ed.*

ed is the original UNIX editor, and it has changed very little. Even though *ed* has been superseded by newer editing programs, there are many reasons to learn it thoroughly. *ed* is a simple, line-oriented text editor, which is short for "edit." It has relatively few commands, making it easy to learn, and form a subset of the *vi* (editor) commands. It is for these reasons that we have chosen to look at the *ed* editor initially.

INVOKING ed

ed has two modes of operation, command mode and text-entry mode. In *command mode,* the editor is waiting for you to enter *ed* commands. *ed* commands can change lines, print lines, read or write disk files, or initiate *text entry mode.*

In *text-entry mode,* the editor allows you to enter lines of text. Anything you type in text entry mode will be added to the file. You can leave text-entry mode and reenter command mode by entering a line of text that consists of single period (.). The period tells *ed* that you have finished entering text, and you want *ed* to start executing your commands.

When you are in *ed* command mode, all the lines that you type are interpreted as editor commands. However, when you are in text-entry mode, all the lines that you type are added to the file just like the text editors provided with MVS.

To invoke, the *ed* editor, simply enter

ed filename

If the file already exists in your directory, the contents are copied into the buffer area for you to edit. The editor will then respond with the number of characters stored in the file. If the file does not exist, a new file is created, and the editor responds with a question mark and the filename.

Example

ed poem
? poem New file

or

662 Existing file

The editor is now in command mode and ready to accept editor commands. Normally, *ed* issues no prompt character, so commands are entered at the beginning of a blank line. If a prompt is required, then enter *P*; this will cause an asterisk (*) to be displayed whenever *ed* is waiting for a command to be entered.

ed COMMANDS

All *ed* commands are invoked by entering a single-character mneumonic. Most commands refer to either a specific line or a range of lines in the file. For example, the *p* command can print one or more lines in the file; if you enter the command

20p

will print the 20th line in the file.

Lines 20–30 can be printed by using the command

20,30p

The Command Format

A complete *ed* command has three parts:

- *The address,* which informs the editor which line or lines are affected by this command.
- *The command,* which informs the editor what must be done.
- *The parameter(s),* which provide additional information such as what substitution will take place.

However, most commands will have just one or two of these parts:

COMMAND	ACTION	COMMAND USAGE	ADDRESS RANGE	PARAMETER
p	Displays one or more lines.	*1,2p*	1,2	
d	Deletes one or more lines.	*3d*	3	
s	Substitutes one or more occurrences.	*3s/The/the*	3	*/The/the*
p	Displays current line.	*p*	Current line	
d	Deletes up to end of file.	*.,LD*	Up to end of file	

Lines and Line Numbers

Most editor commands operate on lines or groups of lines. Since lines are so important to *ed*, you might expect a lot of ways to identify lines of text. Naturally, you can identify a line by mentioning its line number. The first line of text in a file is line 1, the second line is 2, and so on.

In a small file, it is easy to identify lines by line numbers because there are just a few lines. However, it is cumbersome to use line numbers in a larger file. Therefore, the easier way to identify lines in a large file is by using *relative* line numbers. Whenever a number is preceded by a plus (+) or a minus (-) sign, the editor interprets it as a relative line number. For example,

-5,+5p

will print the five lines before the current line, the current line, and five lines after the current line. At the conclusion, the cursor will point to the last line printed as the current line.

Another way to identify lines is by *context*, such as

/hello/p

in place of a line number. This will print the first line following the current line that contains the text pattern *hello*.

When you enter a context pattern in place of a line number, the editor searches for that pattern at the line after the current line. If the pattern is not found before the end of the file, the editor jumps to the top of the file and searches down from the top to the current line. The first line where the pattern is found is used as the line number. If the text pattern is not found, the editor prints a question mark or a short error message.

Besides the forward search, you can tell the editor to perform a reverse context search by surrounding the text pattern with questions marks, such as

?friends?p

will search backward from the current line to print the first line encountered that contains the pattern *friends*. During a reverse context search, if the editor reaches the beginning of the file without a successful match, the editor jumps to the end of the file and searches from there up to the current line.

LOCATING AND DISPLAYING LINES

Text in the editor buffer is organized into consecutively numbered lines and renumbered whenever a new line is inserted. The editor always maintains a current line which is initially the last line in the buffer after the editor is invoked. Therefore, when you type the command on its own, it performs the action on the current line.

The following examples are methods of accessing different or multiple lines. The print *p* command is used in the examples to display lines.

COMMAND	ACTION
p	Displays the current line.
3p	Displays the third line.
$p	Displays the last line.
+3	Displays three lines after current line.
$-2	Displays two lines from final line.
3,5p	Displays lines 3–5.
1,$p	Displays all lines in the file.
.=	Displays current line number.
=	Displays total line numbers.

TEXT MANIPULATIONS

Pattern Searching

Instead of specifying the line number, it is possible to search for a pattern. This is done by enclosing the pattern in slashes. For example, the following command will perform the pattern search and display the complete line as shown:

/search/

If necessary, the search will wrap around from end of the file back to the beginning. To search through the previous text, question marks are used instead of slashes. For example,

?text?

Stepping Through Text

If you type *return* without entering any other command, the editor will *advance* one line and display it on the screen:

.+1p

Therefore, when you enter the editor, you could read through a file slowly by entering *1p* and then return as many times as necessary. Similarly, you can move *backward* through the text by entering

- (or .-1p)

Adding Text to a File

There are three commands that can be used to add text to the editor's buffer:

a	Append, puts text after the addressed or current line.
i	Insert, puts text before the addressed or current line.
c	Changes the text on the addressed or current line.

ed's insert command (*i*) is used to insert text before the specified line. Inserting is similar to appending (*a*), except that text is added before the specified line rather than after the specified line. If no line is specified, the *insertion* is made in front of the current line.

The insert command causes the editor to enter *text-entry mode*. After entering the insert mode, everything that you type will be interpreted as text, and it will be added to the file. As mentioned earlier, you can stop inserting text by typing a line consisting of a single period (.).

Examples

ed days	Edits file *days*.
12	
1,$p	Prints file *days*. (Starting at line 1 to the end of file)
Monday	
Wednesday	

Thursday

...

The change command (*c*) first removes one or several lines from the text, and then the text is appended in place of the deleted lines. Like the insert and append commands, the change command causes *ed* to enter text-entry mode.

COMMAND	USAGE	ACTION
i	*2i* Tuesday	Inserts "Tuesday" at second line.
a	*26a*	Enters text after line 26.
c	*3c*	Changes line 3 with new text. This command deletes and replaces.

Saving Text

As you are working in a temporary buffer, it is important to remember that to save the contents of the buffer, you must write the file to the disk. Writing out the contents of the buffer into a file on disk is accomplished by using the write *w* command. Following the previous example, to save the buffer contents onto disk, the following should be entered:

w

The system will respond with the number of characters in your file. The write *W* can also be used to copy excerpts from a text file for use in another file. For example,

1,10w filename

This command copies lines 1 through 10 to a file called *filename.*

Leaving the Editor

As the write command is often used to write the contents of the buffer onto the disk regularly during long editing sessions, there also has to be a command to *exit*, or *quit* from the editor. The command used is *q*:

q

If you attempt to exit without saving your file, the system will respond with a question mark. Type *q* again to exit without saving the buffer contents.

Replacing the Text

To make changes within a line, the substitute *s* command is used. Examples of this command are

s/this/these	Deletes the first occurrence of *this* and replaces it with *these.*
s/them/him/p	Replaces *then* with *him* and displays the line after making the substitution.
3s/old/new/p	Replaces the first occurrence of *old* on the third line with *new.*

It is possible to use the substitute command to delete a word. In the following example, we want to delete the word *the* and display the results:

Chief of the Wealthy Corporation
s/the//p
Chief of Wealthy Corporation

A space had to be left after the word to avoid having two spaces between *of* and *wealthy*. It is possible to combine the search and substitute commands, as follows:

/delighted/s/delighted/happy/p

This searches for the next occurrence of "delighted" and replaces it with "happy." As the editor realizes that you want to change the pattern that you searched for, the command can be abbreviated to

/delighted/s/happy/p

Deleting Lines

You have seen that the *s* and *c* commands can be used to delete words within a line. However, to remove one or several lines of text, the delete *d* command is used. For example,

d	Deletes the current line of the buffer.
4d	Deletes line 4.
+4d	Deletes four lines after the current line.
4,7d	Deletes lines 4–7.
1,$d	Deletes all lines from the buffer.
10,/there/d	Deletes line 10 to the line containing pattern "there."

To avoid disastrous deletions, it is good practice to print lines before entering the command. Context line numbers are great for finding text, but because text patterns such as "there" occur many times in most text files, it is risky to use context line numbers when you are altering text.

Moving and Copying Text

To move lines of text around within the buffer, without having to retype them, use the move *m* command. The move command (*m*) is used to move text from one place in a file to another. If no source lines are specified, then the current line is moved after the destination line. If two source lines are specified, then the group of specified lines are moved after the destination. The following commands show all three forms of the move command:

3,6m$	Moves lines 3–6 to the end of the buffer.
8m2	Moves line 8 after line 2.
3,6t$	Copies lines 3–6 to the end of the buffer.
10,15t0	Copies lines 10–15 to the beginning of the buffer.
/hi/,50m0 or 3m0	Moves addressed text after line 0.

The transfer (*t*) command is almost the same as the move command. The only difference is that the addressed text is not disturbed during a transfer. The move (*m*) command takes the addressed text, removes it from one place, puts it back somewhere else; the transfer command makes a copy of the addressed lines of text and places the copy at the destination. The move command has no effect on the size of the file, whereas the transfer command always increases the size of the file.

Global Searches and Substitutions

Normally, the search and substitution commands both look and act on the first occurrence of a pattern. The commands can be made more universal by using the global *g* parameter in the command. The substitute *s* command is used to change one pattern of text on a line to another pattern. The general format of the substitute command is

n1,n2s/pattern1/pattern2/

where *n1* and *n2* are line specifiers and *pattern1* and *pattern2* are text patterns. The command causes *pattern1* to be replaced by *pattern2* in the group of specified lines. The simplest form of the substitute command is

s/pattern1//

which removes the text represented by *pattern1* from the current line.

The substitute command is probably the hardest *ed* command. Changing one word to another on a short line is easy, but changing the third asterisk on a long line in a source program can require more skill than writing the program. The carat and the currency symbols are frequently used to simplify substitute expressions. Consider the following:

1101 1101 1101 1101

If you had to change the last number (field) to *1011*, you could use any of the following substitute commands:

1. *s/1101 1101 1101 1101/1101 1101 1101 1011/*
2. *s/1101$/1011/*
3. *s/.....$/1011/*

The currency symbol in the last two examples forces the regular expression match to occur at the end of the line, so less has to be typed or counted. The second example specifically states that the last four characters should be *1101* and that they should be replaced by *1011*. The third example just replaces the last four characters on the line with *1011*. It should be noted that the first two examples will not work if the line contains trailing blanks or tabs.

The carat (^) forces a match to occur at the beginning of a line, such as *s/^/-/* to place a hyphen at the beginning of a line.

Most *ed* commands pertain to a single line in a file or a local group of lines. *ed*'s global command (*g*) is used to modify commands so that they pertain to all lines that contain a certain text pattern. Suppose you want to print all of the lines that contain the word "dog." The *ed* command

g/dog/p

will print all of the lines containing the word "dog" (or "doggy" or "dogged"). The phrase *g/dog/* modifies the print command (*p*) so that it pertains to all the lines containing the pattern "dog." The *g* character introduces the global modifier phrase, and the text pattern is enclosed in slashes. The global command works in two phases: search phase and command execution phase. There are two ways of using these commands:

g/dog/s//tiger/p	Finds all lines containing the string *dog*, replacing the first occurrence on *each line* with *tiger.*
g/dog/s/tiger/g *1,$s/dog/tiger/g*	Replaces every occurrence of the word *dog* with *tiger.*

It is important to understand the difference between the *g* option to the substitute command and the *g* global command. The *g* option specifies that the editor should perform every possible substitution on a line, whereas the global command specifies a list of lines on which a command should be performed. In the example

g/teh/s/teh/the/g

the leading *g* indicates the global command, which makes a list of all the lines containing a "teh." The substitute command is then performed on every line in the list, and the *g* option specifies that every occurrence of "teh" on the line should be changed to "the."

In all examples of the substitute command, the regular expression and the replacement string have been delimited by slashes. In a substitute command (but not in a context pattern), any character other than space is allowed as a delimiter. The slashes are often used because they clearly delimit the expressions.

Joining Lines Together

The join command (*j*) is used to glue two lines together. The command

-,.j

combines the previous line with the current line. The minus sign is a shorthand notation for the line in front of the current line. A group of short lines can be joined as in

10,20j

MANIPULATING FILES

ed remembers the name of the file that is being edited. The file command *f* is used to either display or change the remembered filename. The *ed* command *f* will cause the editor to print the remembered filename, whereas the command *f myfile* will change the remembered name to *myfile*. There are three commands that can change the remembered filename: f, e, and w. The *r* command has no effect on the remembered filename.

Listing Lines of the File

The list (*l*) command is a variant of the print command. It is used to display special characters that may be hiding in the text. Consider a line of text that contains the following eight characters:

a,b,c, <backspace>,d,<tab>,e,f

If you use the print command to display the line, it will appear as

```
-p
abd     ef
```

The *c* is not visible because the backspace character that follows it essentially erases it, and the tab character is expanded into the appropriate number of spaces. However, the backspace and tab are visible if you display the line using the list command:

```
l
abc\bd\tef
```

The *\b* and *\t* conventions indicate a backspace and a tab character, respectively.

Like the print command, the list command accepts zero, one, or two line numbers. Without an address, the list line lists the current line. When one address is given, it lists that line. When an address range is specified, then that range of lines is listed.

Updating the Original File

Whenever you have made any substantial changes or additions to the workspace, you should use the write *w* command to update the permanent copy of the file. Remember that while you are editing, you are working with a temporary copy of the file. It is necessary to update the permanent copy to save your changes. The write command is used to write the workspace to a disk file. The general format of the write command is

n1, n2w filename

where *n1* and *n2* are line specifiers, and *filename* is the name of the disk file. If no line numbers are specified, all the lines in the file are written. If no filename is specified, the default file is the original file being edited. Therefore, the editor command *w* will write all of the lines of the workspace to the original file. The number of characters in the file will be reported after the write succeeds. You usually use the *w* command before you leave *ed* with the *q* command.

Combining and Replacing Files

More than one file can be combined in the editor by using the read *r* command. This reads a file into the buffer without overwriting anything already there. For example, assuming that the final paragraph of a letter has been created in the buffer and is in file called *report* on the disk,

r report

causes the file to be copied into the buffer, at the end of the text already there. This is equivalent to appending data/file at the end of the existing text. Some additional examples are

0r filename	Inserts a file at the beginning of the buffer.
nr filename	Inserts a file after a particular line, where *n* is the required line number.
e newfile	Replaces the contents of the buffer with another file.

SPECIAL CHARACTERS AND PATTERN SEARCHING

As you will have noticed, certain characters have unexpected meaning within the editor. These characters are called *metacharacters* and can be very useful as short cuts. Although there are many of these, a few of these are:

dot character (.)	Matches any character in a search, or substitute command.
/a.c/	Matches *abc*, *a2c*, ...
circumflex or carat (^)	Signifies the beginning of a line.
/^string/	Searches for any line beginning with *string*.

dollar ($)	Signifies the end of a line.
/string$/	Searches for the occurrence of *string* at the end of the line.
asterisk (*)	Matches any number of occurrences of a character.
*a**	Matches *a*, *aaa*, ...
backslash (\)	Turns off the special meaning associated with the special characters.
end\.	Is the end of the end.
left brace ([)	Introduces a character set and the end of the character set
\[	is indicated by a right square brace.

ENTERING THE UNIX SHELL

To execute a UNIX command from within the editor, simply enter an exclamation mark *!*, followed by the command name:

!who

When the command terminates, control will return to the editor.

The editing session is not affected by the shell escape. You do not have to write the text buffer to a permanent file before using a shell escape. If you want to enter several commands, you can escape from the editor by entering the command

!sh

to create a new shell. This new shell will allow you to enter as many UNIX commands as you like. You might try the UNIX *ps* command to get a list of all the processes you are running. Your original shell, *ed*, your new shell, and the *ps* command will be in the list. It is very useful to invoke another shell in this manner. When these have completed, leave the shell in usual manner by entering **Ctrl-d**. Rather than logging out, the control will return to the *ed* editor.

SUMMARY

ed is the original UNIX editor and it has changed very little. In command mode, the editor is waiting for you to enter *ed* commands. *ed* commands can change lines, print lines, read or write disk files, or initiate text entry mode. Most commands refer to either a specific line or a range of lines in the file.

Even though *ed* has been superseded by *vi* and other newer editing programs, there are many reasons to learn it thoroughly. This chapter has introduced you to a line-based text editor, which will enable you to create, modify, and save files.

9

The vi Editor

INTRODUCTION

There is a large variety of editors on UNIX. Of the two most commonly used UNIX editors, *ed* is a line editor. The most popular editor on UNIX is a full-screen editor called *vi.* The basic editor *vi* is cryptic to learn but very powerful, while other editors, like *pico*, are very easy to learn but have only a limited number of commands. *vi* is the editor that is recommended because of its widespread usage on many UNIX platforms.

vi is a command-driven editor. You do not have to use function keys and menus to tell it what you want, as with other text editors and word processors. Instead, you use commands, many of which are one letter long. The advantage of such an editor is that you can do a lot of different things with very little typing. The disadvantage is that many systems do not indicate when you are in command mode or when you are entering text in insert or replace mode.

Unlike other editors in UNIX, both text editors used in MVS include line numbers next to the text. MVS editors save line numbers in their data sets. However, most TSO/ISPF commands offer an operand that lets you omit the line numbers, especially when printing or copying a numbered data set. Given the choice between the MVS ISPF text editor and the TSO EDIT text editor, virtually everyone chooses the ISPF. The ISPF editor is much more flexible and versatile.

There are a large number of TSO and ISPF edit commands that are not supported in *vi*, and vice versa. However, you will find that *vi* provides much more flexibility and latitude in the syntax and use of the commands. Therefore, you always have to be on your guard in *vi*, in using the proper syntax to avoid disastrous results.

You may find some similarity in the names, syntax, and function, but there are some subtle differences in the manner the three editors work. Therefore, caution must be used in executing *vi* commands.

The objective of this section is to introduce you to the UNIX editor *vi* (vee-eye). At the end of the section, you will be able to

- Start and end a *vi* session.
- Position the cursor, scroll, and page.
- Insert, delete, copy, append, and move text.
- Search and search and replace text.
- Save, undelete, and quit.
- Enter UNIX shell and perform special options.

vi Operation Modes

UNIX was designed to support simple ASCII terminals; thus the original editors (*ed*) were line based. *vi* is supplied with all UNIX systems. Because *vi* uses standard alphanumeric keys for commands, you can use it on virtually any terminal or workstation in existence without having to worry about unusual keyboard mappings. As a point of interest, *vi* is actually a special mode of another UNIX text editor called *ex*.

vi is a command line editor in that it has two basic modes of operation, command mode and edit mode. The default mode for *vi* is the command mode. In this mode, editing of user text cannot be performed. *vi* awaits the appropriate command from the user before performing the operation. In general, *vi* will return to the command mode after executing the command. The commands can be executed from files, and documents can be formatted or rearranged by simply running a menu script of commands in *vi*.

The *command mode* is the mode you are in whenever you begin to use *vi*. In this mode commands are used to move around and edit text objects such as words, sentences, and paragraphs. Pressing the ESC key returns you to command mode. In command mode, characters you type perform actions like moving the cursor, cutting or copying text, or searching for some particular text. When you start *vi*, it is in *command mode*.

The *input mode* is the mode you use to type (*insert state*) text into a buffer. There are several commands that you can use to enter this mode. To switch from *command to input mode*, press the *i* key (you do not need to press RETURN). *vi* lets you insert text beginning at the current cursor location. To switch back to command mode, press ESC. You can also use ESC to cancel an unfinished command in *command mode*.

Unfortunately, *vi* does not normally indicate which mode you are in. If you are uncertain about the current mode, you can press ESC a few times. When *vi* beeps, you have returned to the command mode. Before you start typing text, the command below activates the modeline indicator. You are not required to use it, but it tells you whether you are in command or input mode. Type

:set showmode RETURN

Nothing appears to change. When you are in *command mode*, there is no indicator, but if you enter *input mode*, one will appear in the bottom right-hand corner of the window.

The ISPF EDIT option

ISPF (Interactive System Productivity Facility) uses CUA-compliant definitions of function keys F1–F12, except inside the edit function. The most common keys are F3 for exit, F7 for screen scroll up, and F8 for screen scroll down. You can select option 2 for edit, once in the ISPF menu options. The ISPF EDIT helps you create or change program code, test data, or documentation. Special features of the EDIT include edit macros that eliminate repetitive editing tasks and models that help you create dialog elements.

Like *vi*, there are two kinds of commands in ISPF EDIT options:

- *Primary commands* are commands that you type in on the edit command line at the top of your data. For example, PROFILE, CAPS ON/OFF, UNNUM, NULLS ON/OFF, and RESET.
- *Line commands* are commands that you enter on the edit line numbers, which are located on left side of the data. Line commands are the ISPF editor's counterpart to TSO EDIT (XEDIT) prefix commands. You can add, delete, copy, and move lines. You can enter line command commands in the column to the left of the TOP OF DATA and BOTTOM OF DATA lines as well. In fact, you can enter a *line command* anywhere on the line command area.

You can use the INSERT (*I*) *line command*, as follows:

00100
I 0200 'This line command deleted one line'
00300
I5 400 'This line command inserts 5 lines'
00500

When you press **ENTER**, lines are inserted.

To *delete* a line or a group of lines, type

000100
D 0200 'This line command deletes one line'
000300
000400

000500
D3 600 'This command deletes lines 000600 - 000800'
000700
000800
000900
DD 000 'This pair of line commands deletes line 001000 - 001200'
001000
DD 200
001300
...

The MVS TSO TEXT EDIT

MVS TSO uses command formats like the *vi*. The TSO EDIT (XEDIT) commands edit a data set (sequential or partitioned) and provide subcommands for data set creation, updating, and display. Like *vi*, TSO EDIT also operates in *command* and *input modes*:

- *Edit* or *line mode*, where you can use the edit commands to manipulate text (delete, change, repeat, copy, etc.). *vi command mode* works more like the *edit mode* of TSO EDIT. At any given time, the editor treats one line of your data as the "current" line. Most commands, such as DELETE, LIST, UP, DOWN, or COPY, without any operands default to current line.
- *Input mode*, where you just add new lines and data, is also similar to *vi*'s input mode. The only difference is in the mode of switching. In *vi*, ESC transfers you to command mode, whereas in TSO EDIT, the RETURN or ENTER key is used to return to EDIT mode.

You can switch between *input* and *edit modes* by merely pressing the ENTER key on a blank line to switch to EDIT mode and entering INPUT to switch to input mode, or vice versa. For example,

INPUT
00010 This is in the input mode
00020 This is in the input mode
00030 RETURN/ENTER key
EDIT
list * 'List the current line'
up 2 'Move up two lines'
..
..
INPUT
00030 This is in the input mode (appending each new line of data to the end)
00040 This is in the input mode

You can invoke the TSO Editor by using the following format.

EDIT or E data set[member][/password] [NEW/OLD] [data set type] [NUM/NONUM]....

Like *vi*, most TSO EDIT subcommands can be abbreviated to one to three characters, such as

BOTTOM—B	**INPUT—I**	**SALTER—SA**
CHANGE—C	**INSERT—IN**	**SAVE—S**
COPY—C	**LIST—L**	**SCAN—SC**
DELETE—DEL	**MERGE—M**	**SHIFTR—SR**
DOWN—D	**MODIFY—MOD**	**TABSET—TAB**
END	**MOVE—MO**	
FIND—F	**RUN—R**	

The general format is

Subcommand [* / line-number [line-number] [count]] [{character string....}]]

If operands are omitted, TSO assumes the **current** line or position or character. '*' indicates current position.

About vi Commands

While not entering text, you use *vi* in *command mode* and enter editing commands consisting of one or more characters. The syntax of an editing command is *operator'* 2 spaces, and *object*.

The *operator* is a character—such as *d* for delete—that describes the action to be carried out on the object, a word, sentence, paragraph, or section. To return to command mode from *insert mode*, press the ESC key. If you are already in *command mode*, the terminal will beep at you (or make some similar sound).

Using ex Commands

When in *vi* command mode, typing **:** allows you to access the *ex* editor command set. There are a number of *ex* commands that you will want to use within the *vi* editor. A summary of *ex* commands is listed in the Appendix C. *ex* commands are very powerful and can allow you to make some large changes to your files quite efficiently. *ex* functions in *line mode*. It addresses a line by its line number or a range of lines by a range of line numbers and then performs some function, but it does not display line numbers.

The *ex* editor uses the current line as the default. You can abbreviate the *ex* commands that specify functions to single letters.

Symbols Used

Throughout this chapter, you will see *examples* of commands that you can enter. Enter the text exactly as it appears with the following exception: text in italics means you should substitute the appropriate text (like a filename) for the italicized word.

vi commands are *case sensitive*, which means that uppercase and lowercase commands are not the same command. For example, *j* moves the cursor down, but *J* combines two lines into one line.

The word RETURN represents the action of pressing RETURN key. ESC indicates pressing the ESCAPE key. Also, sometimes you will see a keystroke like Ctrl-f. Ctrl-f means you hold down the key marked CONTROL or Ctrl, and press "f." The Ctrl key acts in a manner similar to the SHIFT key.

Useful vi Options

COMMAND OPTION	DEFAULT	ACTION
autoindent	noai	Automatically indents each line of text.
number	nonu	Prefixes lines with line number.
term	$TERM	Sets type of terminal to use.
scroll	scroll=11	Sets number of lines scrolled with *^d* and *z*.
shell	sh=/bin/sh	Defines the shell used for UNIX commands. This value is taken from the SHELL environment variable.
shiftwidth	sw=8	Sets the number of spaces for use with autoindent.
wrapmargin (wm)	wm=0	Specifies number of spaces lines are broken before right edge of the screen.

vi STATES OF OPERATION

vi has multiple personalities. When you start the edit session, the easiest personality to use is the visual state (command mode). From the *visual state*, the text insertion commands (e.g., the *i* command) causes *vi* to enter the *insert state*. From the *visual state*, you can enter the last-line state to perform read/write operations and search and substitute commands (plus other advanced operations).

The *visual state* lets you move around and look at a file with the arrow or other keys. To put in new text or change old text, you need to first enter the *insert state*. To execute complicated commands such as string searches or repetitive string substitutions, you must enter the last-line state by typing a colon (:), a slash (/), or a question mark (?). When you enter the last-line state, a colon prompt appears at the last line of the screen and the cursor is placed at that line ready for you to type the special command. Most *vi* commands are one or two letters long. The case of the command letter is important; for example, while *u* undoes the last change, *U* restores the current line to the original state.

Visual State Commands

Below is a list of useful commands that work in the *visual state* (line or command mode). Note that almost all *vi* commands may be preceded by a positive repeat factor (e.g., typing *20w* is just like typing *w* 20 times). Arrow keys move the cursor left, down, up, and right.

ISPF EDIT COMMAND	TSO EDIT SUBCOMMAND	ACTION	*VI* COMMAND
left, down, up, right	**shiftl, down, up, shiftr**	Move the cursor **left**, **down**, **up**, and **right**, respectively. Use when arrow keys are not available.	***h j k l***
right arrow	**right arrow**	Move forward to next word.	***w***
right arrow	**right arrow**	Move forward to next word, skipping punctuation.	***W***
left arrow	**left arrow**	Move backward to beginning of previous word.	***b***
left arrow	**left arrow**	Move backward to beginning of previous word, skipping punctuation.	***B***
right arrow	**right arrow**	Move forward to the end of next word or punctuation string.	***e***
right arrow	**right arrow**	Move forward to the end of next word.	***E***
left arrow	**left arrow**	Move to the beginning of current line.	***0***
right arrow	**right arrow**	Move to the end of current line.	***$***
m, mm	**DOWN** *n*	Move forward one sentence.	***)***
m, mm	**UP** *n*	Move backward one sentence.	***(***
F *n* (find)	**DOWN** *n*	Move forward to next blank line.	***}***
up arrow	**UP** *n*	Move backward to previous blank line.	***{***
up arrow	**UP** *n*	Move to the beginning of top (home) line on screen.	***H***
down arrow	**DOWN** *n*	Move to the beginning of middle line on screen.	***M***
down arrow	**DOWN** *n*	Move to the beginning of bottom line on screen.	***L***
F8	**B** (bottom)	Move cursor to last line in file.	***G***
F7	**TOP**	Move cursor to first line in file.	***1G***
down arrow	**DOWN** *n* or **UP** *n*	Move cursor to *n*th line in file.	***nG***
down arrow	**DOWN** *n*	Move forward half a screen page.	***Ctrl-d***
up arrow	**UP** *n*	Move backward half a screen page.	***Ctrl-u***
down arrow	**DOWN** *n*	Move forward one screen page.	***Ctrl-f***
up arrow	**UP** *n*	Move backward one screen page.	***Ctrl-b***
		Mark current cursor location with the character *x*.	***mx***
FIND *x*	**F (find)** '*x*'	Move to cursor location marked by character *x*.	***`x***
FIND *x*	**F (find)** '*x*'	Move to beginning of line of location marked by *x*.	***'x***
FIND pattern	**F** '*pattern*'	Move forward to next occurrence of pattern.	***./pattern***
FIND pattern **PREV RFIND**		Move backward to next occurrence of pattern. *n* Repeat previous search in same direction.	***?pattern***

ISPF EDIT COMMAND	TSO EDIT SUBCOMMAND	ACTION	VI COMMAND
		N Repeat search in opposite direction.	
		% Move to parenthesis, brace, or bracket matching the one at the current cursor location.	

Insert State Commands

The main way to put text into your buffer in *vi* is in the *insert state*. While you are in the *visual state*, several commands cause you to enter the *insert state*:

ISPF EDIT	TSO EDIT	ACTION	VI OPERATOR
I (insert)	**I** (input)	Enter insert mode. Characters you type are inserted before the current cursor location.	***i***
left arrow + I	**left arrow + I**	Enter insert mode after moving to beginning of the current line.	***I***
type	**type**	Enter insert mode after moving one character to the right.	***a***
I (insert)	**IN** (insert)	Enter the current insert mode	***A***
I (insert)	**IN** (insert)	Create blank line below current line, and enter insert mode at the beginning of the new line.	***o***
up arrow + I (*insert*)	**UP** *1* **+ IN** (insert)	Create blank line above current line, and enter insert mode at the beginning of the new line.	***O***

The *insert* state is terminated with the ESC key. Note that the *insert state* is line oriented; when you have finished inserting each line, that line cannot be backed over.

Several control sequences have special meaning to *vi* when you insert text, so they will cause actions rather than be inserted. The following key combinations work within the insert state:

ISPF EDIT	TSO EDIT	ACTION	VI OPERATOR
F3 or **end**	**END**	Terminate insert mode and exit to edit mode.	***ESC***
backspace	**shiftl + DEL**	Delete the last character typed. Characters may not disappear instantly for optimization purposes.	***BACKSPACE or DELETE***
DEL	**DEL** *line-num*	Erase this entire insert line currently being typed.	***Ctrl-u***
backspace	**backspace**	Delete the last word typed or word currently being typed.	***Ctrl-w***
RETURN	**RETURN**	Create a new blank line at the point of text insertion.	***RETURN***

INVOKING vi

To enter *vi*, just type *vi* followed by the name of the file to edit:

vi filename RETURN

where *filename* is the name of the file you want to edit. If the file does not exist, *vi* will create it for you. You can also start *vi* without giving any filename. In this case, *vi* will ask for one when you *quit* or *save* your work.

If it is a new file, it does not contain any text. *vi* uses the *tilde* (~) character to indicate lines on the screen beyond the end of the file. *vi* uses a *cursor* to indicate where your next command or text insertion will take effect. The *cursor* is the small rectangle, which is the size of one character, and the character inside the rectangle is called the *current character*. At the bottom of the window, *vi* maintains an announcement line, called the *modeline*. The modeline lists the current line of the file, the filename, and its status.

This will cause *vi* to read the file into its memory and allow you to edit it. If the file does not exist, *vi* will tell you so and then proceed to edit a new file that will be created when you exit the editor.

There are command options to *vi* that allow you to start up your editing session while placing the cursor at different locations in the file:

ISPF EDIT	TSO EDIT	FUNCTION	VI COMMAND
edit *dsname*	**EDIT***dsname*	Edit file placing the cursor at the beginning of file.	***vi*** *file*
down arrow	**DOWN** *n*	Edit file placing the cursor at line *n* of the file.	***vi*** *+n file*
F8	**B** (*bottom*)	Edit file placing the cursor at the last line of the file.	***vi*** *+$ file*
F '*pattern*'	**F** '*pattern*'	Edit file placing the cursor at the first occurrence of the string matched by pattern.	***vi*** *+/pattern file*
		Edit file for purposes of reading and not modifying the file.	***vi*** *-R file*
		Edit file but store file in encrypted form. Encryption key must be supplied.	***vi*** *-x file*
		Invoke editor on last version of file that might have been saved when the system crashed during editing session.	***vi*** *-r file*
		Edit all files in the current directory.	***vi*** *

While using *vi* to edit an existing file, you are actually working on a copy of the file that is held in a temporary buffer. If you invoked *vi* with a new filename (or no filename), the contents of the file exist only in this buffer. Saving a file writes the contents of this buffer to the permanent file, replacing its contents. You can write the buffer to a new file or to some other file. You can also decide not to write the contents of the buffer and leave your original file unchanged.

To get into the **ISPF** editor, you must first enter ISPF by typing *ispf* at the TSO command prompt. This displays the main ISPF menu. Entering *2* (*Edit*) at the OPTIONS menu or the command ispf 2 will put you in the **EDIT** mode. The EDIT entry panel will point you to various ISPF options to select. To move your cursor forward from field to field, press your **TAB** key. To move your cursor in the other direction, press **BACKTAB (SHIFT + TAB key on PCs)**.

The only crucial fields on this entry panel are related to the data set to be edited, either sequential or partitioned. The *vi* does not expect the data set to exist, but in case of ISPF, the data set *must exist* even if it is empty. Therefore, even a new data set must be allocated prior to invoking ISPF. On the other hand, in TSO, EDIT will allocate and create the data set if it does not exist.

Examples of Starting vi, ISPF EDIT, and TSO EDIT

EXAMPLES	ISPF	TSO	VI
1. Open an existing file for editing.	**ispf edit** osc.text	**EDIT** osc.text	***vi*** *osc*
2. Create a file to edit.	file must exist	**EDIT** osc.text	***vi*** *osc*
3. Simply start the editor.	**ispf** 2	**EDIT + INPUT**	***vi***

Ending the vi Session

There are several ways in which you can end your editing session, leave *vi*, and return to the shell. The commands used to leave *vi* are

ZZ Write latest version to file being edited and *exit* (*quit*) the editor.
:wq Same as ZZ.
:q! *Quit* vi without saving changes made during this session.

EXAMPLES	ISPF	TSO	VI
1. Quit and save the contents to a new file.	**END** *dsname*	**SAVE** *dsname* **END**	**:w** *filename* **:q**
2. Quit and save the contents of the file that is being edited.	**END** {saves data in file}	**END** *save*	***ZZ* or *:wq***
3. Quit without saving the contents.	**CANCEL**	**END** *nosave*	***:q!***

MOVING THE CURSOR

When *vi* is loaded on a new file, the cursor is restricted to the upper left position on the screen and cannot be moved using the cursor keys. You will clearly need to move the cursor around your file. You can move the cursor in command mode. *vi* has many different cursor movement commands. The four basic keys appear below. You can also use the backspace key (but not the DELETE key) and spacebar to move left and right, respectively.

Notice that *vi* has its own definitions of sentences and paragraphs, so understanding how *vi* recognizes them is useful.

A sentence is all the characters between normal sentence punctuation marks: period (**.**), question mark (**?**), and exclamation point (**!**). A blank line also ends a sentence.

The text between two RETURN characters forms a line. Hence, it is possible to have lines which are wider than the *vi* display.

A paragraph is a sequence of lines that are not interrupted by any blank lines.

The following keys control cursor movement. *Do not try to use the cursor arrow keys to move the cursor!*

MVS: ISPF TEXT EDITOR		TSO EDIT	FUNCTION	*VI* EDITOR	
up	up 10 - up 10 lines	**UP**	Move the cursor to the previous line.	***k***	up
down	down 1 - down 1 lines	**DOWN**	Move the cursor to the next line.	***j***	down (return)
left	left 1 - left 1 positions	**shiftl**	Move the cursor 1 space to the left.	***h***	left (backspace)
right	right 1 - right 1 positions	**shiftr**	Move the cursor 1 space to the right.	***l***	right (space)

ISPF uses the commands UP, DOWN, RIGHT, and LEFT on the command line. In ISPF, the TAB key is used more frequently to move the cursor around more quickly. TAB and BACKTAB keys are used to jump cursor to the command line, and vice versa, whereas *vi* has adopted the convention of using **hjkl** keys (which are next to each other on the keyboard) for moving the cursor. ISPF uses the facilities of the terminal keyboards (for example, 3270) to move cursor around the screen.

In *vi*, there are other useful commands to control the cursor. The following are used to move the cursor a word at a time, even if this means going to the next line:

w Moves the cursor to the next word.

e Moves the cursor to the end of the current word.

b Moves the cursor to the beginning of the current word.

Certain characters are recognized as being word separators (punctuation characters, for example), in which case the above commands stop when they encounter one of these. If the uppercase versions of the characters are used, then the cursor will move to the next white space character. There are also commands to position the cursor at the beginning or end of the current line:

$	Moves the cursor to the end of the current line.
0 **(zero)**	Moves the cursor to the beginning of the current line.
^ **(carat)**	Moves to the first nonwhite space character.

vi offers a range of commands that provide a great degree of flexibility in how you move around the contents of the file you are editing. Many of these commands can be combined with a numerical value to extend their functionality.

Move the Cursor Along a Line

Press the ESC key to enter command mode before using these commands:

ISPF EDIT	TSO EDIT	CURSOR MOVES TO	vi COMMAND
right arrow	shiftr	Next character.	***l***
left arrow	shiftl	Previous character.	***h***
right arrow	shiftr	Next word.	***w***
right arrow	shiftr	Next n words.	***w****n*
left arrow	left arrow	Previous word.	***b***
left arrow	left arrow	Previous n words.	***b****n*
right arrow	shiftr	End of current word.	**e**
left arrow	shiftl * *column-count*	Start of current line.	***0*** **(zero)**
right arrow	shiftr * *column-count*	End of current line.	***$***

Move the Cursor Between Lines

Press the ESC key to enter command mode before using these commands:

ISPF EDIT	TSO EDIT	CURSOR MOVES TO	*vi* COMMAND
down	DOWN	Next line down (same column).	***j***
down	DOWN	Start of next line down.	**+**
up	UP	Previous line (same column).	***k***
up	UP	Start of previous line.	**-**

Move Between Text Blocks

Press the ESC key to enter command mode before using these commands:

ISPF EDIT	TSO EDIT	CURSOR MOVES TO	*vi* COMMAND
right arrow	shiftr	Beginning of next sentence.	*)*
	shiftl	Beginning of previous sentence.	*(*
down	DOWN *line-count*	Beginning of next paragraph.	*}*
	up *line-count*	Beginning of previous paragraph.	*{*

A full stop followed by two or more spaces is treated as the end of a sentence. All text to the next empty line is treated as belonging to the current paragraph.

Move Between Screens

Press the ESC key to enter command mode before using these commands:

ISPF EDIT	TSO EDIT	CURSOR MOVES TO	*vi* COMMAND
DOWN *page*	DOWN *n*	Next screen.	*^F*
UP *page*	UP *n*	Previous screen (up).	*^B*
DOWN *half*	DOWN *n*	Next half screen (down).	*^D*
UP *half*	UP *n*	Previous half screen (up).	*^U*
UP *data*	UP *n*	Top line on screen.	*H*
right arrow	**shiftr**	Middle line on screen.	*M*
DOWN *data*	DOWN *n*	Bottom line on screen.	*L*

SCREEN SCROLLING AND PAGING

The commands to scroll the screen up and down a page at a time (12 lines) are

Ctrl-d Scrolls down.
Ctrl-u Scrolls up.

For very long files, *vi* provides a goto line number command:

3000G *goto line 3000*

To position the cursor at the last line in the file, type

G

To position the cursor at the beginning of the file, type

1G

This command displays the line number of the cursor position

Ctrl-g Displays current line number.

In summary, the following commands facilitate screen scrolling:

ISPF EDIT	TSO EDIT	ACTION	*vi* COMMAND
down arrow	**DOWN** *n*	Move the cursor down the file.	***Ctrl-d***
up arrow	**UP** *n*	Move the cursor up the file.	***Ctrl-u***
DOWN *page*	**DOWN** *n*	Move forward one screen.	***Ctrl-f***
UP *page*	**UP** *n*	Move backward one screen.	***Ctrl-b***
LOCATE *1400*	**UP** *n*	Move to line 1400.	*1400**G***
F7	**TOP**	Move to line 1.	*1**G***
F8	**B (bottom)**	Move to end of file.	***G***

Another method of positioning within a file is to search for a string of characters. When in command mode, any string preceded by a / indicates a search forward command. The cursor is positioned at the first occurrence of the text string. The command *n* will search forwards for the next occurrence. To search backward, the *?* command is used.

ENTERING UNIX SHELL

It is possible to execute a UNIX shell command from within *vi*. This is accomplished by entering the command mode and hitting the colon (:) key. This will return a prompt at the bottom left-hand corner of the screen. To run a single UNIX command, use the command

:! UNIX_command

:!sh will temporarily take you out of the editor, and into the Bourne shell, where you can perform any desired function. The type of shell that is started is determined by the *$SHELL* variable. You can specify that some other shell is to be started by setting the *vi* shell option. **Ctrl-d** will return you to the editor.

:!Who Will tell you who is logged on

To insert the output from a UNIX command into a file, immediately after the cursor:

:r! command

For example, this facility would be very useful if you were using *vi* to document a UNIX command and you wanted to include examples of the output from this command. To include the output from the executed command within the buffer, enter two exclamation marks, and no colon, as in

!!who

SUMMARY

Throughout the history of UNIX, there have been several common programs for editing text. The UNIX system's first text editor was *ed*. *ed* is a powerful program, but it is best used by the programmers or technically inclined people. Another derivative of the *ed* is *vi* editor. *vi* is also called a *visual* (or screen-oriented) *editor*, because it portrays on your terminal's screen, a picture of the file being edited.

The overriding goal in the design of the *vi* commands was to make them mnemonic. With just a few exceptions, each command letter or symbol is reminiscent of the command name. *a* for append, *i* for insert, **<ESC>** to escape from text-entry mode. Some of the exceptions have other organizing principles; for example, the **hjkl** keys have a layout on the keyboard that makes them easy to remember, and the < shift operator looks like what it does.

For most lowercase commands, there is an uppercase variant. For example, the *w* command moves forward one word, but *W* moves forward one larger word. Another example is that both *a* and *A* lead into text entry; *a* adds text after the cursor position, and *A* adds text at the end of the current line.

Many *vi* commands accept numeric prefixes. For most commands, a numeric prefix means repeat the command that many times. For example, if you type *50j*, you will move the cursor down **50 lines**. On the other hand, a few commands do interpret the numerical prefixcs uniquely. For example, the unadorned *G* command goes to the end of the file, whereas *50G* goes to **line 50.**

The *vi* editor does present an uncanny flexibility in command usage, challenging you from time to time. Therefore, you should be on your guard while attempting the subtle variations.

In this chapter, you should have been able to understand the following concepts about using and manipulating the *vi* editor commands:

- Start and end a *vi* session.
- Position the cursor, scroll, and page.
- Insert, delete, copy, append, and move text.
- Search, search, and replace text.
- Save, undelete, and quit.
- Enter the UNIX shell.
- Using *ex* commands from *vi*.

10

Text Manipulations

INTRODUCTION

Although *vi* has hundreds of commands, you can get by with just a handful. In this chapter, we will concentrate on a subset of *vi* commands that will enable you to perform simple text editing, to create, change, delete, and manipulate text and text files.

TEXT MANIPULATIONS

Text Input Modes

Besides insert mode, *vi* employs a few other input modes. They all let you enter text; the only difference is where the insertion point is. The table below describes the three most common modes: *append*, *insert*, and *open*. Two other text input modes are *change mode* and *replace mode*. The mode indicator displays the current mode.

Input Modes

ISPF EDIT	TSO EDIT	ACTION	*vi* COMMAND
F8 + **I** (insert)	**B** (bottom) + **IN** (insert)	Appends to the last line of the file (inserts text after the cursor).	*a*
left arrow + **I**	**IN**	Inserts at the current cursor position (inserts text before the cursor).	*i*
I	**IN**	Opens a line *below* the cursor, allowing text to be entered at the start of the next line.	*o*
up arrow + **I**	**up** + **IN**	Opens a line *above* the cursor, allowing text to be entered at the start of the next line.	*O*
F11, type	**right arrow** + **I**	Appends text at the end of the current line.	*A*
left arrow	**left arrow** + **I**	Inserts text at the start of the current line.	*I*

Inserting Text

To type text into the buffer you must enter the *insert mode*. Choose the command that is best suited to the present position of the cursor and the editing task you want to do. As the text you are typing in begins to approach the right-hand side of the screen, press RETURN to start a new line.

To enter input mode, press

i

Note that in the bottom right-hand corner, *vi* indicates that you are in *input mode*. Then enter the following text, and remember to press RETURN at the end of each line. You can use the special keystrokes if you make a mistake. After entering this text, press ESC to return to *command mode*.

In **ISPF**, simply move the cursor to the place where you want to insert it and press the INSERT key. On a 3270 terminal, this key has the letter "a" with a carat (^) symbol over it. When you press it, a carat symbol should appear at the bottom of your screen indicating that you are in insert mode. Pressing the RESET key will return you to noninsert mode.

While in input mode, you can enter text by typing normally. *vi* recognizes a few special key strokes as you type.

Commands to Insert Text

ISPF EDIT	TSO EDIT	ACTION	*vi* COMMAND
backspace	**left arrow**	Erases the previous character.	**BACKSPACE or DELETE**
backspace	**left arrow**	Erases the previous word.	**Ctrl-w**
d	**DEL** (delete)	Erases the current line.	**Ctrl-u**
i	**IN** (insert)	Starts a new line.	**RETURN**

Insert the Contents of Another File

To insert the contents of another file, use the command

:r filename

This inserts the file immediately after the current line.

EXAMPLES	ISPF EDIT	TSO EDIT	*vi* COMMAND
1. Insert a file immediately after the line containing the cursor.	**MOVE** *dsname*	**M** (merge) *dsname*	**:r** *osc.txt*
2. Insert the contents of another file after line 23 in the current file.	**down arrow +** **MOVE** *dsname*	**D** (down) + **M** *dsname*	*23:***r** *osc.txt*
3. Use the **append** command to create a new file of text.	**edit** *osc.text*	**E** *dsname*	**vi** *osc* **a**

Examples Using input Modes

Use file *osc* and assume that the cursor is positioned above 't' in word "time." Enter the string *999*, and the text will look as follows by using the four *input mode* commands:

EXAMPLES	ISPF EDIT	TSO EDIT	*vi* COMMAND
1. What is the t**999**ime? Midday	**CHANGE** 'time' 't999ime'	**C** 'time' 't999ime'	***a***
2. What is the **999**time? Midday	**backspace + type** '999'	**backspace + type** '999'	***I***
3. What is the time? 999 Midday	**right arrow + I** 999	**right arrow + IN** 999	***o***
4. 999 What is the time? Midday	**up arrow + I** 999	**up + IN** 999	***O***

Line Numbers

Many *vi* commands use line numbers, which simply count the number of RETURN characters in a file. You can cut and copy text by line number or jump to a certain line. Line numbers can be useful when you receive error messages during program compilation. Frequently, compilers will print the line number, so you can use *vi* to jump to the appropriate line and look for the errors.

Example

To display the line numbers, enter the following command:

:set number RETURN

This command will immediately display the line numbers in the left margin of your *vi* window. It may cause long lines to wrap around the right edge of the window, but they will not be damaged. The *G* movement command lets you jump to any line within a file. First, type the line number, followed by *G*. If you do not type any line number, *vi* jumps to the end of the file. Thus, *1G* takes you to the beginning, and *G* takes you to the end. Another command reports the current line number and the status of your file. When you type *Ctrl-g*, *vi* displays the filename, whether it has been altered since it was last saved, and the current line number along with the percentage of the text of the file representing all the lines up to the current one.

EXAMPLES	ISPF EDIT	TSO EDIT	*vi* COMMAND
1. Jump to line 1.	**F7**	**TOP**	*1G*
2. Jump to end of the document.	**F8**	**B** (bottom)	*G*
3. Jump to line 6.	**down**	**DOWN** n	*6G*

- After typing each of these "go to" commands, notice that the cursor jumps to the desired line. You can type a multiple-digit line number, of course. Next, turn off the line numbers by entering

  :set nonumber RETURN

- Finally, press **Ctrl-g**, and the modeline should look something like

  'sample' [Modified] line 6 of 13 --46%--

View and Display a File

You can look at a file without the risk of altering its contents by using *vi* in "read-only" mode. To do this, use the command:

EXAMPLES	ISPF EDIT	TSO EDIT	*vi* COMMAND
The message [Read only] is displayed at the bottom of the screen. You can then use the same commands as you would in *vi* to move around, search for text and quit view.		**list** or **list** *dsname*	***view*** *filename*

Display vi Option Values

To display the current value of all options, enter the command

:set all

To display the value of those options whose values have been reset from their default, enter the command

:set

Repeating a Command

Often you will want to act on more than one character, word, or line. For example, suppose you want to delete three words. Rather than type *dw* three times, you can type *3dw*, and *vi* will execute the command three times. Many *vi* commands can be repeated in this manner. Just type a number (it can be more than one digit); then type the command. If you want to abandon the number, press ESC to cancel it.

EXAMPLES	*vi* COMMAND
1. Start with the sample document.	*vi sample RETURN*
2. Turn on the modeline.	*:set showmode RETURN*
3. Move to the "e" in "echoed overhead and up ahead lay sa...," then type.	*3dw* {*vi* deletes three words at once.}
4. Undo previous action.	*u* {*vi* restores.}
5. Move to the blank line after "echoed overhead and up..." and enter.	*5iBOOM:! ESC* {*vi* adds "BOOM!" five times.}
6. Try canceling a number. Move to the word "up" on the last line and type (ignore the beep).	*15 ESC 3x* {ESC cancels the number 15, so *vi* only deletes "up" instead of the 15 characters "up ahead lay sa."}

Markers

During an editing session, you may grow weary of typing lengthy cursor moves or having to remember lots of line numbers. *vi* lets you set markers anywhere in a file. These markers make movement, copying, and cutting text much easier. Markers are named from *a* to *z*, where the letter distinguishes them from each other. When you quit *vi*, the markers vanish, so you must set them each time you start *vi*. Setting markers is easy. Just move the cursor where you want to place the marker, then type *mletter* where letter specifies the marker name. Letter can be any lowercase letter from *a* to *z*. Regrettably, *vi* does not indicate that you just set a marker. You can set markers in any order. You do not have to label them sequentially (*a*, *b*, *c*, etc.).

EXAMPLES	*vi* COMMAND
1. Move the cursor to the word "weathered" in text "The navy ship... bolt... weathered... island..."; then set a marker there.	***mw***
2. Now move over to the word "bolt" and set a marker.	***ma***
3. Next go to "island" and type	***ml***

Once you have set a marker, you can return to that line or exact character quickly. To jump to the marker letter type *`letter*. (Use an accent grave (`).) To jump to beginning of the line containing the marker, type *'letter*. (Use the single quote (').)

Example

Move to the first line of the document; then jump among your markers by typing the following:

`w
`l
`a
'l
'a
'w

Last, try to jump to an undefined marker by typing

'c

vi just beeps at you because it doesn't know where to jump since *mc* was not defined as a marker.

Saving Your Work

vi provides several means of saving your changes. Besides saving your work before quitting, it's also a good idea to save your work periodically. Power failures or system crashes can cause you to lose work. From command mode, you type

:w RETURN or
:w filename RETURN {Saves to a specific file.}

to save your work ('w' is for 'write'). Similarly, to quit *vi* use the command

:q RETURN

Examples

In command mode, type

:w RETURN

To enter the write command. After a moment, *vi* gives you a report at the bottom of its window:

'sample' 13 lines, 539 characters

Don't worry if the line and character numbers differ a bit from yours. Most important, you just saved your work. Now you are ready to quit *vi*. From command mode, type

:q

Again the colon signals an *ex* command at the bottom of the *vi* display. Press RETURN to finish entering the command and to exit *vi*. You can combine these two commands at once to write-and-quit by entering command mode and typing

:wq RETURN
:x RETURN {Exits the ex editor, saving any changes made}.

A shorthand for the command mentioned above is "ZZ" (*SHIFT ZZ*). In some cases, you will want to abandon your changes since the last time you saved your work (the last :w command). To do so, type

:q! RETURN

which tells *vi* to quit without saving. Use caution when abandoning *vi* in this manner because any changes you made will be permanently lost.

PATTERN SEARCHING

Press the ESC key to enter command mode before using these commands.

ISPF EDIT	TSO EDIT	SEARCH	*vi* COMMAND
FIND 'pattern'	**F** 'pattern'	forward for a pattern	**/pattern** RETURN
FIND 'pattern' **PREV**	**TOP, F** 'pattern'	backward for a pattern	**?pattern** RETURN
RFIND		repeat previous search	**n**
RFIND		repeat previous search in reverse direction	**N**

As files become longer, you may need assistance locating a particular instance of text. *vi* has several search and search-and-replace features.

Simple Search

vi can search the entire file for a given string of text. A string is a sequence of characters. *vi* searches forward with the slash (**/**) key or backward with the question mark key (**?**). You execute the search by typing the command key, then string followed by RETURN. To cancel the search, press ESC instead of RETURN. You can search again by typing *n* (forward) or *N* (backward). Also, when *vi* reaches the end of the text, it continues searching from the beginning. This feature is called wrapscan.

Example

Start *vi* as usual and try a simple search. Type

/and

and press *n* and *N* a few times to see where the cursor goes.

Special Characters

vi supports a few special characters, which act as wildcards or search-exclusions. These special characters and their use are summarized below. Note that *cccc* stands for any number of characters; it could be *g*, *gefha*, or *23CG-4*. The special characters are *$. * [ ] ^ *.

When specifying search strings, you will sometimes want to search for one of the special characters. To do so, type a backslash (\\) immediately before the special character. For example, *\\$5* matches *$5.00*. To specify a single backslash, type \\\\ . The table below summarizes the special characters. Note that the slash (/) starts a forward search. You can replace it with a question mark (?) to search backward.

Searching with Special Characters

USAGE	ACTION	EXAMPLE	MATCHES
[cccc]	Match any of the characters cccc.	**/sa[fn]**	safe, sanctuary
[^cccc]	Match all characters except cccc.	**/[^a]nd**	behind, ground
[c1-c2]	Match any characters between c1 and c2.	**/[d-h]er**	thunder, weathered
\\<cccc	Match words beginning with cccc.	**/\\<eac**	each
cccc\\>	Match words ending with cccc.	**/und\\>**	ground
^cccc	Match lines beginning with cccc.	**/in...**	in foot and
cccc$	Match lines ending with cccc; match any single character.	**/slow$...** **/i.l**	We scrambled grimly, hills

Searching with Special Characters *(cont.)*

USAGE	ACTION	EXAMPLE	MATCHES
c*	Match the character c zero or more times; match any characters.	**/mb*d**	scrambled, rumbled
.*		**/b.*k**	back, scram[bled to strik]e

Example

Try some of the search strings in the preceding table; then try the following combinations:

/\<*s.o* {words starting with *s*, any letter, then *o* (shook, slow)}

/\<*h.*s*\> {words starting with *h* and ending with *s* with any number of characters in between (heavens, hills) */o.[rtk]* words containing *o*, any letter, and *r*, *t*, or *k* (bolt, foot, poor, shook)}

Search and Replace

vi can also search and replace, which means finding instances of a given string and replacing them with a new string. This search-and-replace operation is actually an *ex* command, and it has the following form:

: line1, line2s/ oldstring / newstring

You specify the range of text for the search-and-replace command with the line numbers *line1* and *line2*. If you only give *line1* and omit the comma, then the command only affects that line. If you give no line numbers, the command affects the current line. The search-and-replace command only finds the first occurrence of oldstring on the line. You can repeat a search-and-replace on the current line by typing an ampersand (&). To repeat it on a different line or group of lines, type

: linenumber&

or

: line1,line2&

Example

Let's replace the word "heavens" with "sky." Move to the last line ("Our heavens fell..."), and press Ctrl-g to see the line number. Note this line number (probably 16). Next move to the line ("Our heavens darkened..."), where we'll do the first search and replace. Type

:s/heavens/sky

and press RETURN. The first instance of "heavens" becomes "sky." Now press the ampersand (**&**) to repeat the command. Nothing happens; in fact, *vi* says

Substitute pattern match failed

because *vi* looks for "heavens" on the current line. Instead use the line number from the beginning and type

:16 &

Press RETURN and *vi* replaces the occurrence of "heavens" on line 16.

Special Flags

You can add a flag to the search-and-replace command; the flag tells *vi* to replace every occurrence or to ask for confirmation before each replacement. To add a flag, use the following form:

: line1, line2s/ oldstring / newstring / flag

Flag is an optional parameter. If flag is *c*, then *vi* will show you each instance of oldstring and wait for confirmation; type *y* (for yes) or *n* (for no) followed by RETURN. A *flag* of *g* requests a global search and replace, without confirmation. Global in this case means every occurrence of oldstring on the current line.

Example

Execute a search and replace with confirmation. Press **Ctrl-g** and note how long the text is (probably 17 lines). Then enter

:1,17s/Our/The/c

and press RETURN. *vi* will prompt you with each instance of the word "Our" and await a response. The first time ("Our sky darkened..."), press

y RETURN

The second time ("Our weathered tent..."), press

n RETURN

The third time ("Our sky fell..."), press

y RETURN

Press RETURN once more (*vi* prompts you at the bottom of the screen), and *vi* updates the screen. Check your screen against the one below; then save your work and quit *vi*.

A Powerful Search and Replace

The *ex* command *g* (for global) can be used with *s* (substitute) to find and replace every occurrence of a string pattern in an entire file. The syntax of the global command is

:g/string/commands

The global command finds each line in the file that has string in it and then applies the commands to it. You can combine the global and substitute it in the following manner:

:g/oldstring/s//newstring/g

You don't need to put oldstring in the search string part of the substitute command because the editor already has the pattern from the global command. When specifying oldstring, you can use the special characters as explained in the section entitled "Special Characters." *vi* does not recognize special characters in newstring, since it is performing a replacement, not a search.

Replacing Text

Press the ESC key to enter command mode before using these commands.

:s/pattern1/pattern2	{pattern1 with pattern2 on the same line}
:g/pattern1/s//pattern2/g	{every occurrence of pattern1 with pattern2}

EXAMPLES	ISPF EDIT	TSO EDIT	*vi* COMMAND
1. To replace one word in the current line with another, type	**change** 'that' 'which'	**C** 'that' 'which'	***:s/that/which*** {This replaces the first instance of the word "that" in the current line with the word "which."}
2. To replace every instance of one word in the current line with another, type	**change** 'destroy' 'delete'	**C** * line-count 'destroy' 'delete'	***:s/destroy/delete/g*** {This replaces every occurrence of the word "destroy" with the word "delete" in the current line.}
3. To replace every occurrence of a word throughout the file, with another, type	**F7** **change** 'insert' 'add' all	**TOP** **C** * line-count 'insert' 'add' **all** {line-count is some number larger than the lines in data set.}	***:g/insert/s//add/g*** {This replaces every occurrence of "insert" with "add."}

EXAMPLES	ISPF EDIT	TSO EDIT	*vi* COMMAND
4. To interactively replace every occurrence of a word throughout the file, with another, type	**F7** **change** 'in conjunction with' 'with' all	**TOP** **C** * line-count 'in conjunction with' 'with' **all**	***:g****/in conjunction with/s//with/gc* {Option used in conjunction with the ls command.}

This displays the first line containing an occurrence of the pattern "in conjunction with" and identifies this occurrence by underlining each character with a ^ (carat). Entering *y* (yes) replaces this instance of "in conjunction with" by "with" and proceeds on to the next. Pressing RETURN leaves this instance unchanged and proceeds to the next.

DELETING AND CHANGING TEXT

Sometimes you will want to delete some of the text you are editing. To do so, first move the cursor so that it covers the first character of the group you want to delete. The letter *d* is the delete operator in *vi*. Because it is an operator, it has no effect by itself, but requires a motion command to tell it the scope of the deletion. As a special case, *dd* deletes the entire current line.

So, what can we do with the delete operator? Basically, *d* followed by any command that would move the cursor deletes text up to and including where the cursor would have gone for that motion. For example,

ISPF EDIT	TSO EDIT	FUNCTION	*vi* COMMAND
CHANGE 'word' ''	**C** 'word' ''	Deletes to the end of the current word.	***de***
left arrow + d	**shiftl + DEL**	Deletes back to the beginning of the line.	***d0***
d n	**DEL** *n*	Deletes to the bottom of the screen.	***dL***
CHANGE 'word' ''	**C** 'word' ''	Deletes all characters from the current cursor location to the next word.	***dw***
d, dd	**DEL** *n*	Deletes all characters from the current cursor location to the next blank line.	***d}***
CHANGE 'xxx' ''	**Carriage forward**	Deletes all characters from the current cursor location to the end of the line.	***D***
CHANGE 'x' ''	**Carriage forward**	Deletes only the single current character.	***x***
d	**DEL**	Deletes the whole current line.	***dd***
d, dd	**DEL** *n*	Deletes current line and the following *n* - 1 lines.	***ndd***
CHANGE	**Carriage forward**	Deletes from the current character to the beginning of the current word.	***db***
CHANGE	**Carriage forward**	Deletes to the end of the sentence.	***d)***
CHANGE 'xxx' ''	**Carriage forward**	Deletes to the beginning of the sentence.	***d(***

ISPF EDIT	TSO EDIT	FUNCTION	*vi* COMMAND
up + d, dd	**TOP + DEL** *n*	Deletes to the top of the screen.	***dH***
FIND 'the' + d,dd	**F** 'the', **DEL** *n*	Deletes to the next occurrence of "the."	***d/****the*
CHANGE	**Carriage forward**	Deletes to the end of line.	***d$***

Note: The *d* (delete) operator can precede most movement commands, in which case, all characters between the current location and the destination location of the movement command would be deleted. In TSO and ISPF, the characters or character strings can be deleted via the keyboard DELETE key.

Notice that the second letter of the command specifies the same chunk of text that the cursor movement commands do. In fact, you can use delete with all of the cursor movement specifiers (e.g., *dH* would delete from the top line on the screen) to delete the desired chunk of text. Also, *D* is equivalent to *d$*.

Example

Try using the cursor movement keys to place the cursor on the word "hands." Move the cursor onto the *s*. Press *x* to delete it. Now let's delete the word "loudly." Move to the beginning of the word. Although you could press *x* seven times to delete the word and its trailing space, it is quicker to delete it by typing *dw*. Finally, remove the line "It just wouldn't stop raining." Move the cursor anywhere on that line, and type *dd*. The line vanishes.

Deletions are saved in a queue of 10 buffers, numbered 1 through 10. The most recent deletion is always in 1. You can get back your most recent deletion with *p* and other deletions with *np*, where *n* is the number of the buffer.

Deleting Text

Text is deleted by combining the delete commands *x* and *d* with the type of text object to be deleted. Numbers can also be used with both the *x* and *d* commands to delete multiple instances of a text object. For example,

5dw

This deletes the current word and the following four words.

Deleting Words and Lines

Press the ESC key to enter command mode before using these commands.

dw	Deletes current word.
db	Deletes current word.
dd	Deletes previous word.
d$	Deletes to end of line.
d0 (zero)	Deletes to start of line, next *n* lines.

Deleting Characters

Press the ESC key to enter *command mode* before using these commands.

x	Deletes current character.
dh	Deletes previous character.

Deleting Sentences and Paragraphs

Press the ESC key to enter command mode before using these commands.

d)	Deletes to end of sentence.
d(	Deletes to beginning of sentence.
d}	Deletes to end of paragraph.
d{	Deletes to beginning of paragraph.

The three most used commands to alter text are

x	Erases the character at the cursor.
r	Replaces the character at the cursor.
dd	Deletes the entire line where the cursor is.

All three commands are executed in command mode and return to the command mode after executing.

Delete, Yank, Put, and Change Operators

In this section, the operators delete, change, and yank will be discussed, and the scopes will be words, lines, sentences, and paragraphs. These commands will be used to delete, duplicate, change, and rearrange text. The following tables summarize the operators and scopes discussed in this section.

ISPF EDIT	TSO EDIT	ACTION	*vi* COMMAND
c	**CO** (copy)	Yanks a copy of text into a temporary buffer. The copy is then pasted using the *put* command.	***y***
Edit COPY	**EDIT COPY**	Puts whatever last deleted or yanked after or below the cursor.	***p***
CHANGE, I	**MO** (move)	Same as delete followed by insert. Performs the delete operation then enters text insert mode. Must press ESC to go back to command mode	***c***
		from the cursor to the end of the current word;	***e***
		from the cursor to the beginning of the next word, including the space;	***w***
		from the letter before the cursor backward to the beginning of the word;	***b***
		from the cursor to the end of the line;	***$***

ISPF EDIT	TSO EDIT	ACTION	*vi* COMMAND
		from just before the cursor to the beginning of the line;	***0***
		from the cursor to the beginning of the next sentence;	*)*
		from just before the cursor backwards to the beginning of the sentence;	*(*
		from the cursor to the end of the paragraph;	*}*
		from just before the cursor backwards to the beginning of the paragraph.	*{*
d	**DEL**	Deletes the entire line where the cursor is.	***dd***

The *dd*, *cc*, and *yy* commands affect the entire line.

Yank and Put

When deletes are made, they are stored in a temporary buffer. The contents of this buffer can be accessed and "put" or "pasted" anywhere in the text.

Unnamed Temporary Buffers

The temporary buffers are numbered 1 to 9 and hold each preceding deletion. Thus, buffer 1 holds the last deletion, buffer 2 the next previous, and so on.

The temporary buffers can be accessed using the *put command*, by preceding the command with the buffer number preceded by a double quote ("*np*).

Using the *put command*, restore the last deletion of "white rabbit." to its original place in the text. Enter the command you used in the space provided below.

....

The *yank* command copies the specified text into temporary buffers, leaving the original text present in the text file.

Position the cursor over the first letter of the word "rabbit." Type the following command to *yank* the word into the temporary buffer.

yw

Named Buffers

There are 26 named buffers for use by the *yank command*. These buffers are named *a* to *z*.

"ay} *Yanks* from cursor to end of paragraph into buffer *a*.

Changing Text Around

There are several ways in which you can change the structure and the content of the file you are editing. *Repeat* parts of the text or *insert* the contents of another file.

You can reuse a piece of text in another part of the file by yanking it into a temporary buffer and then putting the contents of this buffer back into the file. The command *y* yanks the text into the temporary buffer. Combined with other commands that are used to move around text objects, the yank command can be used to pull any part of a file into the buffer. The command *p* pastes the contents of the temporary buffer back into the file immediately after the cursor.

EXAMPLES	*vi* COMMAND
1. Yank the current sentence into the temporary buffer.	*y)*
2. Yank the text from the present cursor position to the beginning of the current paragraph into the temporary buffer.	*y{*
3. Place the contents of the temporary buffer after the current cursor position.	*p*

Saving the Buffer

You are strongly encouraged to save editing changes regularly. The command to write the editor buffer is

:w

If you decide that you do want to overwrite the existing file, but rather save the changes to a new file, then follow the *:w* command with the name of the new file, *:w newfile2.*

MOVING BLOCKS

The move command moves a block of lines from one point in the source file to another. This option works on line numbers. To turn on the display of line numbers within *vi*, type

Ctrl-n

The format of the move command is

startline,endline mafterdestline

thus the following command moves lines 1 to 3 to the end of the file.

1,3m$

TSO EDIT subcommands **MOVE, SALTER,** and **MODIFY** can accomplish similar functions but are not as versatile as the *vi* commands.

Moving Around the Screen

There are commands for moving around the screen you are viewing and for moving around the file using the screen view of the file.

Move around the screen

Move between screens

Cut and Paste Text

Moving pieces of text around within a file is referred to as cut and paste. Doing this in *vi* is a three-stage process:

1. Cut the text you want to move with one of the commands used to delete text.
2. Move the cursor to where you want to paste the text into the file using one of the commands for moving around the text.
3. Paste the text into the file with the command:

   p

Replacing Text

In other cases you will only need to change a single character or word rather than delete it. *vi* has *change* and *replace* functions, too. First, move to the position where the change should begin (the desired line or the beginning of the desired word). Next, type the proper command from the table below. Finally, enter the correct text, usually concluded with ESC (except for *r*).

Correction/Replacement Commands

ISPF EDIT	TSO EDIT	ACTION	*vi COMMAND*
CHANGE *string-1 string-2*	**C** 'word' 'yyy'	Change word. *vi* displays a dollar sign ($) marking the end of the change portion.	***cw***
CHANGE *string-1 string-2*	**C** 'xxx' 'yyy'	Overwrite to the end of the line.	***C***
CHANGE '*x*' '*y*'	**SAlter**	Replace a single character with another one. (No ESC necessary.)	***r***
CHANGE *string-1 string-2*	**C** 'xxx' 'yyy'	Overwrite characters starting from the current cursor position.	***R***
	SAlter	Substitute one or more characters for a single character.	***s***
CHANGE *string-1 string-2*	**SAlter**	Substitute the current line with a new one.	***S***

The change command *c* works like the delete command; you can use the text portion specifiers (e.g., *dH* would delete from the top line on the screen) that act as cursor movement commands to replace the selected text. *C* is equivalent to *c$*.

Example

Let's correct some words. To maintain proper verb tense, "flashes" should be "flashed." Move the cursor to the last **"s"** in "flashes." To enter replace mode, type

r

and notice that the modeline says *REPLACE 1 CHAR*. Next type the letter

d

to make the change. Notice that you do not need to press ESC or RETURN when replacing just one character. Next change "safety" to "sanctuary." Move to the beginning of the word "safety"; then type

cw

vi shows a dollar sign ($) indicating the end of the text being corrected. Type

sanctuary ESC

Now move the cursor to **"do."** We'll change all the text from **"do"** to the end of the line. Start the correction by pressing

C

Again *vi* shows a dollar sign (this time at the end of the line). Make the change by typing

reach that island ESC

If the number *n* is left off, the command only applies to one object.

ISPF EDIT	TSO EDIT	ACTION	*vi* COMMAND
CAPS		Switch case of character at current cursor location, ignoring punctuation.	**~**
CHANGE *string-1 c 'x'*	**C**	Replace character at the current cursor location with new character *x*.	***rx***
CHANGE *string-1 'newtext'*	**SAlter**	Clear current line and replace with newtext.	***S****newtextESC*
DELETE *n* **l**	**C**	Clear *n* lines, starting at current line, and replace with newtext.	*n***S***newtextESC*

ISPF EDIT	TSO EDIT	ACTION	*vi* COMMAND
CHANGE *string-1 'newtext'*	**SAlter**	Replace characters from current cursor location to end of line with newtext.	*CnewtextESC*
CHANGE *string-1 '',* **I**	**SAlter**	Replace characters from current cursor location to end of word with newtext. Text is entered in insert mode.	***cw****newtextESC*

Note: The *c* (change) operator can precede most movement commands, in which case, all characters between the current location and the destination location of the movement are replaced with the new text.

Relocating Text

Text can be relocated by first yanking into a buffer.

vi COMMAND	ACTION
Y	Yank current line into temporary buffer. Unlike *d,* line is not deleted.
yw	Yank a word.
yy	Yank a line.
y$	Yank to the end of the line.
nY	Yank current line and the following *n* - **1** lines into temporary buffer. Unlike *d,* lines are not deleted.
n"xY	Yank current line and the following *n* - **1** lines into buffer named *x* (any letter can be a valid buffer name).
p	Put contents of temporary buffer after current cursor location.
"xp	Put contents of buffer *x* after current cursor location.
P	Put contents of temporary buffer before current cursor location.
"xP	Put contents of buffer *x* before current cursor location.
J	Join next line to the end of current line.

CUT, COPY, AND PASTE

Frequently you'll need to cut or copy some text, and paste it elsewhere in your document. First you cut or copy the text into temporary storage; then you paste it into a new location. Cutting means removing text from the document and storing it, while copying means placing a duplicate of the text in storage. Finally, pasting just puts the stored text in the desired location.

MOVE, SALTER, and **MODIFY** subcommands allow most of the cut and paste functions in **TSO Edit.**

Buffers

vi uses a buffer to store the temporary text. There are nine numbered buffers in addition to an undo buffer. The undo buffer contains the most recent delete. Usually buffer 1 contains the most recent delete, buffer 2 the next most recent, and so forth. Deletions older than 9 disappear. However, *vi* also has 26 named buffers (*a–z*). These buffers are useful for storing blocks of text for later retrieval. Buffer letters are independent of marker letters, so buffer *k* and marker *k* are unrelated. To retrieve text from a buffer, see the section, "Cut and Copy (*Delete* and *Yank*)." The content of a buffer does not change until you put different text into it. Unless you change the contents of a named buffer, it holds its last text until you quit. As with markers, *vi* does not save your buffers when you quit.

By Line Numbers

Two simple commands from the *ex* command set let you cut and copy text by entering the range (in lines) and the destination line. The *m* command moves (cuts and pastes) a range of text, and the *t* command transfers (copies and pastes) it. *t* is a synonym for *c* (copy). The commands have the form shown below.

EXAMPLES	ISPF EDIT	TSO EDIT	*vi* COMMAND
1. Move (cut) line number, *line1*, to the line just below line number, *destline*.	**m** 00100 **a** 00200	**move** *line1* *line1 destline*	*line1,line1mdestline*
2. Move (cut) lines between *line1* and *line2* below line number, *destline*.	**mm** 00100 **mm** 00500 **a** 00900	**move** *line1* *line2 destline*	*line1,line2mdestline*
3. Transfer (copy) line number, *line1*, to the line just below line number, *destline*.	**c** 00100 **a** 00700	**copy** *line1* *line1 destline*	*line1tdestline*
4. Transfer (copy) lines between *line1* and *line2* below line number, *destline*.	**cc** 00100 **cc** 00500 **a** 00800	**copy** *line1* *line2 destline*	*line1,line2tdestline*

First start *vi* as in the previous sections, then try these commands. Move to the line "Take a step" and press **Ctrl-g**. Note the line number (probably 3). Then move to the line "A safe haven," press **Ctrl-g**, and note this line number (probably 11). Now you are ready to copy "move") "Take a step" to another line. Type

:3m11

and press RETURN to finish the command.

Cut and Copy (Delete and Yank)

vi has its own terminology for "cut" and "copy," "delete," and "yank," respectively. Note that the delete command is the same one you have already used; every time you delete text, *vi* changes the automatic buffer and pushes the previous delete into the next numbered buffer. When you delete or yank, the desired text enters a buffer. If you do not specify a named buffer, *vi* uses the automatic buffer (buffer 1). The delete and yank commands take the following form:

Move the cursor to one end of the desired text. If desired, specify a named buffer by typing *'letter* where letter is a letter from a through z. If you do not give a named buffer, *vi* uses the automatic buffers 1–9.

- Type *a* repetition number, if needed (to copy five words or eight lines, for example).
- Type *d* to delete text, or type *y* to yank text.
- Type *a* cursor movement key (*b*, *e*, *w*, etc., see Table 2) to determine the text unit.

If you type *d* or *y* instead, *vi* uses the "line" unit. The cursor key completes the delete or yank and stores the text in the desired buffer.

Using Markers

Markers also let you specify a range of text for cutting or copying without having to count words or lines. The next procedure shows you how to delete or yank text by using markers.

- Move the cursor to one end of the selection.
- Type *mletter* to set a marker.
- Move the cursor to the other end.

If desired, specify a named buffer by typing *'letter*. If you do not give a named buffer, *vi* uses the automatic buffers. Type *d* or *y* to *delete* or *yank* text, respectively. Using letter from the marker, type

`letter

to *delete* or *yank* the text between the marker and the cursor. You may instead type

'letter

to *delete* or *yank* the text by line.

Paste

If retrieving text from a named buffer, specify the buffer by typing *'letter*. Otherwise, *vi* uses the automatic buffers.

Move the cursor to the desired pasting location. Type *p* to paste the buffered text just after the current character or type *P* to paste it just before the current character. If the buffered text is stored by line, it will be pasted below or above the current line.

Example 1

This performs a standard copy and paste. It uses the automatic buffer and does not use any markers. Move to the first line of text ("We scrambled..."); then yank three lines of text by typing

3yy

Nothing appears to happen, but *vi* has put the first three lines into its automatic buffer. The message "3 lines yanked" appears at the bottom of the screen. Now move to the line "A safe haven" and paste the lines in place. To do so, just type

p

Example 2

You use *markers* to identify the text you want to cut, as well as perform a normal cut.

a. First, move to "Glancing" and put a marker there by typing

   mx

   Then move to the "B" in the fourth "BOOM!." Cut the text and place it in buffer *e* by typing:

   'ed`x

b. The text vanishes, but *vi* has put it into buffer *e*. Second, copy the remaining "BOOM! BOOM!" into the automatic buffer. Just type

   dd

c. Third, paste the contents of the automatic buffer. Move to the second instance of "We scrambled..." and type

   P (capital '*P*')

d. Fourth and finally, move to the blank line below "Take a step...". Paste the text from buffer

   e

   by typing:

   'ep

After the previous two examples, the screen should look like that below. Once again, end the session examples by saving your work with

:wq RETURN

We scrambled to strike camp. Water crashed down upon us, far too slow in foot and hand to reach that island. I saw everything spinning wildly.

Our heavens darkened grimly. Thunder echoed overhead and shook the clouds, even the ground rumbled as each clap exploded. Our weathered tent was a poor shelter tonight. As a lightning bolt flashed over the hills, we made out a small cave on the mountainside. A safe haven, thought I. BOOM! BOOM! We scrambled to strike camp. Water crashed down upon us, far too slow in foot and hand to reach that island. I saw everything spinning wildly.

Take a step and fall. Glancing back, I saw an ocean rising behind us. BOOM! BOOM! BOOM! Our heavens fell down, but just ahead lay sanctuary. We crawled in, and wept.

UNDOING CHANGES

Occasionally you will accidentally issue a command or delete some text and want to restore your text to the way it was before you issued that command. *vi* lets you undo the last text change with the undo command, which you execute by typing *u*. Note, however, that *vi* will only recover the last text change.

The *U* command undoes all the changes made on the current line. If you make a mistake, and wish to restore the current line to its original state, the command to use is,

Undeleting Text

To get back a word or line that you have just deleted enter the command

p

The *dd* command has already been covered. This command deletes the current line. The *dw* command deleted the current word. Note that the delete command begins with *d*, followed by the scope of the command (*d* for a line, *w* for a word).

Example

Move to the line "flashed over the hills…" and delete it by typing

dd

Bring back the line by pressing

u

which undoes the last text change. Press *u* a few more times, and watch what happens. When you *undo* something, you change the text, so your *undo* becomes the last text change! That explains why undoing appears to flip between two displays. Leave the line "flashed over..." on the display.

The following commands help when you delete too much or provide shortcuts.

ACTION	ISPF EDIT	*vi* COMMAND
Undo last change. Only one level of undo is provided.	**UNDO**	***u***
Restore current line to its original state. Cursor must remain on the line between changes and recovery.		***U***
Deleted text is inserted after current cursor location.		***h***
Repeat most recent modification command (including inserts, but excluding plain movement commands).		**. (dot)**

JOINING LINES

Occasionally you will want to link two or more lines of text together, usually because deleting text has created a lot of empty space. The *J* command combines the current line with the line below it.

Example

Move to the blank line just after "in foot and hand." Press

i

and insert the following text:

I saw everything spinning wildly. RETURN

Press ESC to return to command mode. Now move to the line "in foot and hand" and press

J

to join it with the line you just typed. At this point the *vi* screen should look like

We scrambled to strike camp. Water crashed down upon us, far too slow in foot and hand to reach that island. I saw everything spinning wildly.

~

The **MERGE** subcommand in **TSO Edit** allows to merge complete data sets or parts of data sets by line numbers.

ADVANCED TOPICS

Variables

vi maintains several variables that control different aspects of its appearance. You have already used a few of these (*:set* number, *:set* showmode).

Toggle and Numeric Variables

The two types of variables are *toggle variables* and *numeric variables. Toggle variables* turn an option on or off (like displaying line numbers), while *numeric variables* take a number as their argument (like tab width). You turn on a *toggle* variable with

:set variable

and you turn it off by typing

:set novariable

Numeric variables are set with an equals sign (=) and the corresponding value. For example, to set tab stops every six spaces, you would enter:

:set tabstop=6

Variable Settings

VARIABLE	DEFAULT	DESCRIPTION
ignorecase	noignorecase	Do not distinguish between capital and lowercase letters during searches.
number	nonumber	Display line numbers.
showmode	noshowmode	Displays the input mode, blank for command mode.
wrapscan	wrapscan	When a search reaches the end of the file, it wraps around back to the beginning and continues the search.
report	report=5	When more than this number of lines are modified, deleted, yanked, or pasted, *vi* will print a message. This option alerts you to large modifications.
tabstop	tabstop=8	Sets tab stops to multiples of this value. Normally 8 works fine.
wrapmargin	wrapmargin=0	Sets the right margin. When you pass the margin set by wrapmargin, *vi* automatically creates a new line.

Useful Variable Examples

To see a list of all the variables and their settings, enter

:set all

Example

You already know how to turn line numbers on and off with number, and you have already used the *showmode* variable, too. Now try a *numeric* variable. From *command mode*, type

:set wrapmargin=5

This command sets the right margin of the file to five characters from the right edge. Unfortunately, it does not affect existing lines, only new text that you enter. Move the cursor onto the "I" in "I saw everything." Enter insert mode by pressing

i

and then type

Staggering like a drunken bum, each step a wicked dance, ESC

Notice that your line wraps around the edge of the window, but *vi* automatically makes a new line for text beyond the right margin.

Special Keys and Ctrl-v

Before proceeding further, you need to learn more about control characters. Control characters are invisible characters which computers use to manage communication protocol. The RETURN key is a control character (**Ctrl-m**), as is the ESC key (**Ctrl-[**). Function keys are usually a sequence of control and regular characters. *vi* lets you put a control character into text by preceding it with **Ctrl-v** (which is also a control character).

Example

Move to the first line of sample and press

O {capital **"O,"** not zero}

to create a new input line. Then type (do not type any spaces):

Ctrl-v RETURN **Ctrl-v Ctrl-t**

Notice that when you first press **Ctrl-v**, *vi* displays a *caret (^)* character, which indicates that the next character will be a control character. Next type a few more control characters (again do not type any spaces):

Ctrl-v Ctrl-v Ctrl-v F1 **Ctrl-v** ESC

Observe that you just inserted a Ctrl-v, an ESC, and the F1 sequence into your text. Don't worry if the F1 sequence looks like garbage. Now erase the control characters (and first three lines of text), by typing

ESC **4dd**

Mapping Keys

You can map a single keystroke into several characters with the *:map* command. It lets you assign functions to the function keys. This command takes the form

:map keystroke result

where *keystroke* is a single character or function key, and the result is the character sequence that should be triggered. The key map remains in effect until you quit *vi.*

Example

This maps function key F1 to mean "Go to beginning of file." From *command mode*, type (_ means a space):

:map_Ctrl-v F1_1G

Before you press RETURN, make sure you understand what is happening: *:map* gives *vi* the *'map'* command. **F1** is the keystroke, but since it starts with a control character, **Ctrl-v** must precede it. Finally, *1G* is the result, which is just the *vi* command to move to the first line of the file. Now try your key map. Move to a different line and press the **F1** key; the cursor should jump to the first line of the file. Try it again.

Macros

You can execute a *vi* macro, which means that *vi* reads the contents of a named buffer (*a–z*) and executes them as if they were commands. Because a macro is just text treated like *vi* commands, macro *g* and buffer *g* are the same buffer. To set up a macro, *delete* or *yank* the macro text into a named buffer. Execute the macro by typing *@char.*

Example

Here you make a macro that finds lines beginning with "BOO" and deletes them. First, go to the end of the document; then enter open mode by pressing

o

Now you are ready to type the commands for the macro. Type (without any spaces)

/^BOO Ctrl-v RETURN dd ESC

You delete (cut) the macro text into buffer *z* just like ordinary text. Type:

'zdd

Now you are ready to execute the macro; just type

@z

and the first line of "BOO" vanishes. Execute the macro again with *@z*.

Using fmt

The *fmt* command lets you format a range of text to fit certain margins. If you have a very raggedy document, *vi* can improve its appearance. *fmt* is actually another UNIX command. You will be using a feature of *vi* that lets you access other UNIX commands to use *fmt*. *fmt* has several options, and the two most important appear below. First, the *-s* option: it preserves short lines of text, which keeps program code from becoming crammed together. Second, the *-width* option: it makes all lines shorter than the specified number, width. *fmt* has the following structure:

:line1,line2 !fmt options

where options can be *-s* or *-width*. Suppose that you are formatting a program segment, lines 8 through 27, with a file width of 68 characters. Because you are formatting program code, you should use the *-s* option with the *-68* option. Then you would enter

:8,27!fmt -s -68

Example

Before you can clean up the file, you need to mess it up a little. Move to the line "in foot and hand"; then join some lines together by pressing

J

three or four times. Your file is quite messy now. Prepare to correct the margins. Press **Ctrl-g** to see the file length (about 16 lines), then enter

:1,16!fmt -72

That should clean up the file. Once again, write and quit with

:wq RETURN

You can also format from the current line to the end of the current paragraph with the following:

!}fmt

The **!** is a *vi* command to filter the specified text through a command. The '}' is the text portion (i.e., paragraph, you could use ')' to refer to sentence), and *fmt* is the command. There is a slight difference between

:line1,line2!cmd

and

!textportion cmd

The first is an *ex* command to pass text to another command, the second is a *vi*-only command to do a similar thing. The commands are not interchangeable. In other words, the following line will not work:

!line1,line2cmd

The last screen of this example looks like

The sky darkened grimly. Thunder echoed overhead and shook the clouds even the ground rumbled as each clap exploded. Our weathered tent was a poor shelter tonight. As a lightning bolt flashed over the hills, we made out a small cave on the mountainside. A safe haven, thought I. We scrambled to strike camp. Water crashed down upon us, far too slow in foot and hand to reach that island. Staggering like a drunken bum, each step a wicked dance, I saw everything spinning wildly. Take a step and fall. Glancing back, I saw an ocean rising behind us. The sky fell down, but just ahead lay sanctuary. We crawled in, and wept.

Saving a *vi* Configuration

You have learned to turn on the mode indicator and set the right margin by typing

:set showmode
:set wrapmargin=5

These two features are very useful, but you probably do not want to type them each time you start *vi*. Fortunately, you can save commands in a file called *.exrc*. Each time you start *vi*, it reads *.exrc* and executes all the commands inside *.exrc*. *.exrc* can contain *:map* and *:set* commands. Each one should be on a separate line, but most important, you should omit the colons in your *.exrc*. With a little work, you can map the function keys into your own functions: cursor movement, cut and paste, and write and quit.

Example

In this example, you'll create a basic *.exrc* file in your home directory, which you can update as you become more adept with *vi*. Enter insert mode and set up two default variables with the text (notice the absence of the colons):

i
set showmode RETURN
set wrapmargin=5 ESC

Save this file. Now, whenever you start with any filename, *vi* will invoke these two commands.

Customizing vi

You can customize *vi* by setting certain options while in the *vi* edit session. Just type colon to enter the Last-line state, and type

:set option

Numerical options are followed by a =number. Boolean options are reset by preceding their names with a no (e.g., nomagic). For a complete list of options, get into *vi* and type

:set all

Here is a list of useful options:

vi COMMAND	FUNCTION
autowrite	Writes buffer before changing files.
lisp	Sets up file.
ignorecase	Ignores case of letters in searches.
number	Numbers lines (numbers are not part of the file).
showmatch	Shows matching parentheses as they are closed.
wrapmargin=n	Wraps lines when typing enters the nth screen column.

You can also create a file called *.exrc* in your home directory and put the set commands in it:

:set option1 option2 option3=n

MACROS concept in **TSO Edit** is similar to what *vi* allows.

SUMMARY

You have witnessed the various ways a UNIX user may create or modify contents of a file. Typical of UNIX are the variety and complexity of editors. The editors *vi*, *ed*, and *ex* are available for line editing. *ex* is a superset of *vi* and *ex*. *ex* has some similarities to the MVS **ISPF** and **TSO** editors in line mode. One fundamental difference is that *ex* or *vi* do not display line numbers, but these may be turned on with the command *set number*.

vi is flexible and comes closest to offering the functionality of the **ISPF** editor. *ex* and *vi* are both interactive, whereas **MVS** editors are not quite emanable for that mode. *vi*, *ed*, and *ex* are case sensitive, whereas the **MVS** editors are not.

11

The Bourne Shell

INTRODUCTION

The most frequently used utility on a UNIX system is the shell, the program that is executed when a user logs onto the system. This chapter describes the basic features of the Bourne shell */bin/sh*, which is a standard shell (command interpreter) for most UNIX systems. Many of the features covered in this section are provided by the shell itself. The shell provides a great deal of functionality on top of UNIX itself.

The shell is not only an interpreter for your interactive commands, which you type at the prompt. The shell also provides you with a programming environment with features similar to those of a high-level programming languages. In addition, it allows you to write shell scripts, to "batch" several shell commands together in a file. Use of shell scripts is a very powerful tool, which will allow you to automate and expand your usage of UNIX. MVS users will recognize the similarity to "batch files" or "TSO CLISTs."

The UNIX shell provides the similar facilities and programming environments as are afforded by the **TSO CLISTs**. CLISTs allow you to use built-in functions, use and create *symbolic* and *control variables*, communicate with terminal users, and perform I/O.

The UNIX Shell

Once you are logged in, you are ready to start using UNIX. As mentioned earlier, you interact with the system through a command interpreter program called the *shell.* The **shell** runs automatically when you log in. Most UNIX systems have two different shells, although you will only use one or the other almost all of the time. The shell you will find on most systems supported networks is the *C shell.* It is called the C shell because it has syntax and constructs similar to those in the C programming language. The C shell command prompt often includes the name of the computer that you are using and usually ends with a special character, most often the percent sign (%).

Another common shell is the *Bourne shell*, named for its author. The default prompt for the Bourne shell is the dollar sign (*$*). If the prompt is neither one of these, a quick way to check which shell you are using is to type the C shell command alias: if a list appears, then you are using the C shell; if the message, "Command not found" appears, then you are using the Bourne shell. Modified versions of these shells are also available. TC shell (*tcsh*) is C shell with additional filename completion and command line editing features (default prompt: >). The GNU Bourne Again shell (*bash*) is basically the Bourne shell with the same features added (default prompt: *bash$*).

In addition to processing your command requests, UNIX shells have their own syntax and control constructs. You can use these shell commands to make your processing more efficient or to automate repetitive tasks. You can even store a sequence of shell commands in a file, called a shell script, and run it just like an ordinary program.

The two common shell types are the C shell and the Bourne shell.

C Shell

/bin/csh, preferred for interactive work,

- Maintains environment variables.
- Locates commands; passes arguments and control to command.
- Performs I/O redirection (<, >, etc.).
- Handles pipes.
- Provides job control.
- Maintains command history.
- Provides alias facility.
- Edits files.

Bourne Shell

The Bourne shell, */bin/sh*, preferred for programming, is the original UNIX shell. It is faster and less complex than C shell, but it does not have the C shell's editing power nor its programming structures (discussed in the later sections). The Bourne shell is a program that interprets commands and arranges for their execution. The Bourne shell displays a character called the prompt (or primary shell prompt) whenever it is ready to begin reading a new command from the terminal. By default, the Bourne shell prompt character is set to the dollar sign (*$*). Some of the main features of the Bourne shell are

FUNCTION	DESCRIPTION
Interactive processing	The shell handles communication between the user and the UNIX system.
Background processing	The system can perform more than one task on behalf of a single user.
Shell variables	The shell provides string variables that can be used interactively to provide abbreviations for frequently used strings, as well as having a number of other uses.
Programming language constructs	The shell supports many of the high-level language programming constructs. UNIX system command can be incorporated into conditional test, loops, and case statements.
I/O redirection	Programs that, by default, take input from the terminal, can easily be instructed to take input from elsewhere. Similarly, output from a program can be directed to another device or to a file on disk.
Pipes and filters	Pipes are used to connect the standard output of one command to the standard input of another. Pipes are frequently used with filters and can provide very elegant solutions.
Wildcards	We have already seen examples of wildcards that enable a user to perform operations on one or more files.
Shell scripts	A sequence of commands can be stored in a file and executed with a single command. MVS/TSO also affords such facility via CLISTs.

Which Shell?

The type of shell that you decide to use is mostly a religious issue. Some folks prefer the Bourne shell syntax with the advanced features of *Bash*, and some prefer the more structured C shell syntax. As far as normal commands, such as *cp* and *ls*, are concerned, the type of shell you're using doesn't matter—the syntax is the same. Only when you start to write shell scripts or use some of the advanced features of the shell do the differences between shell types begin to matter.

COMMAND EXECUTION AND PROCESSES

The user interacts with UNIX via a shell that needs command lines from the user's terminal and interprets them as requests to execute other programs.

A command line consists of the command name, followed by its arguments, separated by spaces. The name is assumed to be a file that is loaded into memory and executed under the auspices of the shell. Rather than forcing you to specify exactly which command is to be executed, the shell uses the variable PATH to specify a list of directories to be searched to find the program. To find out how your PATH is set, you may enter

$ echo $PATH
:/usr/training/bin:/usr/bin:/usr/1bin:/usr/informix:/bin

Similarly, since the arguments are often filenames, the shell will find them as well. If the command name does not contain the '/' character, the shell will search for a command with the same name in each of the directories specified in the PATH and will return a message "not found" only if it cannot find the command in any of the directories.

In the example above, the first character in the PATH is the **:**, which implies that the shell should search the current directory first. If two colons (**::**) occur together in the middle of the path, the current directory will be searched at that point. Similarly, if the colon comes at the end, the current directory will be searched last. If the command name includes a /, the shell searches downward from the current directory unless the pathname begins with /, signifying the root directory. To find

/usr/training/course/practice

the shell starts at the root looking for a directory *usr*. *usr* should contain a directory *training*, which in turn should contain a directory *course* containing a file *practice*. To find file specified as

course/practice

the shell starts at current directory looking for a subdirectory *course* that contains a file called *practice*. When a file has been found, the shell forks and executes (*exec*) the file to load it as a process into memory. A process consists of the program code, either in its read-only segment or shared with other processes, and its own data, plus stack segments. When the command has finished executing, the shell resumes and indicates its readiness to accept another command by returning a prompt character **$** at the terminal.

More than one command can be entered on a line, using a semicolon **;** as the delimiter. The commands are still executed sequentially, and the prompt is output when the last program has terminated. For example,

$ pwd
/usr/training
$ cd course;rm practice
$ pwd
/usr/training/course
$

Commands can also be grouped using parentheses, in which case they are executed as a separate process:

$ pwd
/usr/training
$ (cd course;rm practice)
$ pwd
/usr/training
$

PROFILES

Before issuing the first prompt, the shell checks for a file */etc/profile*. If it exists, just like a **TSO CLIST**, the shell reads and executes the commands in it. This is how the shell automatically notifies you whether you have mail, bulletins, and displays the date and a header, and so on. The shell then checks the user's home directory for a *.profile*, and if one exists, it reads and executes the commands in the *.profile*. In this way, you can have the environment set up the way you prefer. Here is an example of a typical profile:

MVS TSO PROFILE	UNIX PROFILE SETTINGS
PROFILE CHAR(0) LINE(0) PROMPT INTERCOM NOPAUSE NOMSGID NOMODE NOWTPMSG NORECOVER PREFIX(USERID)	*TERM=vt100* *PATH=:$HOME/bin:/usr/bin* *export TERM PATH*
{To change your profile, enter PROFILE command with changed operands:}	*PS1="Brian:"* *PS2=" >"*
PROFILE changed operands	*E=$HOME/unixfun/editor*
PROFILE CHAR(**$**) LINE(>) PAUSE PREFIX(newid)	*S=$HOME/unixfun/shell*
{Change delete character to $, line delete character to >, prefix to newid, and pause to answer questions}	*stty erase "^ H"^ X"* *date* *pwd*

The profile essentially sets up the PATH and TERM variables; sets the prompt strings and a couple of other variables; sets the terminal characteristics; and notifies the user of the date, time, and current directory.

SHELL VARIABLES

Every shell has an environment that is used by the shell and by other programs as well. This environment can be thought of as a set of *variables*. The shell provides string-valued variables whose names begin with a letter and consist of letters, digits, and underscores. Each variable, or key has zero or more values associated with it. These variables may be given values, such as

$ C=/usr/training/course

Having created a variable, we can display the value of the variable by entering

$ echo $C
/use/training/course
$

Once a variable has been established, it is possible to use it in a command line. The more general notation for variable substitution is to enclose the name in braces ({ }), when other characters are to be appended, such as

$ D=/bin/date
$ echo $D2
$ echo ${D}2
/bin/date2
$

In a similar way, the output of a command can be assigned to a variable or parameters, and then substituted:

$ D='date'
$ echo $D at Training
Thu July 27 17:15:36 GMT 1995 at Training

Common Variables

MVS/TSO provides a rich set of symbolic and control variables. There is no one-to-one correlation with UNIX shell variables; however, the method of assigning values and processing is similar. A symbolic variable can be created as

> **SET** PAY_RAISE = 20 /*Set the value of PAY_RAISE equal to 20 defines the variable as **&**PAY_RAISE.

Like the **$** in UNIX, **&** means "the value of" in MVS/TSO. The ampersand (**&**) is not part of a variable name; it simply tells the CLIST to use the value of the variable. The variable **&**PAY_RAISE now is capable of being assigned a different value, when executed in a CLIST. In a CLIST, you can use symbolic variables to include variable data on TSO commands and subcommands, on JCL statements, and many of the CLIST statements. Of course, the symbolic variables have a number of rules that must be followed, such as length in naming such variables.

MVS/TSO **control variables** provide information about MVS, TSO, and the current session, such as levels of software available, the time of day, and the date. In comparison, UNIX basic commands can accomplish some of the same functions, such as *cal*, *date*, *time*, and so on. Similar to UNIX, the control variables are also divided into the following categories:

- Current date and time
- Terminal related
- System related
- User related
- CLIST related

- Input/output related
- Return codes

In UNIX, some variables have a special meaning to the shell–some of these appeared in the example of the *.profile*:

VARIABLE	DESCRIPTION
MAIL	The file which stores mail for the user.
HOME	The user's home directory.
PATH	The list of directories to be searched in order to find a command: **PATH**=/bin:/usr/bin
TERM	The name of the type of terminal being used
PS1	The primary shell prompt: **PS1="$"**
PS2	The secondary shell prompt: **PS2=">"**

PATH is an important variable. The path tells your shell where to look for programs you try to execute. When you start up a shell, it builds a table (called a hash table) based on your path, so it knows where to look for any application you might want to run. This is faster than having it search your path for a command every time you input something. Because this hash table is built when you start up a shell, if you make any changes to your path environment variable, or add a program to one of the directories in your path, and you want the shell to notice right away, you need to have the shell rebuild the hash table. The command for doing this in the Bourne shell is *hash -r*.

Some variables are set automatically when you log on. One such variable is called *HOME*, which indicates your home directory, and another is *TERM*, which gives the *tty* that is sending output to your screen the information it needs to display properly. If you dial up from home using a modem, you need to set your terminal type, so the shell can look for the corresponding terminal behavior entry in the file */etc/termcap*.

Each shell gets its global environment from the shell that spawned it. For the Bourne shell, they are all specified in the *.profile*, which is read by the login shell.

Sometimes in a shell script you'll want to save state information. For example, a process' exit status may be important, so you might want to save it. This kind of state information is most easily kept in variables, although you could conceivably save it into a file instead. Scripts which run in their own shell have their own variables, which are stored separately from those of the shell that you start them from. When the script exits, those variables are forgotten.

There is one command to set a normal variable, and one command to make any variable into an environment variable. In *sh*, to set a key equal to a value, the syntax is

$ key=value

Note that it is important that no spaces be included between the variable and the value to which it is being set. To make a variable visible to the environment, it must be "exported." The shell built-in *export* is designed for this task. One possible syntax follows:

```
$ EDITOR=/usr/local/bin/gnuemacs export EDITOR
```

These commands needn't follow each other on the same line, or even be in the order given in the example above. Here is an example where the environment is alerted to the existence of a global variable before that variable is set:

```
$ export PAGINATOR
$ env | grep PAGINATOR
$ PAGINATOR=/usr/5bin/pg
$ env | grep PAGINATOR
PAGINATOR=/usr/5bin/pg
```

The Bourne shell is flexible in its treatment of variables. If an unset variable is referenced, its value is assumed to be null. In fact, there are operators that are used specifically in conjunction with variables whose status as set or unset is not known.

Given these rules, it is easy to set a variable without going to a lot of trouble to find out which variables are set and which aren't first. Say we want to find out who the user running our script is. We could use something like

```
$ PERSON=${USER:-${LOGNAME:-`whoami`}\}
```

This sets the variable *PERSON* to be *$USER* if that is set; otherwise, it uses *$LOGNAME*, unless that is not set either, in which case it uses the command *whoami*, which should return the effective current username. If the first part of the search works, as it does in this case when the *$USER* variable is set, the rest of the expression never gets called. Thus there's no penalty for using increasingly convoluted and time-consuming commands as you move to the right, since the first successful (nonnull) entry will prevent the others from being executed.

There are some variables the Bourne shell sets automatically. All these variables contain state information of some kind or other.

Here are some more examples of setting Bourne shell variables:

```
$ TERM=vt100 export TERM
$ TIME=`date | awk '{print $4}'`
$ foo="foo is a commonly used variable name in UNIX..."
$ TIME=${TIME:-"No time."}
```

Variables and the Environment

In the same manner as MVS, the UNIX shell also allows you to define variables, as most programming languages do. A variable is just a piece of data which is given the name. When you assign a value to a variable (using the = operator), you can access the variable by prepending a $ to the variable name (& for most MVS variables), as demonstrated below:

MVS VARIABLE	SHELL VARIABLE
SET FOO = "hello there"	*/home/larry# foo="hello there"*

The variable *foo* is given the value "hello there." You can now refer to this value by the variable name, prefixed with a **$** character. The following example illustrates the command usage:

MVS VARIABLE EXAMPLES	SHELL VARIABLE EXAMPLES
&FOO hello there	*/home/larry# echo $foo* *hello there* */home/larry#* produces the same results as */home/larry# echo "hello there"* *hello there* */home/larry#*

These variables are internal to the shell. This means that only the shell can access these variables. This can be useful in shell scripts; if you need to keep track of a filename, for example, you can store it in a variable, as above. Using the command set will display a list of all defined shell variables.

However, the shell allows you to export variables to the environment. The environment is the set of variables which all commands that you execute have access to. Once you define a variable inside the shell, exporting it makes that variable part of the environment as well. The *export* command is used to export a variable to the environment. Again, here we differ between *Bash* and *Tcsh*. If you're using *Tcsh*, another syntax is used for setting environment variables (the *setenv* command is used).

The environment is very important to the UNIX system. It allows you to configure certain commands just by setting variables which the commands know about.

Here's a quick example. The environment variable *PAGER* is used to display man pages one screenful at a time. If you set *PAGER* to be the name of a command, it will use that command to display the *man* (manual) *pages*, instead of more (which is the default).

Setting *PAGER* to "*cat*" will cause output from man to be displayed to the screen all at once, without breaking it up into pages.

/home/larry# PAGER="cat"

Now, you can export *PAGER* to the environment, with

/home/larry# export PAGER

Try the command man *ls*. The man page should fly past your screen without pausing for you. If we set *PAGER* to "more," the *more* command will be used to display the man page.

/home/larry# PAGER=more

Note that we don't have to use the *export* command after we change the value of *PAGER*. We only need to export a variable once. Any changes made to it thereafter will automatically be propagated to the environment.

The man pages for a particular command will tell you if the command uses any environment variables; for example, the man page explains that *PAGER* is used to specify the pager command. Some commands share environment variables. For example, many commands use the EDITOR environment variable to specify the default editor to use when one is needed.

The environment is also used to keep track of important information about your login session. An example is the *HOME* environment variable, which contains the name of your home directory.

/home/larry/papers# echo $HOME
/home/larry

Another interesting environment variable is *PS1*, which defines the main shell prompt. For example,

/home/larry# PS1="Your command, please: "
Your command, please:

STANDARD I/O AND REDIRECTION

Input can be redirected with the less than sign (<), and output can be redirected with either one or two greater than signs (> or >>). To append the standard output to an existing file, you must use two greater than (>>) signs in a row. If the file will be created by the redirected output, use one (>). Using an example of input/output (I/O hereafter) redirection to make the program *sort* read input from a file called "input" and write to a file called "output," rather than reading from the keyboard device and writing to a *tty*:

$sort < input > output

UNIX maintains a couple of conventions regarding where input to a program or command comes from and output from that program or command goes. In UNIX, the standard input is normally the keyboard, and the standard output is normally the screen.

Standard Input: This is the place from which a program expects to receive input. For commands that expect a file as standard input, if no file is specified, the keyboard will be taken as standard input.

Standard Output: This is the place to which a program sends its output. This is usually the terminal screen. Both standard input and output can be changed from their default values. Standard input can come from a file and standard output can be written or appended to a file. These capabilities are called *I/O redirection*. To tell the operating system to redirect input or output, certain operators must be placed in the command. Examine the examples below to learn how three of the I/O redirection operators work.

UNIX is very flexible and it allows you to change or redirect where the input comes from and where the output goes. First, any command that would normally give results on the screen can be directed instead to send the output to a file with the > (output redirection) symbol. Thus,

$date > file

directs the system to put the output from the *date* command, which merely reports the time and date as the system knows it, into the file named file rather than printing it to your screen. One thing to keep in mind about > is that each successive redirection to a particular file may overwrite all of the previously existing data in that file.

Another redirection is < which tells the command to take its input from a file rather than from the keyboard. For example, if you have a program that requires data input from the keyboard, you may find that you have to type the same data a large number of times in the debugging stage of program development. If you put that data in a file and direct the command to read it from there you will only have to type the data once, when you make the data file.

$program < datafile

If you do this, you would see the same response from the program as if you had typed the data in from the keyboard when requested. You can also combine both kinds of redirection as in

$program < datafile > outputfile

The data in the file *datafile* will then be used as input for the program, and all output will be stored in the outputfile. If you want to accumulate output from different sources in a single file, the symbol < > directs output to be appended to the end of a file rather than replacing the previous (if any) contents, which the single > redirection will do.

A final I/O redirection is the pipe symbol, |. The | tells the computer to take the output created by the command to the left of it and use that as the input for the command on the right. For example, we could type

$date | program

This would use the output of the date command as input to another program. Some typical examples are

EXAMPLE	DESCRIPTION
$ **who** > users	<-- of who to the file "users."
$ **who** >> users	<-- who to the end of "users."
$ **mail** crc1 < users	<-- Mails "users" to user crc1
$ **sort** < users > file9	<-- Multiple redirection precedes from left to right

PIPES AND FILTERS

UNIX can do even more for you to ease the task of running programs and capturing their output. Suppose you wanted to find items (i.e., lines) in the sorted list prepared in the last section which start with the string "smith." One thing you can do after you run the previous command to produce *sorted.list* is to run the *grep* command (or program) on it:

$ grep "smith" < sorted.list > filtered.list

Now you may remove the original file *sorted.list*, since what you want is already in the file *filtered.list*. This three-stage procedure can be simplified with the piping operator | as follows:

$ sort names | grep "smith" > filtered.list

Here you don't delete any files, because none were created. UNIX has mechanisms to buffer the (standard) output of one program and channel (redirect) it to the (standard) input of another. Here is another example that will allow you to produce a sorted display of the names of these who have sent you electronic mail:

cat ~/mbox | grep "From:" | sort > forgotten_people

This mechanism is known as *piping*, and the programs that can be used with the pipe operator (|) on both ends are called *filters*. These programs are written to read their input from the standard input and write it to the standard output, and are usually noninteractive in nature.

Pipes

UNIX systems offer true pipelining. This feature is extremely powerful. It means that the output of one utility can be fed directly into the input of another. The | symbol indicates pipelining in UNIX systems. To illustrate how this works, consider the following command.

pr -2 -n temp | wc -l

This creates a pipe between the output of the *pr* utility and the input of the utility *wc*. The command runs *pr*, which takes the file temp, adds line numbers to it, and formats it using two columns per line, feeding the output into *wc* which prints the line count on the standard output.

A pipe interconnects two programs. Pipes connect the output of one command to the input of another using the | character. Pipelines can be arbitrarily long. They allow you to "filter" the output from commands to suit your needs. For example, if you wanted to see the first 10 words beginning with the letters "ri," try the following:

look ri | head

The *look command* looks for words in the system dictionary. In the above example a list of all the words beginning with the letters "*ri*" is produced with *look* and is sent "through the pipeline" to the *head* command which pares off all but the first 10 lines. As another example, try

look ri | wc

Filter Commands

Some useful filter commands are

MVS/TSO COMMAND	DESCRIPTION	UNIX COMMAND
<ENTER>	Breaks up output into screen-sized pieces for easier reading.	***more***
TSOSORT	Sorts lines into alphabetical order.	***sort***
FIND	Extracts lines containing word.	***grep***
EDIT	Displays only the first 10 lines.	***head***
EDIT	Displays only the last 10 lines.	***tail***
	Shows the number of lines, words, and characters in the input.	***wc***

The filter commands described above are all normal UNIX commands—there is nothing about them which is inherently special to UNIX. Just as the first item typed at the UNIX prompt must be a UNIX command, the first item typed after each pipe symbol (|) must be a UNIX command, not an argument or option.

SHELL SCRIPTS

What is a script? A *script* is a set of commands, either in a file or typed at the command line, that performs multiple operations on a file or files. Another term for scripts that might be familiar to you is a "macro" or a CLIST in MVS/TSO.

How do they work? To run a file as a script, the file must have the execution bit set. This means the file has the *x*, which stands for *e-x-ecution* bit, set:

```
$ ls -l
-rwxr-xr-x 1 joeuser 60 Apr 9 01:57 shellscript
```

If the execution bit is set, what happens next depends on the first line of the file. If the first two characters are anything other than **#!**, the file is interpreted as a Bourne shell script. If the characters **#!** are followed by an explicit program location, such as */usr/bin/awk*, that program is run as an interpreter on the contents of the file.

As an alternative to setting the execution bits on a file and then running that file directly, it is also possible to source a nonexecutable file. This runs the current shell as an interpreter on the file being sourced, and thus should be used very carefully, since any environment variables set or changed in the script will be altered in the current shell. As a result, it is safer to run the script in its own subshell.

Building Shell Scripts

Let us say that you use a series of commands often, and would like to shorten the amount of required typing by grouping all of them together into a single "command." For example, the commands

```
/home/larry# cat chapter1 chapter2 chapter3 > book
    /home/larry# wc -l book
    /home/larry# lp book
```

would concatenate the files *chapter1*, *chapter2*, and *chapter3* and place the result in the file book. Then, a count of the number of lines in the book would be displayed, and finally the book would be printed with the *lp* command. Instead of typing all these commands, you could group them into a shell script. The shell script used to run all of these commands would look like

```
#!/bin/sh
# A shell script to create and print the book
    cat chapter1 chapter2 chapter3 > book
    wc -l book
    lp book
```

If this script was saved in the *file makebook*, you could simply use the command

```
/home/larry# makebook
```

to run all of the commands in the script. Shell scripts are just plain text files. You can create them with an editor such as *emacs* or *vi*. Creating CLIST scripts in **MVS/TSO** is a bit more complex.

Let us look at the above shell script. The first line, *#!/bin/sh*, identifies the file as a shell script, and tells the shell how to execute the script. It instructs the shell to pass the script to */bin/sh* for execution, where */bin/sh* is the shell program itself. On most UNIX systems, */bin/sh* is a Bourne-type shell, such as *Bash*. By forcing the shell script to run using */bin/sh*, we are ensuring that the script will run under a Bourne syntax shell (instead of, say, a C shell). This will cause your script to run using the Bourne syntax even if you usc *Tcsh* (or another C shell) as your login shell.

The second line is a comment. Comments begin with the character # and continue to the end of the line. Comments are ignored by the shell—they are commonly used to identify the shell script to the programmer.

The rest of the lines in the script are just commands, as you would type them to the shell directly. In effect, the shell reads each line of the script and runs that line as if you had typed it at the shell prompt.

To make sure that your shell script is always run from a standard Bourne shell, have the line

```
#!/bin/sh
```

as the first line of the script.

Passing Arguments to the Shell

Shell scripts can act like standard UNIX commands and take arguments from the command line. Arguments are passed from the command line into a shell program using the positional parameters *$1* through to *$9*. Each parameter corresponds to the position of the argument on the command line.

The positional parameter *$0* refers to the command name or name of the executable file containing the shell script. Only nine command line arguments can be accessed, but you can access more by using the *shift command.* All the positional parameters can be referred to using the special parameter *$**. This is useful when passing filenames as arguments. For example,

```
$ cat printps
# {This script converts ASCII files to PostScript}
# {and sends them to the PostScript printer ps1}
# {It uses a local utility "a2ps"}
a2ps $* | lpr -P ps1
$ printps elm.txt vi.ref msg
```

This processes the three files given as arguments to the command *printps.*

Permissions

Permissions are important for shell scripts. If you create a shell script, you must make sure that you have execute permission on the script in order to run it. The command

```
/home/larry# chmod u+x makebook
```

can be used to give yourself execute permission on the shell script makebook.

Reading User Input

To read standard input into a Bourne shell script, use the *read command.* For example,

```
echo "Please enter your name:"
read name
echo "Welcome to Edinburgh $name"
```

This prompts the user for input, assigns this to the variable name, and then displays the value of this variable to standard output. If there is more than one word in the input, each word can be assigned to a different variable. Any words left over are assigned to the last named variable. For example,

```
echo "Please enter your surname\n"
echo "followed by your first name: \c"
read name1 name2
echo "Welcome to Glasgow $name2 $name1"
```

Printing Commands

MVS	DESCRIPTION	UNIX
PRINTDS {[dsname] [filename/ddname]} [options]	Print a file.	***lpr*** *filename*
	Check print queue.	***lpq***
	Remove a job from the print queue.	***lprm*** *job_number*

You might need to indicate a specific printer for *lpr* to send your document to. To do this, use the *-P* option. So your print command may look something like this:

$ lpr -Pprinter filename

SUMMARY

MVS/TSO COMMAND	MEANING	UNIX COMMAND
	This null command has no effect; the command is a *noop*. A zero exit code is returned.	*:*
EX clistname 'parm1 parm2(value)'	Read and execute commands from file and return. The search path specified by PATH is used to find the directory containing file. Note that the dot command does not spawn a subshell.	***.file***
	Exit from the enclosing for or while loop, if any. If *n* is specified, break *n* levels.	***break*** *[n]*
	Change the current directory to *arg*. The environment variable HOME is the default *arg*. The environment variable CDPATH defines search path for the directory containing *arg*. If *arg* begins with /, the search path is not used. Otherwise, each directory in the path is searched for *arg*.	***cd*** *[arg]*
DO-END	Resume the next iteration of the enclosing for or while loop. If *n* is not specified, resume at each *n*th enclosing loop.	***continue*** *[n]*
READ &NAME	Read arguments as input to the shell and execute the resulting commands.	***eval*** *[arg...]*
EX {dsname} [options] {LIST/NOLIST}	Execute the command specified by the arguments in place of this shell without creating a new process. I/O arguments may appear and if no other arguments are given, cause the shell I/O to be modified.	***exec*** *[arg...]*

MVS/TSO COMMAND	MEANING	UNIX COMMAND
EXIT [CODE(expression)] [QUIT]	Cause the shell to exit with the exit status specified by *n*. If *n* is omitted, the exit status is that of the last command executed. An *eof* will also cause the shell to exit.	***exit*** *[n]*
	Mark names for automatic export to the environment of subsequently executed commands. If no arguments are given, a list is printed of all names exported in the current shell. Function names may not be exported.	***export*** *[name...]*
	For each name, the location in the search path of the command specified by name is determined and remembered by the shell. The *-r* option causes the shell to forget all locations.	***hash*** *[-r] [name...]*
LISTCAT	Print the current working directory.	***pwd***
	Read one line from the standard input and assign the first word to the first name, the second word to the second name, and so on to the last name. The exit status is 0 unless an *eof* is encountered.	***read*** *[name...]*
Used in a **CLIST** procedure	Cause a function to exit with the return value specified by *n*. If *n* is omitted, the exit status is that of the last command executed.	***return*** *[n]*
SET NAME=JOHN	*-a* Mark variables that are modified or created for export. *-e* Exit immediately if a command terminates with a nonzero exit status. *-f* Disable filename expansion. *-h* Locate and remember function commands as functions that are defined. *-k* Place all keyword arguments in the environment for a command, not just those that precede the command name. *-n* Read commands but do not execute them. *-t* Exit after reading and executing one command. *-u* Treat unset variable as an error when substituting. *-v* Print shell input lines as they are read. *-x* Print commands and their arguments as they are executed. -- Do not change any of the flags; useful in setting $1 to -. Using **+** rather than **-** causes these flags to be turned off.	***set*** *[[-] [-aefhkntuvx] [arg...]]*
	Change names of the positional parameters *$n* + 1 ... to $1... If *n* is not given, it is assumed to be 1.	***shift*** *[n]*

MVS/TSO COMMAND	MEANING	UNIX COMMAND
TEST	Evaluate conditional expressions. Test evaluates the expression *expr*, and if its value is true, returns a zero (true) exit status; otherwise, a nonzero (false) exit status is returned. Test also returns a nonzero exit status if there are no arguments. The following primitives are used to construct exp.: *-r file* True if file exists and is readable. *-w file* True if file exists and is writable. *-x file* True if file exists and is executable. *-f file* True if file exists and is a regular file. *-d file* True if file exists and is a directory. *-c file* True if file exists and is a character special file. *-bfile* True if file exists and is a lock special file. *-p file* True if file exists and is a named pipe (FIFO). *-u file* True if file exists and its set user ID bit is set. *-g file* True if file exists and its set group ID is set. *-k file* True if file exists and its sticky bit is set. *-s file* True if file exists and has a greater size than zero. *-t [fields]* True if open file whose file descriptor number is fields (1 by default) and is associated with a terminal device. *-z s1* True if length of string *s1* is zero. *-n s1* True if length of string *s1* is non-zero. *s1 = s2* True if strings *s1* and *s2* are identical. *s1!= s2* True if strings *s1* and *s2* are not identical. *s1* True if *s1* is not the null string. *n1 -eq n2* True if integers *n1* and *n2* are algebraically equal.	***test*** *[expr]*
TIME	Print the accumulated user and system times for process run from shell.	***times***
	Read the command *arg* and execute when the shell receives signal(s) *n*. Trap commands are executed in order of signal number. If the *arg* is absent, all trap(s) *n* are reset to their original values. If *arg* is the null string, this signal is ignored by the shell. If *n* is 0, the command *arg* is executed on exit from the script.	***trap*** *[arg] [n]*
	Set the file-creation mask to *nnn*. The three octal digits refer to read/write/execute permissions by the owner, group, and others, respectively.	***umask*** *nnn*

12

Shell Programming and Utilities

INTRODUCTION

The shell provides many mechanisms to customize your work environment, just as MVS/TSO via terminal session, CLISTs, and symbolic variables. MVS has no such concept as shells in UNIX.

The shell is more than a command interpreter—it is also a powerful programming language. While writing shell scripts is an extensive subject, we would like to introduce you to some of the ways that you can simplify your work on a UNIX system by using these advanced features of the shell.

Different shells use different syntax's when executing shell scripts. For example, *Tcsh* uses a C-like syntax, while *Bourne shells* use another type of syntax. In this section, we will not be discussing the differences between the two, but we will assume that shell scripts are executed using the Bourne shell syntax.

The objectives of this chapter are to make you familiar with the programming techniques and structure using some of the more powerful UNIX facilities, like the "UNIX Bourne SHELL."

Categories of Shells

In general, there are two main classes of shells. The first class are those shells derived from the Bourne shell which includes *sh*, *ksh*, *bash*, and *zsh*. The second class are those shells derived from C shell and include *csh* and *tcsh*. In addition there is *rc*, which most people consider to be in a "class by itself," although some people might argue that *rc* belongs in the Bourne shell class. With the classification above, using care, it is possible to write scripts that will work for all the shells from the Bourne shell category, and write other scripts that will work for all of the shells from the C shell category.

Changing Shells

The UNIX shell is most people's main access to the UNIX operating system, and as such any improvement to it can result in considerably more effective use of the system and may even allow you to do things you could not do before. Primarily, most of the new-generation shells give you increased speed. They require fewer key strokes to get the same results due to their completion features, they give more information (e.g., showing your directory in your prompt, showing which files it would complete), and they cover up some of the more annoying features of UNIX, such as not going back up via symbolic links to directories.

The C shell */bin/csh* was born at UC Berkeley. This shell included several concepts which were new (the majority of these being job control and aliasing) and managed to produce a shell that was much better for interactive use. But as well as improving the shell for interactive use, they also threw out the baby with the bath water and went for a different input language. The theory behind the change was fairly good, the new input language was to resemble C, the language in which UNIX itself was written.

Eventually the *Korn shell /bin/ksh* made its appearance. This quite sensibly junked the *C shell* language and reverted back to the *Bourne shell* language, but it also added in the many features that made the C shell good for interactive work (you could say it was the best of both worlds). It also added some features from other operating systems. The *Korn shell* became part of System V.

The search for the perfect shell still goes on, and the latest entry into this arena is *zsh*. It is based roughly on the Bourne shell (although there are some minor but important differences) and has so many additional features.

Which of the many shells you choose depends on many different things. The main reason for switching shells is to gain extra functionality. Switching between certain shells of the same syntax is a lot easier than switching between shells of a different syntax. So if you do not have much time, a simple upgrade (e.g., *csh* to *tcsh*) may be a good idea. If you ever look at a UNIX manual page it will say that to change your shell use *chsh* or passwd -*s*; unfortunately, it often is not as simple as this, since it requires that your new shell is recognized as a valid shell by the system and at present many systems do not recognize the newer shells (the normal selection is */bin/sh*, */bin/csh*, and possibly */bin/ksh*). You may be left only with the choice of changing your effective login shell without changing your official entry in */etc/passwd*.

You may also be left with the problem that there isn't a compiled binary on your system, so you will have to get hold of the shell's source and compile it yourself (It's generally best to ask around to see if anyone's done this already, since it isn't that easy). Once done you should add in code to your old shell's login file so that it overlays your official login shell with your new shell (remember to add the login flags to the command line and with *csh/tcsh* ensure that the overlay doesn't happen recursively since they both read the same *.login file*).

The shell can be recognized as a valid shell if the system administrator puts it in the file */etc/shells*. If this file does not exist, it must be created and should contain all valid shells.

Warning

If you do decide to change your shell you must be very careful—if handled wrongly, it can be almost impossible to correct, and will almost certainly cause you a lot of hassle. Never make a new shell a login shell until you have tested its new configuration files thoroughly and then tested them once again. It is also important that you make a full backup of your previous settings if you have to change any of them (which you will probably have to do if you can't change your shell entry in */etc/passwd*).

SPECIAL SHELL VARIABLES

All of the major shells other than *sh* have aliases, but they do not all work the same way. For example, some do not accept arguments. Although not strictly equivalent, shell functions (which exist in most shells from the Bourne shell category) have almost the same functionality of aliases. Shell functions can do things that aliases cannot. Shell functions did not exist in Bourne shells derived from Version 7 UNIX, which includes System III and BSD 4.2. BSD 4.3. and System V shells do support shell functions.

The shells from the C shell category use *"set variable=value"* for variables local to the shell and *"setenv variable value"* for environment variables. To get rid of variables in these shells, use *unset* and *unsetenv*. The shells from the Bourne shell category use *"variable=value"* and may require an *"export VARIABLE_NAME"* to place the variable into the environment. To get rid of the variables, use *unset*.

Special Variables

Like control variables in MVS/TSO, there are some UNIX shell variables which are set internally by the shell and are available to the user.

NAME	DESCRIPTION
$1–$9	The positional parameters.
$0	The name of the command currently being executed.
$#	The number of positional arguments given to this invocation of the shell.
$?	The exit status of the last command executed is given as a decimal string. When a command completes successfully, it returns the exit status of 0 (zero); otherwise, it returns a nonzero exit status.
$$	The process number of this shell—useful for including in filenames, to make them unique.
$!	The process ID of the last command run in the background.
$-	The current options supplied to this invocation of the shell.
$*	A string containing all the arguments to the shell, starting at $1.
$@@	Same as above, except when quoted.

NOTE #	DESCRIPTIONS
1	$* and $@@ when unquoted are identical and expand into the arguments.
2	$* is a single word, comprising all the arguments to the shell, joined together with spaces. For example, '1 2' 3 becomes "1 2 3."
3	$@@ is identical to the arguments received by the shell, the resulting list of words completely match what was given to the shell. For example '1 2' 3 becomes "1 2" "3."

Evaluating Shell Variables

The following set of rules govern the evaluation of all shell variables.

DEFINITION	DESCRIPTION
$var	Signifies the value of *var* or nothing, if *var* is undefined.
${var}	Same as above except the braces enclose the name of the variable to be substituted.
${var-thing}	Value of *var* if *var* is defined; otherwise, *thing*. *$var* is not set to *thing*.
${var=thing}	Value of *var* if *var* is defined; otherwise, *thing*. If undefined *$var* is set to thing.
${var?message}	If defined, *$var*; otherwise print message and exit the shell. If the message is empty, print a standard message.
${var+thing}	Thing if *$var* is defined; otherwise nothing.

CREATING COMMANDS AND PROGRAMS USING THE SHELL

When using the shell to run commands, you can use its built-in programming language to write your own commands or programs. You can put commands into a file—known as a shell script—and then execute that file as you would a command or program.

The use of the Bourne shell (*sh*) is illustrated as this is available on all UNIX systems. Bourne shell scripts will also work under the Bourne Again Shell (*BASH*). The *C* and *TC* shells use a programming language which is similar to the C programming language.

Conditional Execution

Every UNIX command returns a value on exit which the shell can interrogate. This value is held in the read-only shell variable $?.

A value of 0 (zero) signifies success; anything other than 0 (zero) signifies failure.

- The *if* statement
- The *&&* operator
- The || operator

The *if* Statement

The *if* statement uses the exit status of the given command and conditionally executes the statements following. The general syntax is

MVS (IF-THEN-ELSE)	**UNIX** (IF-THEN-ELSE-FI)

IF conditional **THEN +**
  DO
  action or commands (if condition is true)
  END
ELSE +
  DO
  action or commands (if condition is true)
  END
	if *test*
	  then
	  commands (if condition is true)
	  else
	  commands (if condition is false)
	  fi

then, *else*, and *fi* are shell reserved words and as such are only recognized after a newline or ; (semicolon). Make sure that you end each *if* construct with a *fi* statement.

if statements may also be nested:

```
if ...
  then ...
  else if ...
         ...
       fi
  fi
```

The *elif* statement can be used as shorthand for an *else if* statement. For example,

```
if ...
   then ...
   elif ...
          ...
          ...
        fi
   fi
```

Example of Using an *if* Construct

To carry out a conditional action,

```
if who | grep -s keith #/dev/null
   then
   echo keith is logged in
   else
   echo keith not available
   fi
```

This lists who is currently logged on to the system and pipes the output through *grep* to search for the username *keith*. The *-s* option causes *grep* to work silently, and any error messages are directed to the file *#/dev/null* instead of the standard output.

If the command is successful, that is, if the username *keith* is found in the list of users currently logged in, then the message *keith* is logged on is displayed; otherwise, the second message is displayed.

The && Operator

You can use the **&&** operator to execute a command and, if it is successful, execute the next command in the list. For example,

```
cmd1 && cmd2
```

cmd1 is executed and its exit status examined. Only if *cmd1* succeeds is *cmd2* executed. This is a terse notation for

```
if cmd1
   then
   cmd2
   fi
```

Example of Using the && Operator

To notify the user about the outcome of a previous command,

```
$ cat deliver
   #!/bin/sh
```

```
# usage: deliver username filename
{cat $2 | write $1;} && echo done
```

The first command *{cat $2 | write $1;}* concatenates and displays the message held in the file greeting and *pipes* the output through *write* command whose argument is the name of the user to whom the message is to be sent.

Note the use of the positional parameters $1 and $2. The ; (semicolon) is needed to sequentially execute the preceding pipeline. If this command is successful, the message done is displayed on standard output.

The || Operator

You can use the || operator to execute a command and, if it fails, execute the next command in the command list. For example,

```
cmd1 || cmd2
```

cmd1 is executed and its exit status examined. If *cmd1* fails, then *cmd2* is executed. This is a terse notation for

```
cmd1
  if test $? -ne 0
  then
cmd2 </I>
  fi
```

Example of Using the || Operator

To send a message to a user using the appropriate utility,

```
$ cat writemail
# usage: writemail user message
echo "$2" |{write "$1" || mail "$1" ;}
```

The user types a command such as

```
$ writemail sarah 'call me'
```

The message entered by the user is through the command *{write "$1" || mail "$1" ;}*. If the message cannot be sent to the user's terminal (they are not logged on) with the command write "$1," then the message is sent to the user by mail.

Testing for Files and Variables with the Test Command

The shell uses a command called *test* to evaluate conditional expressions. For example,

```
if test ! -f $FILE
  then
```

```
if test "$WARN" = "yes"
then
echo "$FILE does not exist"
     fi
fi
```

First, we test to see if the filename specified by the variable **$FILE** exists and is a regular file. If it does not then we test to see if the variable **$WARN** is assigned the value *yes*, and if it is a message that the filename does not exist is displayed.

Flow of Control Statements

The Bourne shell provides several flow of control statements. These are

- The *case* statement.
- The *for* statement.
- The *while* and *until* statements.
- The *break* and *continue* statements.

The CASE Statement

case is a flow control construct that provides for multiway branching based on patterns. Program flow is controlled on the basis of the *word* given. This *word* is compared with each pattern in order until a match is found, at which point the associated command(s) are executed.

FUNCTION	MVS	UNIX

Format	**WHEN** SYSRC (operator-integer) (command/END)
	  WHEN expression1 action
	  WHEN expression2 action
	  WHEN expression3 action
	
	  [**OTHERWISE**} action
	  ...
	END
		case
		  test command1
		  test command2
		  test command3
		ecas

Example	**WHEN** (&RTNCODE = 0) CALL 'A.B.LOAD(PGM)'
	WHEN (&RTNCODE = 1) +
	  DO
	    SET &X = X + 1
	    SET RETRY = &STR(YES)
	  END
	OTHERWISE SET &MSG = &STR(SEVERE_ERROR)
	END
		case *word in*
		  pattern1 command(s)
		  ;;
		  pattern2) command(s)
		  ;;
		  patternN) command(s)
		  ;;
		  esac

As in MVS, when all the commands in UNIX are executed, control is passed to the first statement after the *esac*. Each list of commands must end with a double semicolon ;;. A command can be associated with more than one pattern. Patterns can be separated from each other by a | symbol. For example,

```
case    word in
pattern1 | pattern2)    command
...                            ;;
```

Patterns are checked for a match in the order in which they appear. A command is always carried out after the first instance of a pattern. The * character can be used to specify a default pattern as the * character is the shell wildcard character.

Example of Using the CASE Statement

To specify an action when a word matches the pattern:

```
$ cat diary
   today='date +%m/%d` (presents the date in the format 01/31)
   case $today in
   07/18)      echo    "Antonio Maher"
   ;;
   07/21)      echo    "Ben Wyvis"
   ;;
   08/02)      echo    "Beverly Maher"
   ;;
   08/03)      echo    "Slouch"
   ;;
   *)          echo    "Wet..low level today"
   esac
$ date +%m/%d
   07/18
   $ diary
   Antonio Maher
   $
```

The value for the word *$today* is generated by the *date* command. This is then compared with various patterns so that the appropriate commands are executed. Note the use of the pattern *; this can be used to specify default patterns as the * character is the shell *wildcard* character.

Looping with FOR Statement

The *for* loop notation has the general form:

FUNCTION	MVS	UNIX
Format	**DO** **UNTIL** Condition action ... **END**	***for*** *var in list-of-words* ***do*** *command (s)* ***done***
Example	**DO** **UNTIL** &INPUT = YES /* Perform action until condition is YES ... action ... WRITE Type YES if you are finished READ &INPUT **END**	*# do something to each subdirectory found* ***for*** *i in `for i in ** ***do*** ***if*** *test -d $i* ***then*** *echo $i* ***fi*** ***done`*** ***do*** ... ***done***

commands/action is a sequence of one or more commands separated by a newline or ; (semicolon). The reserved words *do* and *done* must be preceded by a newline or ; (semicolon). Small loops can be written on a single line. For example,

for var inlist; do commands; done

Examples of Using the FOR Statement

1. To take each argument in turn and see if that person is logged onto the system.

```
$ <B>cat snooper
   # see if a number of people are logged in
   for i in $*
   do
   if who | grep -s $i #/dev/null
   then
   echo $i is logged in
   else
   echo $i not available
   fi
   done
```

For each username given as an argument, an *if* statement is used to test if that person is logged on and an appropriate message is then displayed.

2. To go through each file in the current directory and compare it with the same filename in another directory:

```
# compare files to same file in directory "old"
  for i in *
  do
  echo $i:
  cmp $i old/$i
  echo
  done
```

3. If the list of words is omitted, then the loop is executed once for each positional argument (i.e., assumes $* in the for statement). In this case the loop will create the empty files whose names are given as arguments.

```
# create all named files
  for i
  do
  &#62 $i
  done
```

4. Some examples of command substitution in *for* loops are

```
# do some thing for all files in current
# directory according to time modified
  for i in 'ls -t'
  do
  ...
  done

# do something for all non-fred files.
  for i in 'cat filelist | grep -v fred'
  do
  ...
  done
```

The WHILE and UNTIL Statements

The *while* statement has the general form

FUNCTION	MVS	UNIX
Format	**DO WHILE** condition action **END**	***while*** *command-list1* ***do*** *command-list2* ***done***

FUNCTION	MVS	UNIX
Example	SET &COUNTER = 5 /* initialize /* Perform action while counter is greater than 0 */ **DO WHILE** &COUNTER > 0 (&RTNCODE = 0) CALL 'A.B.LOAD(PGM)' (&RTNCODE = 1) + ... set of instructions ... SET COUNTER = &COUNTER - 1 /* Decrease counter by 1 */ **END**	# display calendar by month ***set*** *I = 1* ***while*** *($I != 13)* *cal $I 1994* *@ I = ($I + 1)* ***end*** *echo "calendar complete"* ***exit***

The commands in *command-list1* are executed, and if the exit status of the last command in that list is 0 (zero), the commands in *command-list2* are executed. The sequence is repeated as long as the exit status of *command-list1*.

This is identical in function to the *while* command except that the loop is executed as long as the exit status of *command-list1* is nonzero. The exit status of a *while/until* command is the exit status of the last command executed in *command-list2*. If no such command list is executed, a *while/until* has an exit status of 0 (zero).

Examples of Using the WHILE and UNTIL Statements

1. To wait for someone to log out,

```
while who | grep -s $1 #/dev/null
   do
   sleep 60
   done
   echo "$1 has logged out"
```

   This script checks to see if the username given as an argument to the script is logged on. While they are, the script waits for 60 seconds before checking again. When it is found that the user is no longer logged on, a message that they have logged out is displayed.

2. To declare when a file has been created,

```
until test -f $FILE
   do
   sleep 60
   done
   echo "$FILE now exists"
```

   This tests every 60 seconds until the filename represented by the variable **$FILE** exists. A message is then displayed.

3. To watch someone for logging in,

```
# make sure we pick up the correct commands
  PATH=/bin:/usr/bin
  # remember $# is number of positional arguments
  case $# in
  1) ;;
  *) echo 'usage: watch for username' ; exit 1
  esac
  until who | grep -s "$1" #/dev/null
  do
  sleep 60
  done
  echo "$1 has logged in"
```

If more than one username is given, one "watch for username" is displayed and the command fails.

The BREAK and CONTINUE Commands

It is often necessary to handle exception conditions within loops. The statements *break* and *continue* are used for this. The *break* command terminates the execution of the innermost enclosing loop, causing execution to resume after the nearest done statement. To exit from **n** levels, use the command

```
break n
```

This will cause execution to resume after the done *n* levels up.

The *continue* command causes execution to resume at the *while*, *until*, or *for* statement which begins the loop containing the continue command. You can also specify an argument *n|FR* to continue which will cause execution to continue at the *n|FRth* enclosing loop up.

Example of Using the BREAK and CONTINUE Commands

To prompt for a command, enter

```
while echo "Please enter command"
  read response
  do
  case "$response" in
  'done') break # no more commands
          ;;
            "") continue # null command
          ;;
```

```
        *) eval $response # do the command
                ;;
    esac
    done
```

This prompts the user to enter a command. While the user enters a command or null string, the script continues to run. To stop the command, the user enters *done* at the prompt.

SHELL INITIALIZATION SCRIPTS

In addition to shell scripts that you create, there are a number of scripts that the shell itself uses for certain purposes. The most important of these are your initialization scripts, scripts automatically executed by the shell when you login.

The initialization scripts themselves are simply shell scripts, as described above. However, they are very useful in setting up your environment by executing commands automatically when you log in. For example, if you always use the mail command to check your mail when you login, you place the command in your initialization script so it will be executed automatically.

Both *Bash* and *Tcsh* distinguish between a *login* shell and other invocations of the shell. A *login* shell is a shell invoked at login time; usually, it is the only shell that you'll use. However, if you "shell out" of another program, such as *vi*, you start another instance of the shell, which isn't your login shell. In addition, whenever you run a shell script, you automatically start another instance of the shell to execute the script.

The initialization files used by *Bash* are */etc/.profile* (set up by the system administrator, executed by all Bash users at login time), *$HOME/.bash_profile* (executed by a login *Bash* session), and *$HOME/.bashrc* (executed by all nonlogin instances of *Bash*). If *.bash_profile* is not present, *.profile* is used instead.

Tcsh uses the following initialization scripts: */etc/csh.login* (executed by all *Tcsh* users at login time),

$HOME/.tcshrc

(executed at login time and by all new instances of *Tcsh*), and *$HOME/.login* (executed at login time, following *.tcshrc*). If *.tcshrc* is not present, *.cshrc* is used instead.

To fully understand the function of these files, you'll need to learn more about the shell itself. Shell programming is a complicated subject, far beyond the scope of this book.

EXTENDED SHELL SCRIPTS

This section provides you with information about several functions which can be used within a shell script.

- Doing arithmetic.
- Including text in a shell script.
- Forcing evaluation of commands.
- Executing a command without creating a new process.
- Controlling when to exit a shell script.
- Trapping operating system signals.

Doing Arithmetic

There are a number of operators which are utilized in manipulating data and arithmetic operations. A list of the arithmetic, bitwise, and logical operators is listed below. The arithmetic operators only apply to integer values. The shift operators **>>** and **<<** shift the value on the left side left or right by the number of bits specified by the value on the right side of the expression. The 1's complement operator ~ inverts the bits (changing 1's to 0's and 0's to 1's) in its expression. The operator **!** merely inverts the logical result of its expression—its value can only be 0 or 1. Similarly, the operators |, ^, and & perform bitwise operations (or, exclusive or, and) on their values.

<table>
<tr><th>SYMBOL</th><th>MEANING</th><th>EXAMPLE (NUM = 10)</th><th>ECHO $r</th></tr>
<tr><td>+</td><td>addition</td><td>r = $num + 4</td><td>14</td></tr>
<tr><td>-</td><td>subtraction</td><td>r = $num - 5</td><td>5</td></tr>
<tr><td>*</td><td>multiplication</td><td>r = $num * 10</td><td>100</td></tr>
<tr><td>/</td><td>division</td><td>r = $num / 6</td><td>1</td></tr>
<tr><td>%</td><td>modulo</td><td>r = $num % 3</td><td>1</td></tr>
<tr><td>>></td><td>right shift</td><td>r = ($num >> 2)</td><td>2</td></tr>
<tr><td><<</td><td>left shift</td><td>r = ($num << 3)</td><td>80</td></tr>
<tr><td>~</td><td>1's complement</td><td>r = ~ $num</td><td>-11</td></tr>
<tr><td>!</td><td>logical negation</td><td>r = ! $num</td><td>0</td></tr>
<tr><td>|</td><td>bitwise "inclusive or"</td><td>r = ($num | 7)</td><td>15</td></tr>
<tr><td>^</td><td>bitwise "exclusive or"</td><td>r = ($num ^ 7)</td><td>13</td></tr>
<tr><td>&</td><td>bitwide "and"</td><td>r = ($num & 6)</td><td>2</td></tr>
<tr><td>||</td><td>logical "or"</td><td>r = ($num > 8 || $num < 4)</td><td>1</td></tr>
<tr><td>&&</td><td>logical "and"</td><td>r = ($num > 4 && $num < 8)</td><td>0</td></tr>
</table>

Note: Although C shell has numeric operators, it stores all variables as strings.

The *let* command in the *ksh* shell provides integer arithmetic operations using long arithmetic. You can represent a named variable internally by using the *typeset -i* command, as in the following example:

```
# Declare num as an integer variable
  typeset -i num
```

A base between 2 and 36 may be specified with the *typeset -i* command to represent the notation the number should take, as in

```
# Declare binary as a base 2 integer
   typeset -i2 binary
```

You can provide arithmetic functions on declared integer variables by using the let command, as in the following example:

```
   typeset -i num1 num2 ans
   num1=5
   num2=8
   let ans= "$num1 * $num2"
   print $ans
40
```

Many of the arithmetic operators for the *let* command (*, <, >, etc.) require quoting to prevent the shell from interpreting them.

The notation ((...)) can be used in place of the *let* command, as used for the C shell. For example, the following can be used in place of the previous example:

```
   ((ans = $num1 * $num2))
   Print $ans
40
```

Including Text in a Shell Script

Text can be included in the shell script by using a *here document*, a special form of input redirection. The ## symbol is used to indicate that text should be read up to a given mark. For example,

```
# this script outputs the given text before it runs
cat ## EOF
```

This shell script is currently under development, please report any problems to Harry:

```
(harry@cornflake.com)
EOF
exec /usr/local/test/bin/test_version
```

The text is read from the script until a pattern is found which matches that after the ## symbol; execution then proceeds as normal.

Forcing Evaluation of Commands

Another built-in function is *eval*, which takes the arguments on the command line and executes them as a command. For example,

```
echo "enter a command:"
  read command
  eval $command
```

Execute a Command Without Creating a New Process

The *exec* statement causes the command specified as its argument to be executed in place of the current shell without creating a new process. For example,

```
$ exec zmail -visual
```

This runs just the *zmail* program without a shell. When you quit the application, the current shell also exits.

Controlling When to Exit a Shell Script

The *exit* statement will exit the current shell script. It can be given a numeric argument which is the script's *exit status*. If omitted the *exit status* of the last run command is used. 0 (zero) signifies success; nonzero signifies failure. For example,

```
if [ $# -ne 2 ]
  # "$#" is the number of parameters- here we test
  # whether it is not equal to two
  then
  echo "Usage $0 \#file1\# \#file2\#" # not two parameters
  # so print message
  exit 2                              # and fail ($0 is
  # name of command).
  fi
    # rest of script #
```

This script is supposed to take two positional arguments. It will exit with status 2 (error) rather than 0 (success) if it is not called with two parameters.

Trapping Operating System Signals

Shell procedures may use the *trap* command to catch or ignore UNIX operating system signals. The form of the trap command is

```
trap 'command-list' signal-list
```

Details of the most common signals to be caught are here. Several traps may be in effect at the same time. If multiple signals are received simultaneously, they are serviced in ascending order. To check what traps are currently set use the trap command.

The command list is placed between single quotes, as the command line is scanned twice, once when the shell first encounters the *trap* command and again when it is being executed. The single quotes inhibit immediate command and variable substitution but are stripped off after the first scan, so that the commands are processed when the command is actually executed.

If *command-list* is not specified, then the action taken on receipt of any signal in the *signal-list* is reset to the default system action.

If *command-list* is an explicitly quoted null command (' ' or " "), then the signals in *signal-list* are ignored by the shell. The *command-list* is treated like a subroutine call. The commands in the list are executed when the signal is trapped, and control is then returned to the place at which it was interrupted.

here DOCUMENTS

The C shell allows in-line input redirection using symbols <<. We call such input a *here document.* The C shell calls the program and passes text from your script directly to it as a standard input. The format for a here document is as follows:

```
command [argument (s)] << word
        command input
        .....
        .....
word
```

The << symbol specifies input in-line redirection. The marker **word** indicates the beginning and end of the input. It can be a single character or a *word.* You should select something that does not appear in the text. The ending word should be on a line by itself (no spaces before or after it). If we quote *word*, the shell does not perform command substitution or file or variable expansion on the input. Otherwise, it does, and you must quote special characters (such as **$** and *) with \. Using a *here document*, let us send a message to Teri.

```
mail teri << +
I just installed the modem you wanted. You can locate the pertinent information
relating to drivers in the /usr/include/src directory. It is called remote.c.
+
```

Here we use **+** as the marker word; the second **+** terminates the *mail* command. Suppose you are writing a script that sends mail to a list of users. It contains the statement:

mail $user < message

This means that you must create and maintain the message file. *here documents*, on the other hand, allow you to put the message text directly into the script as illustrated in the example above.

ERROR HANDLING

The treatment of errors detected by the shell depends on the type of error and on whether the shell is being used interactively. Execution of a command may fail for any of the following reasons:

- The I/O redirection may fail if a file does not exist or cannot be created.
- The command itself does not exist or cannot be executed.
- The command terminates abnormally, for example, with a bus error or memory fault signal.
- The command terminates normally but returns a nonzero exit status.

In most cases, the shell will display an error message and go on to execute the next command. If the command is a shell script, nonzero exit status or abnormal termination of a command may allow the script to continue to execute the next command.

Other types of errors, such as failed I/O redirection, invalid command, syntax errors such as *if then done*, an interrupt signal that was not trapped, or failure of any of the built-in commands usually cause a script to terminate. The shell flag *-e* causes the shell to terminate if an error is detected.

To make your shell scripts more robust, you will want to add error checking. For example, a script can verify that you gave it the correct number of arguments. If arguments are files, a script can verify that they exist and are readable or writable. This avoids unexpected side effects caused by typing errors or misreadings.

INTERRUPT HANDLING

You can interrupt most (foreground) UNIX commands with a single keystroke. The DELETE key terminates a command and returns control to the shell. You may, however, want to transfer control to a different place in your script when an interrupt occurs. Here you can execute statements before returning control to the shell. Such statements are referred to as *interrupt handlers*.

Typically, you would display messages, or, more often, remove temporary files created by the script. This allows "clean up" before returning to the shell. In addition, you can always use *exit* with a nonzero status to indicate abnormal termination.

C Shell Interrupts

The **C** shell provides the *onintr* (on interrupt) command to process interrupts within shell scripts, such as

onintr label

transfers to *label* when an interrupt occurs. This command usually appears at the beginning of a script. It is in effect only while the script is executing. If the interrupt does occur and you need to transfer control to *label*, include the following somewhere in your script:

```
label:
        commands
        ........
        ........
```

label: should be on a line by itself. Any number of commands may follow it. Typically an exit statement with nonzero status is the last command.

C shell also allows you to disable interrupts using the notation

onintr -

placed on a separate line. If this is the first statement, the entire script will be impervious to interrupts. You can also use *onintr* - to shield part of a script.

There are varied uses of the interrupts, such as

- Removing temporary files if an interruption occurs.
- Shielding critical code.
- Preventing users from interfering with one another.

Examples of Interrupt Handling with C Shell

Let us examine a simple program to shield critical code from uncontrolled interrupts.

% NUM SHIELD

```
#
# build new directories
#
onintr remove                      # prepare to catch interrupts
set tf = /tmp/$$                   # build temp filenames
cd ~/list                          # go to list directory
echo "building list"               #
for each file (?.words)            # expand file
```

% NUM SHIELD

```
 9.    echo $file\:                                # reverse fields using awk
10.    awk -F: '{print $2 ":" $1}' Sfile > $tf$file
11. end
12. onintr -                                       # disable interrupts
13. echo "rename original files"
14. for each file (?.words)                        # move all tmp files to current
                                                   directory
15. mv $tf$file $file
16. end
17. exit 0
18. remove:                                        # interrupt handler
19.    onintr -                                    # ignore future interrupts
20.    set nomatch                                 # prevent file expansion errors
21.    rm -f $tf?.words                            # remove temporary files
22.    exit 1                                      # error exit
```

Before the critical move operations begin, line 12 forces the C shell to ignore interrupts. However, you can safely terminate the script any time before line 12. The second *onintr* - command (line 19) prevents the shell from processing multiple interrupts.

Built-in Interrupt Commands

A *trap* is a built-in instruction whose effect is somewhat similar to that of a hardware interrupt. The trap leads to a change in context, and it often causes the calling process to be suspended or even swapped out. System calls on many versions of UNIX system work by means of a *trap instruction.*

trap sets up a command to be executed when the shell receives a signal. With no arguments, *trap instruction* displays the traps currently in effect. If no command is specified, all traps for signal are reset. If the command is null (:, ' ', or " "), this shell and all commands it invokes ignore the signal. If the signal is 0, command is executed when it exits the shell.

trap commands are executed in order of signal number. If a signal that is ignored on entry to the current shell is trapped, the command is not executed. The following signals are often used with the *trap* command:

SIGNAL	MEANING
0	Special signal for the shell. Executes command when shell exits.
1	Hangup. Sent when loss of **DTR** is detected.
2	Interrupt. Sent when user presses **BREAK** key.
3	Quit. Sent when user presses **DEL** key.
15	Software termination. Set when a program **exits**.

The built-in trap command is suitable only for simple signal handling (for example, catching an interrupt from the keyboard to terminate the script). Functions requiring complex signal handling should be implemented as a *C program.* The *trap* command allows you to detect error signals and indicate what action should be taken. The command has the form

trap [command] [number] ....

This is a command string that is read and executed when the shell receives signals whose numbers are given in number. command is scanned once when the trap is set and once when the trap is executed. trap commands are executed in order of signal number. For example,

trap 'rm -f /tmp/junk; 0 1 2 3 15

sets a trap for the specified signals. If any of the signals is received, the shell will execute the script. The primary cleanup action is to remove the file designated by *'junk'.*

You can cause a procedure to ignore signals by specifying the null string as the argument to trap. The fragment

trap ' ' 1 2 3 15

causes the system hangup, interrupt, quit, and software termination signals to be ignored both by the procedure and by invoked commands.

The trap command with no arguments prints a list of commands associated with each signal number.

trap 1 2 3 15

resets the traps for the corresponding signals to their default values.

Examples of Interrupt Handling with Trap Command

1. To use single quotes to inhibit command substitution:

```
trap 'echo `pwd` ##$HOME/errdir' 2 3 15
  for i in /bin /usr/bin /usr/any/bin
  do
  cd $i
  some series of commands in the directory $i
  done
```

The file *errdir* will contain the name of the directory being worked on when the procedure is interrupted. What happens if the same procedure has double quotes around it?

```
trap "echo `pwd` #errdir" 2 3 15
```

The file *errdir* will just contain the name of the directory from which the procedure was invoked because the *pwd* command would be substituted on the first scan by the shell and not when it is invoked in the script.

2. To remove temporary files when a procedure is interrupted:

```
temp=/tmp/file.$$
   trap 'rm $temp; exit' 0 1 2 3 15
   ls # $temp
   .....
```

If any of the named signals are encountered, the command *rm $temp; exit* will be executed. The *exit* command is needed to terminate the execution of the whole procedure.

3. To continue processing commands after a *trap* command:

```
# read and process commands
   dir='pwd'
   for i in *
   do
   if test -d $dir/$i
   then
   cd $dir/$i
   while echo "$i:"
   trap exit 2 # trap ^C
   read x
   do
   trap '' 2 #ignore interrupts
   eval $x
   done
   fi
   done
```

The shell continues to process commands after a *trap* command. The entire procedure is terminated if interrupted when waiting for input, but the interrupt is ignored while executing a command. The command list is an explicitly quoted *null command*, and so the signal is ignored by the shell.

DEBUGGING SHELL SCRIPTS

Debug Options

Several shell options can be *set* that will help with debugging shell scripts. These are

OPTION	MEANING
-e	Causes the shell to exit immediately if any command exits with a nonzero exit status.
-n	Prevents execution of subsequent commands. Commands are evaluated but not executed. This is usually combined with *-v* option when used for debugging. This is very useful for "syntax checking."
-u	Causes the shell to treat unset variables as an error condition.
-v	Causes lines of the procedure to be printed as read. Use this to help isolate syntax errors.
-x	Provides an execution trace. After parameter substitution, each command is printed as it is executed.

These execution options can be turned on with the *set* command:

set -option

You can turn on options either inside the script or before its execution (except *-n*, which freezes the terminal until you send an *eof*). Options can also be turned off by typing

set +option

Alternatively, they can be turned on with the *sh* command if the script is executed this way. To display where a script produces an error, use the command

$ sh -x script argument

The *-x* option to the *sh* command tells it to print commands and their arguments as they are executed. You can then see what stage of the script has been reached when an error occurs. Other debugging options are described here.

Example of Debugging a Shell Script

To print commands and their arguments as they are executed,

```
$ cat example
   TEST1=result1
   TEST2=result2
   if [ $TEST1 = "result2" ]
```

```
then
echo $TEST1
fi
if [ $TEST1 = "result1" ]
then
echo $TEST1
fi
if [ $test3 = "whosit" ]
then
echo fail here'cos it's wrong
fi
```

This is a script called *example*, which has an error in it; the variable *$test3* is not set so the third and last test command will fail. Running the script produces

```
$ sh example
  result1
  [: argument expected
```

The script fails and to see where the error occurred you would use the *-x* option like this:

```
$ sh -x example
  TEST1=result1
  TEST2=result2
  + [ result1 = result2 ]
  + [ result1 = result1 ]
  + echo result1
  result1
  + [ = whosit ]
  example: [: argument expected
```

The error occurs in the command *[= whosit]* which is wrong as the variable *$test3* has not been set. You can now see where to fix it.

SUMMARY

Most of the shell functions can be accomplished in MVS via JCL as well as PROC statements. However, the UNIX shell programming is unique in its characteristics. In this chapter, you have learned some of the programming techniques using UNIX shells.

The UNIX shell is both a command interpreter and a programming language. The UNIX shell(s) can be used to supplement systems programming, such as program debugging. A number of shells can be employed depending upon the development requirements. Two versions of the shell run under UNIX System V: the Bourne shell and the Korn shell. The Korn shell has all the features of the Bourne shell, some of the best features of C shell (BSD developed shell), and many new features of its own.

Shell programming relies to a great extent on the numerous commands provided on a UNIX system. Knowing these commands and their use is invaluable when you develop shell programs.

13

Document Preparation

INTRODUCTION

UNIX has a number of powerful text processing tools that require a skillful programmer to implement. On the other hand, a large number of third-party vendors have developed "easy-to-use" solutions for text processing. MVS also supports a number of text processing applications and tools along with various script and GML languages. IBM has developed a number of document architectures for revised (RFTDCA), mixed text processing (MODCA), and document interchange architectures (DIA).

SCRIPT/VS runs in the TSO foreground. TSO's interactive editing (ISPF/PDF or EDIT) and related facilities provide the text entry, editing, and data set management that are used with SCRIPT/VS for text processing. SCRIPT/VS provides a flexible composition for printing on terminals, impact printers, or nonimpact printers as an alternative to independent typesetting machines. When SCRIPT/VS formats a document, it takes into consideration the characteristics of the specific physical output device. This device may be a terminal, a line printer, a nonimpact page printer, or a PostScript device. SCRIPT/VS can also be used to prepare documents for processing by other programs or applications, such as formatters and photocomposers.

But there is no correlation or similarity in the way MVS and UNIX present text processing facilities to the user. To give you some familiarity, we will restrict our discussion to UNIX features that perform simple text processing.

UNIX provides two basic tools for text processing:

nroff	new runoff
troff	typesetter runoff

troff2 typesetter runoff extension for html (hypertext marking language)

troff is an extension of the *nroff* and supports proportional spacing, multiple fonts, and the like. Many versions of *troff* have been developed to support PostScript, laser, and other printers processing many of the desirable typesetting features.

In this chapter we will discuss a number of powerful UNIX text processing tools which require a skillful programmer to implement. MVS also supports a number of text processing applications and tools along with various script and GML languages. But there is no correlation or similarity in the way MVS and UNIX present text processing facilities to the user. To give you some familiarity, we will restrict our discussion to UNIX features that perform simple text processing.

nroff—FORMAT DOCUMENTS FOR DISPLAY OR LINE PRINTER

Format

nroff [-ehiq] [-mname] [-nN] [-opagelist] [-raN] [-sN] [-Tname] [file]

Description

nroff formats text in the named *files* (standard input by default) for printing on typewriterlike devices and line printers. If no file argument is present, *nroff* reads the standard input. An argument consisting of a "-" is taken to be a filename corresponding to the standard input.

Options

Options may appear in any order so long as they appear before the filenames.

-e	Produces equally spaced words in adjusted lines, using full terminal resolution.
-h	Uses output TAB characters during horizontal spacing to speed output and reduce output character count. TAB settings are assumed to be every eight nominal character widths.
-i	Reads the standard input after the input files are exhausted.
-q	Invokes the simultaneous input-output mode of the *.rd* request.
-mname	Prepends the macro file */usr/share/lib/tmac/tmac.name* to the input files.
-nN	Numbers the first generated page *N* or *start-no*.
-opagelist	Prints only pages whose page numbers appear in the comma-separated list of numbers and ranges. A range *x-y* M means pages *x* through *y*; an initial *-y* means from the beginning to page *y*; and a final *x-* means from *x* to the end.

-raN	Sets the number register referenced by a (one-character) to *N* (integer).
-sN	Specifies the number of pages to print between pauses. Stop every *N* pages. *nroff* will halt prior to every *N* pages (default *N* = 1) to allow paper loading or changing, and will resume upon receipt of a *newline*.
-Tname	Prepares output for a device of the specified name.

Example

The following command

nroff -s4 -me users.guide

formats *users.guide* using the *-me* macro package and stopping every four pages.

Files

/bin/nroff	Executable file.
*/tmp/ta**	Temporary file.
*/usr/share/lib/tmac/tmac.**	Standard macro files.
*/usr/share/lib/nterm/**	Terminal driving tables for nroff.
/usr/pub/terminals	File containing a list of supported terminals.
/usr/share/lib/term/README	Index to terminal description files.

nroff Mode

nroff mode is a mode like text mode but modified to handle *nroff* commands present in the text. Invoke "*M-x nroff-mode*" to enter this mode. It differs from text mode in only a few ways. All *nroff* command lines are considered paragraph separators, so that filling will never garble the *nroff* commands. Pages are separated by *.bp* commands. Comments start with backslash doublequote. Also, three special commands are provided that are not in text mode:

'M-n'	Moves to the beginning of the next line that isn't an *nroff* command (*forward-text-line*). An argument is a repeat count.
'M-p'	Like *M-n* but moves up (*backward-text-line*).
'M-?'	Prints in the echo area the number of text lines (lines that are not *nroff* commands) in the region (*count-text-lines*).

The other feature of *nroff* mode is that you can turn on electric *nroff newline* mode. This is a minor mode that you can turn on or off with *m-x electric-nroff-mode*. When the mode is on, each time you use RET to end a line that contains an *nroff* command that opens a kind of grouping, the matching *nroff* command to close that grouping is automatically inserted on the following line. For example, if you are at the beginning of a line and type ".(b RET," the matching command ".)b" will be inserted on a new line following point.

troff—TEXT FORMATTING AND TYPESETTING

Format

troff [-olist] [-nN] [-mname] [-raN] [-] [-i] [-q] [-z] [-a] [-Tdest] [-sN] [-Tname] [-e] [-h] [file]

Description

troff formats text in the named files for printing on a phototypesetter; *nroff* for typewriterlike devices. If no file argument is present, the standard input is read. An argument consisting of a single minus (-) is taken to be a filename corresponding to the standard input.

Options

The options, which may appear in any order so long as they appear before the files, are

-olist Prints only pages whose page numbers appear in the comma-separated list of numbers and ranges. A range *N-M* means pages *N* through *M*; an initial *-N* means from the beginning to page *N*; and a final *N*-means from *N* to the end.

-nN Numbers first generated page *N*.

-mname Prepends the macro file */usr/misc/lib/tmac/tmac.name* to the input files.

-raN Set register *a* (one character name) to *N*.

- Specifies a filename corresponding to the standard input.

-i Reads standard input after the input files are exhausted.

-q Invokes the simultaneous input-output mode of the *rd* request.

-z Produces no output: diagnostics and *.tm* messages only.

-a Sends a printable ASCII approximation of the results to the standard output.

-Tdest Prepares output for typesetter *dest*. *-Fdir* take font information from directory *dir*.

-sN *nroff* will halt prior to every *N* pages (default *N* = 1) to allow paper loading or changing and will resume upon receipt of a newline.

-Tname Prepares output for specified terminal. Known names include 37 for the (default) Teletype Model 37 terminal, *lp* (line printer) for any terminal without half-line capability, 450 for the DASI-450 (Diablo Hyterm).

-e Produces equally spaced words in adjusted lines, using full-terminal resolution.

-h Uses output tabs during horizontal spacing to speed output and reduce output character count. Tab settings are assumed to be every eight nominal character widths.

Example

The following command

troff -o4, 8-10 -mabc file1 file2

requests the formatting of pages 4, 8, 9, and 10 of a document contained in the files named *file1* and *file2* and invokes the *abc* macro package.

Files

/bin/troff	Executable file.
*/usr/misc/lib/term/**	Terminal driving tables for *nroff.*
/usr/lib/font/dev/**	Font width tables for *troff.*
*/usr/misc/lib/tmac/tmac.**	Standard macro files.
*/usr/misc/lib/term/**	Terminal driving tables for *nroff.*
*/usr/misc/lib/font/**	Font width tables for *troff.*

troff2—TEXT FORMATTING AND TYPESETTING IN AN html ENVIRONMENT

Format

troff [-olist] [-nN] [-mname] [-raN] [-] [-i] [-q] [-z] [-a] [-Tdest] [-sN] [-Tname] [-e] [-h] [file]
troff2 [arguments] input files ...

Description

troff2 is the program to convert *troff* markup to html (hypertext markup language) for the World Wide Web. *troff2* only supports the *me* macros.

- Understands *-me* macros.
- Understands strings and sourced files.
- Permits output from preprocessors (eqn, tbl, etc.) to be run through *nroff.*
- Translates all iso-8859-1 entities.
- Is table of contents configurable.
- Is navigation bar configurable.
- Is splitting-by-section level configurable.
- Allows you to add your own macros with relative ease.

Options

Options may appear in any order so long as they appear before the files.

-name string Basename for output html files [input filename].

-title string Main title (not header) added to all pages [ ].

-split number Section at which to split html files [999].

-nosplit or -split 0 Gives a single page.

-numbersection Section titles will have *nroff* like numbers.

-nonumbersection No section numbers [default].

-nofill <method> What to do with nofill regions (supported methods are *pre* or *br*. The default is *pre*).

-toc Table of contents generated [default].

-notoc No table of contents generated.

-toc page Table of contents gets separate page, even if *-split 0* [default is top].

-toc bottom Table of contents is on bottom of first page [default is top].

-headerlink Headers are links back to table of contents [default if *split = 0*].

-headerlink explicit Explicit links are put near headers back to table of contents.

-index Include link to index in navigation bar [no].

-noindex Don't print any indices.

-notes Include link to endnotes in navigation bar [no].

-notes <string> The link to notes will be labeled [*Notes*].

-nonotes Don't print any endnotes.

-nav Include a navigation bar on each page [default if *-split > 0*].

-nonav No navigation bar included [default if *-split = 0*].

-nav words Navigation bar will use word links [default].

-nav icons Navigation bar will use icons.

-tbl <method> How to handle tables (*tbl* preprocessor).

-eqn <method> How to handle equations (eqn preprocessor).

-pic <method> How to handle pictures (pic preprocessor) (currently supported: *omit*, *pre*, *nroff*, and *ps*).

-warn Warn about all ignored macros [yes].

-macros Print names of all understood/known macros and exit.

-perl <file> Additional macros defined in *perl* file.

-entity Use entity names, not numbers, for isolation chars [no].

Note: Arguments can be abbreviated, with defaults in square brackets.

troff2html Arguments

All arguments can be abbreviated by their shortest unambiguous string. Thus, split -2 can be abbreviated -s 2.

-name string — If name is not given, the base name for all output files will be the basename (no extension) of the first input file. The top entry point to the document will always be *basename.html*. If you want *troff2html* to read from standard input, supply a *-name* argument so it knows what to call the output files.

-title string — It is useful to have a descriptive html so that browser histories are more meaningful. Normally, files are titled after the basename or after their section title. This argument will be prepended to all document titles, which are normally seen only in a browser window or browser history. This text will not appear in the visible section headers.

-split number — Splits into separate files at this level of section headers.

-split 0 or -nosplit — Means no splitting at all; the resulting document will be a single page. *-split 1* will split at the top-level section headers (*.sh 1* or *.NH 1*). *troff2html* tries very hard not to leave a single header alone on a page if you do something like:

```
.sh 1 Introduction
.sh 2 Once upon a time.
```

Right now, unnumbered headers are always counted as being one below the last numbered header. This should probably be configurable.

-Numbersection — Normally, section numbers in the html document are not numbered.

-numbersection — Turns on explicit section numbering to mimic *troff* behavior.

-nofill method — What to do with the *troff* command *.nf*. Should be one of *pre* or *br*. The default is *pre*, which uses the html command. This will preserve indentation and line breaks, but it will change the font to fixed pitch. Specifying *br* will use the html command to put a line break after each line of the *troff* input. The font thus remains normal and proportionally spaced, but you will lose any indentation, tabs, or internal spacing you had in the *.nf* section.

-toc — Adds a *table of contents* (defined by section headers) to the document.

-notoc — Turns off the table of contents. This is on by default if you have any section headers in your document. If no section headers are present, no table of contents will be printed. You may need to use *-notoc* even if you have no section headers.

-toc page	If you give this option a page argument, the table of contents will have its own page (be a separate file), even if *-nosplit* is defined.
-toc bottom	Places the table of contents at the bottom of the first page instead of the top.
-headerlink	If this option is given, section headings will be hyperlinks back to the table of contents. This is mainly useful for a single page document to jump up to the table of contents and is enabled by default only if *-nosplit*. It is not enabled by default for multifile documents, since each file/page/section has a navigation bar that also jumps back to the table of contents.
-headerlink explicit	If you give this option an explicit argument, the links back to the table of contents are an explicit phrase after each section header, instead of the section header itself. The exact phrase is configurable, but the default is "[To Table of Contents]."
-Index	*troff2html* doesn't know ahead of time if you have an index, so no link to the index is included in the navigation bar on each page. Use this option to include a link to the index on each page. If you have index entries but don't explicitly print the index, *troff2html* will print it at the end of the document.
-noindex	Means do not print this final index, although you can still print one explicitly with *.xp*.
-Notes	*troff2html* does not know ahead of time if you have footnotes or references, so no link to the endnotes is included in the navigation bar on each page. Use this option to include a link to the endnotes on each page.
-nonotes means	Do not print any endnotes.
-notes string	Since all the footnotes and references are put at the end of the document, they are really endnotes. The default name for this section is simply "Notes." If you want something else, use this argument (e.g., *-notes References*).
-Nav	Include a navigation bar on each page (what links are included and in what order is configurable). This is the default if the document is going to be more than one html file (i.e., if -split ⩾1).
-Nonav	Turns off the navigation bar.
-nav method	Method should be words or icons. The words and icons are configurable.
-tbl method	How to treat sections marked for the *tbl* (table) preprocessor. Method should be one of
omit	Omits the section entirely.
pre	Leaves the raw *tbl* commands in the document and include them as a reformatted section.
nroff	Runs it through *tbl* | *nroff* and include as a preformatted section.

ps	Renders as postscript (with *tbl* | *psroff*), use ghostscript to convert to GIF, and include as an inline image.
-eqn method	As *tbl*, for the *eqn* (equation) preprocessor.
-pic method	As *tbl*, for the *pic* (picture) preprocessor.
-Warn	Warns about all unknown macros. Use *-nowarn* to turn warnings off.
-macros	Prints the name of all understood macros and exits. Many macros that deal with formatting are understood in the sense that we know enough to ignore them.
-perl filename	Although you can add your own macro definitions and code when you configure *troff2html*, you can also add *perl* code to be evaluated at runtime with this argument. This is useful, for instance, to add heuristic code to detect section headers from font size changes for a specific file.
-Entity	Many web browsers, Mosaic™ and NetScape™ among them, do support all of the iso-8859-1 character set, but do not support entity names (like *plusnm*; for the plus/minus symbol) for all of this set. By default, *troff2html* translates these entities to their encoded number instead (#177; in this case). Use *-entity* in the future when all the browsers support all the entity names.

The basic syntax is simply *troff2html inputfile.me*. Make sure you're in a separate, writable directory; *troff2html* assumes freedom to write a lot of files. *troff2html* will process all files on the command line as a single document.

Example

A simple document will probably be best translated as

troff2html -nosplit -notoc simple.me

which gives a single page document *simple.html* with no table of contents. It's a good idea to tell *troff2* explicitly *-nosplit -notoc* if that's what you want; strange things may happen otherwise.

Since numeric registers are not supported, using them in section headers with *-numbersection* will not yield the correct results. html has two different fixed pitch modes: a *font* (usually > and some others such as spaces) and >. Using the *font*, multiple spaces are taken as one, like normal in html. In *troff*, fixed font C never eats spaces. If *troff2html* chooses the wrong mode, your output is off. If you have multiple files (i.e., section headers) and some text before the first section header, *-toc page* doesn't work, mostly because that initial matter has no name. Since it will be on a separate page, it needs a link. By default the table of contents will be after the initial matter, and *-toc top* will put it on top of that first page.

Although higher-level markup, such as the *me* and *ms* macros are available, most of the *troff* documents continue to use low-level, presentation-based markup instead of logical markup. For example, people use centering and font size changes instead of *.sh*.

In working with documents in the World Wide Web, keeping them up-to-date is the hardest part. You have two choices: you can change the resulting html, or you can change the *troff* source.

If you even suspect you're going to update the paper (*troff*) copy of your document, it's worth your while to make the translation automatic, so that in the future turning out an up-to-date *html* version is as painless as possible. Editing a raw *html* file every time quickly becomes tedious and gets put on the bottom of the todo list.

eqn—TEXT FORMATTING AND TYPESETTING

Format

eqn [-] [-dxy] [-fn] [-pn] [-sn] [-Tdest] [file] ...

Arguments

-	Causes *eqn* to read the standard input.
-dxy	Sets delimiters to characters *x* and *y* between *.EQ* and *.EN*. The left and right delimiters may be the same character, the dollar sign often being used as such a delimiter. Delimiters are turned off by *delim off*. All text that is neither between delimiters nor between *.EQ* and *.EN* is passed through untouched.
-fn	Specifies the font to be used. Replace *n* with the desired font.
-pn	Specifies the point size of the equation. Replace *n* with a point size.
-sn	Specifies the size of the equation.
-Ttty-type	Causes *eqn* to prepare output for the specified output device, *tty-type.*
file	Specifies the file to be formatted. If this option is not given, *eqn* will read the standard input.

Description

Eqn is a *troff* preprocessor for typesetting mathematics on a phototypesetter. Usage is almost always

eqn [options] file ... | troff [options] | [typesetter]

If no files are specified, these programs read from the standard input. *Eqn* prepares the output for the typesetter.

.EQ marks the beginning of an equation, whereas *.EN* marks the end. Neither of these lines is altered, so they may be defined in macro packages to get centering, numbering, and so on. It is also possible to set two characters as delimiters. Delimiters may be set to characters *x* and *y* with the command line argument *-dxy* or with *delim xy* between *.EQ* and *.EN*. The left and right delimiters may be identical. Delimiters are turned off by *delim off*. All other text that is neither between delimiters nor between *.EQ* and *.EN* is passed through untouched.

Tokens within *eqn* are separated by spaces, tabs, newlines, braces, double quotes, tildes, or circumflexes. Braces { } are used for grouping; generally speaking, anywhere a single character like *x* could appear, a complicated construction enclosed in braces may be used instead. The tilde ~ represents a full space in the output, the circumflex ^ half as much, and the tab represents an ordinary *troff* tab character.

Files

/bin/eqn	Executable file

tbl—TABLE FORMATTER

Format

tbl [-TX] [file] ...

Arguments

-TX	Forces the *tbl* to use only full vertical line motions, as in most printers.
file	Specifies the file to be formatted. If no file is given, *tbl* reads the standard input.

Description

tbl is a preprocessor that formats tables for *nroff* and *troff*. The input files are copied to the standard output, except for lines between *.TS* and *.TE* command lines, which are assumed to describe tables and are reformatted by *tbl*.

The *.TS* command line is followed by global options:

center	Centers the table (default is left adjust).
expand	Makes the table as wide as the current line length.
box	Encloses the table in a box.
doublebox	Encloses the table in a double box.
allbox	Encloses each item of the table in a box.
tab (x)	Uses the character *x* instead of a tab to separate items in a line of input data.

Each line of the table is described by a single keyletter, optionally followed by specifiers that determine the font and point size of the corresponding item, that indicate where vertical bars are to appear between columns, that determine column width, inter-column spacing, and so on. The available keyletters are

c Centers item within the column.
r Right adjusts item within the column.
l Left adjusts item within the column.
n Numerically adjusts the item within the column.
s Spans previous item on the left into this column.
a Centers longest line in this column and then left adjusts all other lines in this column with respect to that centered line.
^ Spans down previous entry in this column.
_ Replaces this entry with a horizontal line.
= Replaces this entry with a double horizontal line.

The characters *B* and *I* stand for the bold and italic fonts, respectively. The character | indicates a vertical line between columns. The format lines are followed by lines containing the actual data for the table, followed finally by *.TE*—a terminator. Within such data lines, data items are normally separated by tab characters.

If the data line consists of only _ or =, a single or double line, respectively, is drawn across the table at that point. If a single item in a data line consists of only _ or =, then the item is replaced by a single or double line.

Example

The following input represents a tab:

```
.TS
center box ;
cB s s
cI cI s
cI | cI s
l | n n
Family | Population
_
City ^I Units
^I Number ^I Size
=
Data1 ^I 819   ^I 2.36
Data2 ^I 1829 ^I 2.26
Data3 ^I 2839 ^I 2.46
Data4 ^I 3849 ^I 2.56
```

Data5 ^I 859 ^I 2.66
.TE

Yields:

FAMILY POPULATION		
	FAMILY	
CITY	NUMBER	SIZE
Data1	819	2.36
Data2	1829	2.26
Data3	2839	2.46
Data4	3849	2.56
Data5	859	2.66

Files

/bin/tbl *Executable file*

SUMMARY

UNIX has a number of powerful text processing tools which require a skillful programmer to implement. MVS also supports a number of text processing applications and tools along with various script and GML languages. But there is no correlation or similarity the way MVS and UNIX present text processing facilities to the user. To give you some familiarity, we have restricted our discussion to UNIX features that perform simple text processing.

SCRIPT/VS provides a flexible composition for printing on terminals. SCRIPT/VS and TSO's interactive editing (ISPF/PDF or EDIT) provide the text entry, editing, and data set management that are used with SCRIPT/VS for text processing. impact printers, or nonimpact printers as an alternative to independent typesetting machines.

In UNIX, *nroff* and *troff* provide basic tools for text processing: *troff* is an extension of the *nroff* and supports proportional spacing, multiple fonts, and the like. Many versions of *troff* have been developed to support postscript, laser, and other printers processing many of the desirable typesetting features.

Unlike MVS/TSO, text processing in UNIX is accomplished by many third party applications.

14

Communicating with Other Users

INTERACTIVE COMMUNICATIONS

Electronic mail (UNIX e-mail) is a good way to keep in touch with coworkers and friends who also have accounts on a network connected to yours. The main benefit of electronic mail over standard mail (aka "snail mail") is that it is delivered very quickly—it should arrive just a minute or two after it was sent. The simple mail utility has the advantage of being available on nearly all UNIX systems, though many users prefer a menu-driven system.

There are a variety of electronic mail systems available to users today. The most commonly used electronic mail on UNIX systems today is the *Internet*. In addition, there are many versions of the "local" mail, one example being Microsoft Mail for the LAN.

Introduction

The role of electronic mail in communication can scarcely be overemphasized; it is generally a more effective and convenient method for reaching members of a community than telephones, paper mail, or attempts to meet in person. Some good things to remember when using e-mail are the following:

- When replying to a message, it is often desirable to include portions of the original message; most mailers provide a way to do this. Keep it within reasonable bounds; most people don't like rereading their entire 57-line mail message to see your 1-line response at the bottom.
- Don't count on mail being secure, and confirm anything that seems odd by some other channel.

There are many ways to communicate with other users in MVS/TSO. You can

- Use the SEND command or the SEND subcommand of EDIT to send to:
  - One or more users.
  - Other users on your system node.
  - A specific operator.
  - The master console operator.
- Use the LISTBC command to see all current broadcast messages.
- Use the TRANSMIT command to send longer messages and data sets to other users.
- Use the RECEIVE command to receive transmitted messages from other users.
- Access the LOG data set that keeps a record of all TRANSMIT and RECEIVE activity.

MVS users can utilize TSO MAIL to send and receive electronic mail messages within the *Internet* networks. The MAIL command is used directly from TSO and ISPF. TSO users are automatically notified at LOGON time if they have mail waiting. To begin, type MAIL at the READY prompt. MAIL responds with an abbreviated index of all messages that have been sent to you, followed by the prompt MAIL. Here you can issue your mail commands.

MAIL:**SEND** userid
MAIL: **PRINT** # DEST(destination)

Users can also invoke MAIL from **ISPF** by entering the command **MAIL** from the command or option line in any ISPF panel. A main menu will be displayed with the options **S** (send), **P** (process), **T** (tutorial), and **X** (exit). The send option sends mail to *Internet* or local TSO users. The process option processes mail from other users. When selected, this option displays an ISPF panel that allows mail to be saved, deleted, read, forwarded, and answered.

With the ***SEND*** option' a panel appears where you must enter the Internet address and the subject line. All other fields are optional. After hitting the *ENTER* key, an edit entry screen is displayed. Because TEXT ENTRY mode is on, enter your message beginning in the blank line beneath the last numbered line. After all text has been entered, on the command line type *SEND* to send the message, *SEND LOG* to send and log the message, or *CANCEL* to cancel before sending.

UNIX mail permits users on UNIX systems to send each other messages, transfer small files, act as personal reminders, and communicate with users on remote systems. The UNIX mail invocation works almost exactly like MVS/TSO. Once you enter *mail username*, the system responds with a prompt for "to" followed by "subject," and so on.

UNIX uses two mailboxes to hold mail messages:

system mailbox (/usr/spool/mail/)
users mail box (.../.../mbox)

Mail arrives in the system mailbox and is saved in your user mailbox after you have read it. The users mailbox is normally located in their $HOME directory.

A UNIX mail message is exchanged between users. Mail messages consist of two parts:

header	Contains information about sender, receiver, and subject.
body	Contains actual content of message.

Mail headers have the following construction:

To:	Specifies the name of the recipients of the message (mandatory).
Subject:	Describes the message (optional).
cc:	Lists users to receive a carbon copy (optional).
bcc:	Lists users to receive blind carbon copy (users do not see user names in the received message (optional).

If the original message contains a subject field, the mailer will automatically fill this in for you, taking the contents of the original message's subject field.

The UNIX mail program operates in two main modes:

compose mode	Messages are created.
command mode	Manages your mail; lists/edits/deletes/prints/saves messages.

If there is mail, *command mode* is entered. If there is no mail, the program returns immediately. *Compose mode* is entered when you invoke the mail program and specify a user as an argument, e.g.,

mail username

The example below invokes the mail program and names the recipient of the message as *joe*. The user is placed into compose mode, where the message content is filled in (*do not* type this example!).

mail joe

For you to become familiar with the features of mail, run the mail program as shown above, but use your login name instead of the user *joe*. This means that the mail will be sent to yourself. This is the best way to learn all the features of mail, without distracting other users. Type

mail your_user_name

where *your_user_name* is the *login* name you used to *login* to the UNIX host.

Using Electronic Mail

When the UNIX mail program starts, it reads a mail script file (if one is present) located in the user's home directory. This specifies options for how the mail program works. One of the options is *asksub*, which tells the mail program to ask for a subject heading. If this option is set, then the mail program prompts you to enter a subject line,

Subject:

Enter the string "Hello" as the subject content for this message. Subject fields are limited to a single line. The mail program is now in *compose mode*. Enter each of the following lines. At the end of each line, press RETURN.

In compose mode, the mail program accepts special key sequences. These commands begin with the tilde (~) symbol. You will note that if you make a mistake on a previous line, you cannot go back and change it (at least not yet).

Using the command sequence *~v* invokes the UNIX editor *vi* and permits you to edit the message you have entered. After exiting *vi*, you are back into mail compose mode, where you continue adding lines or send the message by pressing **Ctrl-d.**

To display a list of available escape sequences, enter the following command while in compose mode.

~?

To list previous entered lines while in compose mode, press *~p.*

You can abort the sending of a message by pressing the interrupt key (either BACKSPACE or Ctrl-BACKSPACE) twice. If you abort a message in this manner, the message is saved in the file *dead.letter* in your $HOME directory.

Note:

- To delete a line in *compose mode*, press Ctrl-u.
- To view the message before sending it, press *~p*.
- To abort the message, press the DELETE key twice (this has been mapped to Ctrl-BACKSPACE on the IBM-PC keyboard, and will save the message in the file dead.letter).
- To send the message, press Ctrl-d.

To finish entering the message, press **Ctrl-d**. The mail message is sent, and the mail program returns you to the shell prompt.

When the mail program starts, it uses the default mail folder, which is the system mailbox. Remember the save mail message command, which saved the mail message to a file. It was stated that the mail program treats this file as a mail folder. By specifying the mail folder on the command line as an argument, mail will use a different mail folder.

mail -f meetings

The UNIX mail command has the following syntax:

mail [-h] [-s] [-w] [-d] [-e] [-f file] [-r] [-p] [-x] [-q] [-t] address

Commonly used mail command options are

m address	Mails the message to the named addresses.
+	Acts as the same as newline.
h	Lists headers.
s filename	Saves current message in the named file [*mbox* is default].
w filename	Saves current message without the header, in the named file [*mbox* is default].
d	Deletes the message and goes on to next message.
e	Causes *mail* not to be printed. An exit value of 0 is returned.
f file	Causes *mail* to use *file* (e.g., *mbox*) instead of the default *mailfile*.
r	Replies.
p	Prints on screen.
x	Exits and discards changes.
q	Puts undeleted mail in the mail file and quits.
t address ...	Causes the message to be preceded by all *addresses* the mail is sent to.
?	Lists mail commands.
!command	Escapes to the shell to perform *command.*

mailx enables you to send and receive messages also. *mailx* allows much more extensive option set. UNIX *mailx* command has the following syntax:

mailx [-d] [-e] [-f [filename]] [-F] [-h number] [-H] [-i] [-n] [-N] [-r address] [-s subject [-u user] [-U] [name] ...

Commonly used *mailx* command options are

d	Turns on debugging output.
e	Tests for the presence of mail.

f filename	Reads messages from *filename* instead of *login name*.
F	Records message in a *file* named after the first recipient.
h number	Specifies the number of network hopes made so far.
H	Prints the header summary only.
i	Ignores interrupts.
n	Does not initialize from system default.
N	Does not print the initial header summary.
r address ...	Passes address to network delivery software.
s subject	Sets the Subject header field to subject.
u user	Reads any incoming mail from a user with the specified login name.
U	Converts uucp-style addresses to Internet standard.
name	Specifies the *login name* of the user you wish to send *mail* to.

The following table displays the close similarities between UNIX and TSO mail systems.

FUNCTION	MVS/TSO	UNIX
Format	**MAIL: SEND** userid	***mail*** [option(s)] username
Example 1	**MAIL: SEND** 'message' userID {Where "message" is an in-line message and userID is the recipient's TSO userid.} {The **RECEIVE** command enables to receive information that is transmitted from another user, system, or yourself.} **TRANSMIT** userID **dataset** (dsname) **msg-dataset** (dsname) {Another way to send a message to appear on someone's screen is with **MSGDATASET** option of the **TRANSMIT** command.}	***mail*** *joe* {Invokes the mail program and names the recipient of the message as *joe* and puts in *compose mode.*}
Example 2	**MAIL: PRINT** # DEST(destination) {Mail message is to be printed and the printer destination.} **LISTBC** {Displays messages stored in a broadcast data set.}	***l*** *joe* {*l* command prints a specified mail message received from the user *joe.*}

Reading or Receiving Mail

Even though the TSO and UNIX mail systems are similar, there are certain subtle differences that must be noticed.

In TSO, when you first enter MAIL, an index of mail messages is automatically listed for you. The list appears in the following format:

M#	DATE	FROM	SUBJECT
*1	31Mar	USERABC	Mail info
*2	15Apr	USERXYZ	Test mail

The number preceding each listed message is the message number. An asterisk (*) preceding the message number indicates that the message has not been read. To see the contents of a particular message, type LOOK # or READ #. MAIL displays the entire contents of the selected message.

To read the current TSO message denoted by the > symbol, press the return key. The mailer displays the message as follows:

Message 1:
From brian Mon May 31 15:00:20 1996
From: brian@cit1.cit.ac.nz (Brian)

To: brianb
Subject: Hello
Date: Mon, 31 May 96 15:00:16 NZT
Message-ID: <9305311500.aa12036@cit1.cit.ac.nz>
Status: RO

This is my first UNIX mail message. I am entering the contents of this message in compose mode.
Once I press the return key I cannot edit previous lines. Have a nice day.

In TSO, read messages are not held in the system mailbox when you exit the mail program. If you want to save these messages after reading them, you must do so before exiting the mail program. To read the next message, press the RETURN key. The mailer responds with

Message 2:
From brianb Mon May 31 15:01:48 1996
From: brian@cit1.cit.ac.nz (Brian)
X-Mailer: SCO System V Mail (version 3.2)

To: brian
Date: Mon, 31 May 96 15:01:47 NZT
Message-ID: <9305311501.aa12046@cit1.cit.ac.nz>
Status: R

Hello and welcome. This message was in a file named tmpfile.

In TSO, the messages can be read or received by activating the RECEIVED command. The TRANSMIT command does not automatically add data sets to the recipients disk space. They wait in a special area until they are pulled in with the RECEIVE command.

In UNIX, to check if you have any new mail use the *from* command. If there is no new mail, you will get an error message; otherwise, *from* will tell you who has sent you new mail and what time it arrived. Some examples are

FUNCTION	MVS/TSO	UNIX
Example 1	**MAIL** **MAIL**: LOOK 1 or **SEND** 'how are you?' **USER**(user2) **SAVE** {Sends the enclosed message and displays only when the user issues LOGON or LISTBC command.}	***from*** *joe* {Invokes the mail program and names the recipient of the message as *joe*.}
Example 2	**MAIL**: READ 2 or **LISTBC** {Displays received messages.}	***mail*** {Reads mail that has been sent.} ***l*** *joe* {*l* command prints a specified mail message received from the user *joe*.}
Example 3	**TRANSMIT** node1.joe da('sys1.xyz') {Transmits a copy of 'sys1.xyz' data set to 'joe' at node1.} **RECEIVE** {'joe' receives the copy of the 'sys1.xyz' data set transmitted above.}	***mail***
Example 4	**TRANSMIT** node1.joe da('sys1.xyz') mem(pay,vacation) {Transmit member's pay and vacation of 'sys1.xyz' data set to 'joe' at node1.} **RECEIVE** {'joe' receives the two members of the 'sys1.xyz' data set transmitted above.} **Note:** You can also RECEIVE network data not sent by TRANSMIT command.	***mail***

MESSAGING

Sending Messages

To send mail, in UNIX, choose the *m* for *(m)ail*. Then you are prompted for the user's address, and subject of the mail message. Once these are entered, you can type your message. When you have entered as much text as you wish to appear in the body of your message, use one of the following to indicate "end of text": **Ctrl-d** or '.' on a new line. If you wish to view other options, type "?."

Example

TSO:

To send mail to another user, enter

MAIL: SEND *userid*

where userid is the recipient's TSO userid.

To send mail to a user on *Internet*, enter

MAIL: SEND *userid@host.domain*

To send mail *from a data set* (which must be text format with a record length of 80 characters), use

MAIL: SEND *userid FROM(dsname)*

or, for partitioned data sets, enter

MAIL: SEND *userid FROM(dsname(membername))*

After entering the SEND command, MAIL responds with the prompt SUBJECT:. Here you can enter the subject of your message. The next prompt is

Enter message: (empty line ends message)

Begin typing on the prompt line. After each line is full, press ENTER, and you will receive another prompt line. Pressing ENTER after an empty message line indicates that the message is finished. MAIL then responds with the *message sent.*

UNIX:

To send a letter to a certain user, use the mail command with the recipient's userid as an argument. Start out by sending yourself an e-mail message with

mail userid
Specify subject:
Type message:
Tilde escapes:

~p	View messages.
~r	Filename inserts file here.
~v	Edits message with *vi*.

~c userid	Adds user to the 'cc:' list.
~?	Lists tilde commands.

Exit with Ctrl-d ("end of text").

You can send mail to other users at remote sites by specifying their specific mail address:

brian@brian.cit.ac.nz
os2user@brian.cit.ac.nz
your_user_name@csc.cit.ac.nz

If the mail message already exists in a file, this is sent to a user by typing the following command:

mail joe < message

which sends the text file *message* to the user *joe*.

The command line option *-s* specifies the subject header for mail to use. The command

mail -s "Meeting today at 11:00 am" joe < message

sends the file *message* to the user *joe* and inserts the text string "Meet...am" into the subject field of the message header.

FUNCTION	MVS/TSO	UNIX
Example 1	Creates a message in a dsname "tmpfile."	***cat*** - > tmpfile {Creates a file named "tmpfile" which contains a message to send.} "Hello and welcome" {This message was in a file named tmpfile.}
	TRANSMIT node1.joe da(tmpfile) {Sends a message file named 'tmpfile' to joe on node1.}	***mail*** *-f* tmpfile
Example 2	**MAIL: SEND** userid FROM(dsname) or for partitioned data sets, enter **MAIL: SEND** userid FROM(dsname(membername))	***mail*** *joe < message* {*Sends the text file message to the user joe*}.
Example 3	**MAIL: SEND** userid@host.domain {Sends mail to a user on Internet.} {After entering the SEND command, MAIL responds with the prompt SUBJECT:. Here you can enter the subject of your message. The next prompt is.} **Enter message**: (empty line ends message)	

FUNCTION	MVS/TSO	UNIX
Example 4	**SEND** 'This is the text message' USER(*) {The message text is sent to your own userID.}	***mail*** *your_user_name* < tmpfile {Sends the file to yourself as outlined above.}
Example 5	**SEND** 'This is the text message' USER(userID) {The message text is enclosed in single quotes.} **SEND** 'This is the text message' USER(user1,user2,..) {The message text is sent to a number of users.} **SEND** 'Please cancel my userID' {The message senr to master console operator.} **SEND** 'Please mount tapes' OPERATOR(7) {The message text is intended for the operator console.}	***mail*** *joe* {Sends mail message to user 'joe' from 'mailfile'.}

Sending a Mail Message Contained in a File

"/usr/spool/mail/brian": 3 messages 3 new

N 3 brian	*Mon May 31 15:02*	*10/299*	*My message3*
N 2 brian	*Mon May 31 15:01*	*9/278*	
N 1 brian	*Mon May 31 15:00*	*12/415*	*My first message*
&			

This initial screen (above) displays the subject fields of messages which have arrived. The format of the display is

Type Message_number From_User Date/Time Subject

N	Denotes a new message.
>	Denotes the current message.
&	Mail prompt symbol.

Note how message number 2 does not have a subject heading. This is because the mail message was sent from a file, and the *-s* option was not specified on the command line when the mail program was invoked.

FUNCTION	MVS/TSO	UNIX
Example 1	**CREATE dataset** {a sequential or partitioned dataset member} **MAIL: SEND** userid FROM(dsname) or for partitioned data sets **TRANSMIT** userID **dataset**(dsname)	***cat*** - > tmpfile {Creates a file named "tmpfile" which contains a message to send.} "Hello and welcome" {This message was in a file named tmpfile.}

FUNCTION	MVS/TSO	UNIX
Example 2	**MAIL: SEND** userid FROM(dsname(membername)) **MAIL: SEND** userid@host.domain {Sends mail to a user on Internet.} {After entering the SEND command, MAIL responds with the prompt SUBJECT:. Here you can enter the subject of your message. The next prompt is.} **Enter message**: (empty line ends message)	***mail*** *joe* < message *{Sends the text file message to the user joe.}*

Saving Messages

Received mail messages are not kept in your catalog. Any messages are kept by the system for a specified number of days. If you want to keep a message longer, you can save it into one of your own data sets.

In UNIX, users will generally save important messages in a file. This is done by using the *save* command and specifying a file to save the message. For example, to save message number 3 into a file, you may enter:

The *hold* or *preserve* command saves the message in the system mail box. This means it will still be visible next time you enter mail.

Leaving mail with the *quit* command normally saves the message in the user's mailbox. It will not appear in the list of mail messages next time the mail program is invoked.

Type the command *hold* to preserve the current message. Follow this command by using the header command to display the message headers. Your screen should look like

```
& hold
& header
N   3 brian    Tue Jun 1 08:43    10/308    My message3
>P 2 brian     Tue Jun 1 08:42     9/287
1 brian        Tue Jun 1 08:41    12/417    My first message
&
```

Note how the *P* symbol highlights the message as being preserved. This message will be available next time you run the mail program, as well as unread messages, but the messages that you have read will not be available.

FUNCTION	MVS/TSO	UNIX
Example 1	**MAIL**: READ 3 INTO(SAVE.MAIL) *{For a sequential data set.}*	***mail*** *-s meetings* {Saves the current message in the file meetings. This file is now treated as a mail folder by the mail program.}
Example 2	**MAIL**: READ 3 INTO(SAVE.MAIL(member)) *{For a partitioned data set.}*	***mail*** *-s 3 welcome* {Saves message number 3 in a mail folder named **welcome**.}

FUNCTION	MVS/TSO	UNIX
Example 3	**RECEIVE** logds(meetings) {Receives the message into data set 'meetings' instead of the default log data set.}	***mail*** *-w meetings* {Saves the message, without header, in file named 'meetings'.}
Example 4	**SEND** 'text' userID SAVE {SEND stores the message in broadcast data set.}	

Deleting Messages

After reading a message, you can delete it from the system mail file. The delete command deletes messages.

FUNCTION	MVS/TSO	UNIX
Example 1	MAIL: DELETE # {*where "#" signifies the mail message number.*}	***mail*** *joe* {Invokes the mail program and names the recipient of the message as joe.}
Example 2	**RECEIVE** delete {Receives the file and deletes without restoring.}	***delete*** *joe* {Deletes the message from user joe.}

HANDLING MAIL

Replying to a Mail Message

In UNIX, the reply command allows you to send a reply to the sender of the message.

Example

mail joe {*Invokes the mail program and names the recipient of the message as joe.*}

reply 2 {*Replies to message number 2.*}

reply {*Replies to current message.*}

If the original message contains a subject field, the mailer will automatically fill this in for you, taking the contents of the original message's subject field.

Forwarding a Mail Message

In UNIX, a message is forwarded (sent on to) another user by using the forward command.

Example

mail joe	{*Invokes the mail program and names the recipient of the message as joe.*}
f 1 brian	{*Forwards message number 1 to user brian.*}
f 2 brian joe	{*Forwards message number 2 to users brianb and joe.*}

PRINTING MESSAGES

In TSO,

MAIL: PRINT # DEST(destination)

specifies which mail message is to be printed and the printer destination, such as R3 (Remote 3). The default print attributes are CLASS(A), DESTINATION(MERRICK), COPIES(1), NOHOLD, FORMS(RGLR).

In UNIX,

The *l* command prints a specified mail message. The following command prints all mail messages received from the user *joe*.

l joe

To print the current message, you do not supply any arguments.

FUNCTION	MVS/TSO	UNIX
Example	**MAIL: PRINT** # DEST(destination) {Mail message is to be printed and the printer destination.} **RECEIVE** userID **DISPLAY** {The transmitted data/message to be displayed at the terminal.}	***l*** *joe* {*l* command prints a specified mail message received from the user *joe*.}

EXITING MAIL

FUNCTION	MVS/TSO	UNIX
Example 1	To terminate the MAIL command, type END at the MAIL prompt.	***mail*** *-x* {Puts all mail in the mailfile unchanged and stops.} ***mail*** *-q* {Puts undeleted mail back in 'mailfile' and stop.}

USING NICKNAME DATA SETS

You can create a nickname data set to establish nicknames for both local and remote users, providing userid and node information, as well as more descriptive information such as full name, address, and phone number. You can establish a nickname the same as your own userid to provide your name, address, and phone number in the header of messages you send. You can also define a nickname for a distribution list.

EXECUTING SHELL COMMANDS

UNIX commands can be executed from within the mailer by preceding them with an exclamation symbol, such as

!ls -la	Does a directory listing.
!sh	Runs a shell.

GETTING HELP

In TSO, type HELP MAIL from TSO or type HELP while executing under the MAIL command. To list HELP information for a mail subcommand, type HELP subcommand after invoking MAIL.

To display *help* (in UNIX) while running the mail program, type a question (**?**) mark.

type [msglist]	Prints messages.
next	Goes to and types next message.
edit [msglist]	Edits messages.
from [msglist]	Gives header lines of messages.
delete [msglist]	Deletes messages.
undelete [msglist]	Restores deleted messages.
save [msglist] file	Appends messages to file.
reply [message]	Replies to message, including all recipients.
reply [msglist]	Replies to the authors of the messages.
preserve [msglist]	Preserves messages in mailbox.
mail user	Mails to specific user.
quit	Quits, preserving unread messages.
xit	Quits, preserving all messages.
header	Prints page of active message headers.
!	Escapes shell.
cd [directory]	Changes directory.

list	Lists all commands (no explanations).
top [msglist]	Prints top 5 lines of messages.
z [-]	Displays next [last] page of 10 headers.

[msglist] is optional and specifies messages by number, author, subject, or type. The default is the current message.

SUMMARY

The mail functions are built into the UNIX systems since UNIX was developed as an interactive operating system. *mail* and *mailx* are the most common UNIX commands used for electronic mail. However, there are many mail programs that are available in the market. UNIX mail can be used to

- Receive or send messages to other users.
- Reply or forward the received messages.
- Messages can be sent or received "in line" or with a file.
- Messages can be saved, printed, or deleted.

MVS offers no built-in mail facility. However, you can buy mail programs separately to run on your MVS systems.

- You can use the SEND command to send a one-line message to someone else's terminal. You can add this SEND operand to the LOGON command. Another way to send a message is with the MSGDATASET option of the TRANSMIT command.
- Data sets can be sent from one ID to another with the TRANSMIT command and received with the RECEIVE command.

15

Processor-to-Processor Communications

INTRODUCTION

Many organizations already have a substantial number of computers in operation, often located far apart. Initially, each of these computers may have worked in isolation from the others. However, in this age of the *Internet* and global markets, it has become imperative to connect them all to extract, share, and correlate information about the entire enterprise.

The primary issue is resource sharing, and the goal is to make all programs, data, and equipment available to anyone on the network without regard to physical location of the resource and the user. It is this concept requirement which leads to processor-to-processor communication or networking. The term network means different things to different people. To PC-only users, it might mean sharing data between a small number of PCs; to wide area network users it might mean connecting together remote offices and e-mail.

In this section, we will explore how various commands of UNIX and MVS facilitate communication among various processors, whether it be for file transfer, file copy, or remote command execution.

REMOTE LOGIN

Sometimes, while you are logged into one workstation, you will find that you would like to be logged in to another workstation, file server, or other UNIX system. *rlogin* and *telnet* will allow you to establish a session on a remote host. *rlogin* can be used for trusted-host access, whereas *telnet* can be used for either trusted or nontrusted Internet host connections. In either case, *login* name and password information is required.

Starting with MVS version 5.2.2, it's simple to run shell scripts from the ISHELL (ISPF shell). On the command line, just type

sh shellscript_name

Of course, you can also run a shell script from TSO, using BPXBATCH or OSHELL. Starting with MVS 5.2.2, if you have accessed the OpenEdition shell using *rlogin* or *telnet*, you can retrieve a command entered earlier. Then, if you want, you can edit it (using *vi*, *emacs*, or *gmacs*) and run it.

The UNIX command *rlogin* allows you to do so provided that you have an account on the other system. Type

rlogin newSystem

You may then have to supply your password. You should also get the messages about logging in that are used on *newSystem*. If your userid is different on *newSystem*, you will have to use the form

rlogin newSystem -l userid

Remote *login* is the simplest form of connection for one person. It allows you to use e-mail, Usenet news, *telnet*, *ftp*, *gopher*, and other usual Internet services. Transfer of files from/to local computer can be made with usage of *ftp* or similar protocol. This kind of connection has minimal requirements on a customer's hardware—any computer with modem and communication software is suitable.

The command *rlogin* establishes a remote login session from your terminal to the remote machine named hostname. It uses the following format:

rlogin [-8] [-ec] [-l username] hostname

Arguments

-8	Passes eight-bit data across the net instead of seven-bit data.
-ec	Specifies a different escape character, *c*, for the line used to disconnect from the remote host.
-l username	Specifies a different username for the remote login. If you do not use this option, the remote username used is the same as your local username.

Description

Hostnames are usually kept in the hosts database, which may be contained in the */etc/hosts* file, the Network Information Service (NIS) hosts database, the Internet domain name server, or a combination of these. Each host has one official name (the first name in the database entry) and, optionally, one or more nicknames. Either official hostnames or nicknames may be specified in hostname.

Each remote machine may have a file named */etc/hosts.equiv* containing a list of trusted hostnames with which it shares usernames. Users with the same username on both the local and remote machine may *rlogin* from the machines listed in the remote machine's */etc/hosts.equiv* file without supplying a password. Individual users may set up a similar private equivalence list with the file *.rhosts* in their home directories. Each line in this file contains two names: a hostname and a username separated by a SPACE.

An entry in a remote user's *.rhosts* file permits the user named username who is logged into hostname to *rlogin* to the remote machine as the remote user without supplying a password. If the name of the local host is not found in the */etc/hosts.equiv* file on the remote machine, and the local username and hostname are not found in the remote user's *.rhosts* file, then the remote machine will prompt for a password. Hostnames listed in */etc/hosts.equiv* and *.rhosts* files must be the official hostnames listed in the hosts database; nicknames may not be used in either of these files.

To counter security problems, the *.rhosts* file must be owned by either the remote user or by root.

The remote terminal type is the same as your local terminal type (as given in your environment TERM variable). The terminal or window size is also copied to the remote system if the server supports the option, and changes in size are reflected as well. All echoing takes place at the remote site, so that (except for delays) the remote login is transparent. Flow control using **^S** (Ctrl-s) and **^Q** (Ctrl-q) and flushing of input and output on interrupts are handled properly.

Files

/usr/bin/rlogin	Executable file.
*/usr/hosts/**	Directory for *rhost* version of the command.

REMOTE SHELL EXECUTION

The command *rsh* connects to the specified hostname and executes the specified command. *rsh* copies its standard input to the remote command, the standard output of the remote command to its standard output, and the standard error of the remote command to its standard error. Interrupt, quit, and terminate signals are propagated to the remote command; *rsh* normally terminates when the remote command does.

Shell metacharacters which are not quoted are interpreted on the local machine, while quoted metacharacters are interpreted on the remote machine. Hostnames are given in the hosts database, which may be contained in the */etc/hosts* file, the NIS hosts database, the Internet domain name database, or some combination of the three. Each host has one official name (the first name in the database entry) and optionally one or more nicknames. Official hostnames or nicknames may be given as hostname.

If the name of the file from which *rsh* is executed is anything other than "rsh," *rsh* takes this name as its hostname argument. This allows you to create a symbolic link to *rsh* in the name of a host which, when executed, will invoke a remote shell on that host. The */usr/hosts* directory is provided to be populated with symbolic links in the names of commonly used hosts. By including */usr/hosts* in your shell's search path, you can run *rsh* by typing hostname to your shell.

Each remote machine may have a file named */etc/hosts.equiv* containing a list of trusted hostnames with which it shares usernames. Users with the same username on both the local and remote machine may *rsh* from the machines listed in the remote machine's */etc/hosts* file. Individual users may set up a similar private equivalence list with the file *.rhosts* in their home directories. Each line in this file contains two names: a hostname and a username separated by a SPACE. The entry permits the user named username who is logged into hostname to use *rsh* to access the remote machine as the remote user. If the name of the local host is not found in the */etc/hosts.equiv* file on the remote machine, and the local username and hostname are not found in the remote user's *.rhosts* file, then the access is denied. The hostnames listed in the */etc/hosts.equiv* and *.rhosts* files must be the official hostnames listed in the hosts database; nicknames may not be used in either of these files.

rsh will not prompt for a password if access is denied on the remote machine unless the command argument is omitted. The type of remote shell (*sh*, *rsh*, or other) is determined by the user's entry in the file */etc/passwd* on the remote system. *rsh* runs the Bourne shell. The command format is

rsh [-l username] [-n] hostname [command]
rsh hostname [-l username] [-n] [command]

Arguments

-l username. Use username as the remote username instead of your local username. In the absence of this option, the remote username is the same as your local username.

-n. Redirect the input of *rsh* to */dev/null*. You sometimes need this option to avoid unfortunate interactions between *rsh* and the shell which invokes it. For example, if you are running *rsh* and start a *rsh* in the background without redirecting its input away from the terminal, it will block even if no reads are posted by the remote command. The *-n* option will prevent this.

Examples

The following command appends the remote file *lizard.file* from the machine called lizard to the file called *example.file* on the machine called example.

rsh	*lizard* cat	*lizard.file*	>> *example.file*
hostname	command	filename	machine or remote host

This example appends the file *lizard.file* on the machine called lizard to the file *another.lizard.file* which also resides on the machine called lizard.

rsh lizard cat lizard.file >> another.lizard.file

FILE TRANSFER

The TRANSMIT command in MVS/TSO allows you to send information (a message) or a copy of information (a data set), or both, to another user. The TRANSMIT command converts these data into a special format so that it can be transmitted to other systems (or users) in the network. RECEIVE command can be used to retrieve the data and restore them to the original format.

UNIX File Transfer Protocol (*ftp*) has had a long evolution over the years. *ftp* is a program for transferring files between two computer systems, a "local host" and a "remote host." While you are logged in on a local host and are running its *ftp* program, you can transfer files to and from a remote host by means of a "server" program that resides on that remote host. *ftp* uses the TCP/IP communications protocol.

The objectives of *ftp* are (1) to promote sharing of files (computer programs and/or data), (2) to encourage indirect or implicit (via programs) use of remote computers, (3) to shield a user from variations in file storage systems among hosts, and (4) to transfer data reliably and efficiently. *ftp*, though usable directly by a user at a terminal, is designed mainly for use by programs. This is to satisfy the diverse needs of users of maxihosts, minihosts, and personal workstations, with a simple, and easily implemented, protocol design.

The file transfer protocol was defined as a protocol for file transfer between HOSTs on the ARPANET, with the primary function of *ftp* defined as transferring files efficiently and reliably among hosts and allowing the convenient use of remote file storage capabilities.

The *ftp* uses the Telnet Protocol on the control connection. This can be achieved in two ways: first, the user or the server may implement the rules of the Telnet Protocol directly in their own procedures, or, second, the user or the server may make use of the existing Telnet module in the system. Ease of implementation, sharing code, and modular programming argue for the second approach. Efficiency and independence argue for the first approach.

ftp, file transfer program, is the user interface to the ARPANET standard File Transfer Protocol (FTP). *ftp* transfers files to and from a remote network site. The client host with which *ftp* is to communicate may be specified on the command line. If this is done, *ftp* immediately attempts to establish a connection to an *ftp* server on that host; otherwise, *ftp* enters its command interpreter and awaits instructions from the user. Options that may be specified are

MVS/TSO	UNIX
TRANSMIT *addressee(s) DATASET (dsname) DDNAME/FILE (ddname) [MEMBER} MESSAGE] [LOG/NOLOG] [NOTIFY/NONOTIFY] [PDS] [SEQUENTIAL] [OUTDDNAME/OUTFILE] [OUTDSNAME/OUTDATASET]*	***ftp*** *[-dgintv] [hostname]*
Addressee(s) specifies the target node, user ID, or node/userid, dist list. **DATASET** specifies the name of the data set to be transmitted. **DDNAME** specifies 1–8 character DD name of a preallocated file to be transmitted. Must specify MEMBER for PDS. The data set must be on DASD. **MESSAGE** specifies to prompt for messages that accompany the transmitted data set. **COPYLIST** specifies the target node, user ID, or node/userid, dist list. **LOG** records the transmission in the LOG data set. **NOTIFY** Notifies sender when the transmitted data set has been received. **PDS** specifies if the data set transmitted is a member of a PDS. **SEQUENTIAL** specifies if the target data set is sequential. **OUTDDNAME/OUTFILE** specifies the target file. **OUTDSNAME** specifies the use of a data set as output data set.	*-d* Enables debugging. *-g* Disables filename "globbing" or file expansion. *-i* Turns off interactive prompting during multiple file transfers. *-n* Does not attempt "autologin" upon initial connection. If autologin is enabled, *ftp* checks the *.netrc* file in the user's home directory for an entry describing an account on the remote machine. If no entry exists, *ftp* will prompt for the login name of the account on the remote machine (the default is the login name on the local machine) and, if necessary, prompts for a password and an account with which to login. *-t* Enables packet tracing (unimplemented). *-v* Shows all responses from the remote server, as well as report on data transfer statistics. This is turned on by default if *ftp* is running interactively with its input coming from the user's terminal. *hostname or remote-system* Specifies the name of the remote system with which *ftp* normally performs upon initial connection. The value of remote system can be host name or the Internet address of a system that is reachable through an Ethernet connection.

Description

The *ftp* specification specifies many parameters which may affect a file transfer. The "file structure" may be one of "file" (no record structure), "record," or "page." *ftp* supports only the default value, which is "file." The "transfer mode" may be one of "stream," "block," or "compressed." *ftp* supports only the default value, which is "stream."

Like MVS/TSO, data are transferred from a storage device in the sending host to a storage device in the receiving host. Often it is necessary to perform certain transformations on the data because data storage representations in the two systems are different. For example, NVT-ASCII has different data storage representations in different systems. DEC TOPS-20s's generally store NVT-ASCII as five 7-bit ASCII characters, left-justified in a 36-bit word. IBM mainframes store NVT-ASCII as 8-bit EBCDIC codes. MULTICS stores NVT-ASCII as four 9-bit characters in a 36-bit word. It is desirable to convert characters into the standard NVT-ASCII representation when transmitting text between dissimilar systems. The sending and receiving sites would have to perform the necessary transformations between the standard representation and their internal representations.

A different problem in representation arises when transmitting binary data (not character codes) between host systems with different word lengths. It is not always clear how the sender should send data, and the receiver store it. For example, when transmitting 32-bit bytes from a 32-bit word-length system to a 36-bit word-length system, it may be desirable (for reasons of efficiency and usefulness) to store the 32-bit bytes right-justified in a 36-bit word in the latter system. In any case, the user should have the option of specifying data representation and transformation functions. It should be noted that *ftp* provides for very limited data-type representations. Transformations desired beyond this limited capability should be performed by the user directly.

Examples

MVS/TRANSMIT	UNIX/FTP
TRANSMIT node1.tsouser1 dataset(oriris.text) Transmit data set 'osiris.text' to userid 'tsouser1' at node 'node1.'	***ftp*** *printit* Connected to *printit.* Name **(printit: jim:) :** Password required for *jim.* Password **:** User *jim* logged in. ***ftp>*** *get james.an* Port command successful. Opening data connection for *james.an.* Transfer complete. Local : *james.an remote* : *james.an nnnnnnn bytes* received in *nnnnn* second. ***ftp>*** *quit.* *Goodbye.*
TRANSMIT node1.tsouser1 dataset(oriris.text) member (nqs, epoch) Transmit members 'nqs and epoch' of a partitioned data set 'osiris.text' to userid 'tsouser1' at node 'node1.'	

Files

/usr/bin/ftp Executable file.

NETWORK FILE ACCESS

The Network File System (**NFS**) permits a UNIX user to access files physically located on disks attached to remote hosts. The access appears to the user as if the devices were attached to the local host. NFS, originally developed by Sun Microsystems, can run on a variety of systems and computer platforms, allowing you to access files on a variety of hardware types.

FILE COPY

UNIX-to-UNIX Copy (uucp)

uucp, which stands for UNIX-to-UNIX copy, is the suite of programs underlying the mail. It is the system of low- to midlevel programs that connect one UNIX machine to another and make such things as networks possible. At the foundation of *uucp* are the low-level programs *uucico* and *uuxqt*, which are never run by the average user. Next are the midlevel programs *uucp*, *uupick*, *uuto*, *uux*, and *uusend*, which are seldom run by the average user. At the top is *mail*, often run by the users. The functions of these programs can be summarized in the table below:

PROGRAM	DESCRIPTION
uucp	Copies files from one system to another system.
uusend	Copies files through a series or routing of UNIX sites to a remote UNIX site.
uuto	Sends files from the local site into the directory of a neighbor UNIX site.
uupick	Interactively retrieves files sent with *uuto*.
uux	Runs UNIX programs on other UNIX machines.
uulog	Views status of *uucp* requests.
uustat	Views and modifies status of queued *uucp* jobs.
uusnap	Views status of current neighbor site connections to the local machine.
uucico	Communicates with neighboring UNIX machines and disposes of queued *uucp* jobs.
uuxqt	Handles received requests for programs to be executed.

The *uucp* is similar to the standard UNIX *cp* program, except that you can refer to a file on a remote system by using *system!* before the filename. For example, to copy the file *notes.txt* to the system *airs*, you would say *uucp notes.txt airs!~/notes.txt*. In this example ~ is used to name the *uucp* public directory on *airs*.

Format

uucp [-cCdfjmr][-g <grade>] [-n <username>] [-x <debug-level>]source-file destination-file

Arguments

-c	Reads the actual source file, rather than a copy. It is a default.
-C	Makes a copy of the source file and transfers the copy.
-d	Makes any intermediate directories at the destination. It is a default.
-f	Prevents making of any intermediate directories that may be necessary to complete copy.

-grade	Specifies a *grade* that is used to prioritize file transfers. The value of *grade* is a string of one or more alphanumeric characters.
-j	Writes the job identification string on the standard output.
-m	Sends mail to the requester when the transfer is complete.
-nlogin-name	Sends mail to *login-name* on the remote system to notify a user that a file has been transferred.
-r	Queues the job, but does not begin the transfer.
-sfile	Writes status information about the transfer into file. This overrides the *-m* option.
-xdebug-level	Writes debugging information on standard output.

uucp copies each *source-file* to the named *destination-file*. A filename may be a path name on your machine, or may have the form

system-name ! *pathname*

where *system-name* is taken from a list of system names that *uucp* knows about. The system-name may also be a list of names such as

system-name ! *system-name* !...! *system-name* ! *pathname*

in which case, an attempt is made to send the file by way of the specified route, to the destination.

If the result is an erroneous pathname for the remote system, the copy will fail. If the *destination-file* is a directory, the last component of the *source-file* name is used. *uucp* preserves execute permissions across the transmission and gives 0666 read and write permissions.

Description

uucp copies files from one system to another.

Examples

The following command transfers the file *myfile*, which resides in the current directory, to the home directory of a user called *dorsey* on a system named *odessy*:

uucp myfile odessy!~dorsey

The following command transfers the files that begin with *R* in the */tmp* directory to the */user/spool/uucppublic* directory on a system named *dolan*. If there are other files queued for *olson*, these files are sent before files of a lower priority. The command also sends mail to the requester when the transfer to *olson* completes and causes mail to be sent to a user called *chris* on *dolan* when the files arrive on *dolan*. The success of this command depends on the ability of the systems named olson and robert to forward files.

uucp -ghigh -m -nchris /tmp/R \olson!robert!dolan!~*

Files

/usr/bin/uucp	Executable file
*/usr/lib/uucp/**	Directory of *uucp* commands and configuration files
/usr/lib/uucp/uucico	Executable file that actually transfers files

Public System-to-System Copy (uuto, uupick)

Format

The public system-to-system file copy has the format

uuto [-mp] source-file ... destination

where

-m Sends mail to the sender when the copy is complete.

-p Copies the source file into the spool directory before transmission.

uupick [-s system] where

-s Searches only the "public UUCP" directory on the local machine for files sent from *system.*

Description

uuto is a simple shell script interface to *uucp*. It will transfer a file, or the contents of a directory, to a remote system and notify a particular user on the remote system when it arrives. The remote user can then retrieve the file(s) with *uupick.*

uuto sends source-files to destination. *uuto* uses the *uucp* facility to send files, while it allows the local system to control the file access. A source-file name is a path name on your machine. Destination has the form

system-name ! *username*

where *system-name* is taken from a list of system names that *uucp* knows about. *Username* is the *username* of someone on the specified system.

The files (or subtrees if directories are specified) are sent to the "public UUCP" directory on the remote machine system-name. Normally, this directory is */usr/spool/uucp-public*. Specifically, the files are sent to *PUBDIR/receive/username/mysystem/file,* where

PUBDIR is the "public UUCP" directory on system-name, *mysystem* is the system from which the files are sent, and file is the file being sent. The destined recipient is notified by mail(1) of the arrival of files.

uupick accepts or rejects the files transmitted to the user. Specifically, *uupick* searches the "public UUCP" directory on the local machine for files destined for the user.

Remote File Copy (rcp)

rcp copies files between two systems. Each filename or directory argument is either a remote filename of the form:

hostname:path

or a local filename (containing no ':' characters, or a '/' before any ':'s).

If a filename is not a full path name, it is interpreted relative to your home directory on hostname. A path on a remote host may be quoted (using \, ", or ') so that the metacharacters are interpreted remotely.

rcp handles third-party copies, where neither source nor target files are on the current machine. Hostnames may also take the form *username@hostname:filename* to use *username* rather than your current local username as the *username* on the remote host. *rcp* also supports Internet domain addressing of the remote host, so that *username@host.domain:filename* specifies the *username* to be used, the *hostname*, and the domain in which that host resides. Filenames that are not full pathnames will be interpreted relative to the home directory of the user named username, on the remote host.

The destination *hostname* may also take the form *hostname.username:filename* to support destination machines that are running older versions of *rcp*. *rcp* command has the following format:

rcp [-p] filename1 filename2
rcp [-pr] filename...directory

Arguments

- *-p* Attempts to give each copy the same modification times, access times, and modes as the original file.
- *-r* Copies each subtree rooted at filename; in this case the destination must be a directory.

Description

rcp copies files between machines. Each *file* or *directory* argument is either a remote filename of the form *rhost:path* or a local filename. *rcp* handles third-party copies, where neither the source nor the target files are on the current machine.

rcp requires that the source host have permission to execute commands on the remote host when doing third-party copies. *rcp* does not detect all cases where the target of a copy might be a file in cases where only a directory should be legal. *rcp* can become confused by output generated by commands in a *.profile*, *.cshrc*, or *.login* file on the remote host. *rcp* requires that the source host have permission to execute commands on the remote host when doing third-party copies.

Examples

rcp recipe sam:cooky — Copies the file *recipe* from the current directory and renames it as *cooky* in the remote login directory on *sam.*

rcp -r sam:mary — Creates a new directory *mary* below the current (local) directory. The local *mary* contains copies of every file and subdirectory contained in the remote *mary* on the machine *sam.*

Files

/usr/bin/rcp — Executable file

Remote File Distribution (rdist)

rdist — distributes remote files.

Format

rdist *[-DFn] [-A num] [-a num] [-d var=value] [-l <local logopts >] [-L <remote logopts >] [-f distfile] [-M maxproc] [-m host] [-o distopts] [-t timeout] [-p <rdistd-path >] [-P <rsh-path >] [name ...]*

rdist *-DFn -c name ...[login@]host[:dest]*

rdist *-Server*

rdist *-V*

rsh *Host [option(s)] command(s)*

Arguments

-A (num) — Sets the minimum number of free files (*i*-nodes) on a file system that must exist for *rdist* to update or install a file.

-a (num) — Sets the minimum amount of free space (in bytes) on a file system that must exist for *rdist* to update or install a file.

-D — Enables copious debugging messages.

-d — *var* = value.

Define *var* to have value. This option is used to define or override variable definitions in the *dist_file.* Value can be the empty string, one name, or a list of names surrounded by parentheses and separated by tabs and/or spaces.

-F — Does not fork any child *rdist* processes. All clients are updated sequentially.

-f (distfile)	Set the name of the distfile to use to be *distfile*. If *distfile* is specified as "-" (dash), then read from standard input (*stdin*).
-l (logopts)	Sets local logging options. See the section Message Logging for details on the syntax for logopts.
-L (logopts)	Sets remote logging options. logopts is the same as for local logging except the values are passed to the remote server (*rdistd*). See the section Message Logging for details on the syntax for logopts.
-M (num)	Sets the maximum number of simultaneously running child *rdist* processes to *num* the default is 4.
-m (machine)	Limits which machines are to be updated. Multiple *-m* arguments can be given to limit updates to a subset of the hosts listed in the distfile.
-n	Prints the commands without executing them. This option is useful for debugging *distfile*.
-o (distopts)	Specifies the *dist* options to enable. *distopts* is a comma-separated list of options for mode.
-p (<rdistd-path>)	Sets the path where the *rdistd* server is searched for on the target host.
-P (<rsh-path>)	Sets the path to the *rsh(1c)* command. The *rsh-path* may be a colon separated list of possible path names. In this case, the first component of the path to exist is used, that is,

/usr/ucb/rsh:/usr/bin/remsh, */usr/bsd/rsh*

-t (timeout)	Sets the time-out period (in seconds) for waiting for responses from the remote *rdist* server. The default is 900 seconds.
-V	Prints version information and exits.

Description

rdist is a program to maintain identical copies of files over multiple hosts. It preserves the *owner*, *group*, *mode*, and *mtime* of files if possible and can update programs that are executing. *rdist* reads commands from *distfile* to direct the updating of files and/or directories. If *dist_file* is -, the standard input is used. If no *-f* option is present, the program looks first for *distfile* and then *Distfile* to use as the input. If no names are specified on the command line, *rdist* will update all the files and directories listed in *distfile*. Otherwise, the argument is taken to be the name of a file to be updated or the label of a command to execute. If label and filenames conflict, it is assumed to be a label. These may be used together to update specific files using specific commands. The *-c* option forces *rdist* to interpret the remaining arguments as a small *distfile*. The equivalent *distfile* is as follows.

(name ...) - > [login @] host install [dest] ;

rdist can use either the *rcmd* function call or the *rsh*, remote shell, command to access each target host. The method used is selected at compile time. If the *rsh* method is used, and the target host is the string local host, and the remote user name is the same as the local user name, *rdist* will run the command

/bin/sh -c rdistd -S

Otherwise, *rdist* run will run the command

rsh host -l remuser rdistd -S

where *host* is the name of the target host, *remuser* is the name of the user to make the connection, and *rdistd* is the *rdist* server command on the target host as shown below.

The *-Server* option is recognized to provide partial backward-compatible support for older versions of *rdist* which used this option to put *rdist* into server mode. If *rdist* is started with the *-Server* command line option, it will attempt to *exec (run)* the old version of *rdist*. This option will work only if *rdist* was compiled with the location of the old *rdist* (usually either */usr/ucb/oldrdist* or */usr/old/rdist*) and that program is available at runtime.

If the *rcmd* method is used, then *rdist* makes the connection to the target host itself and runs the *rdistd* server program as shown below. The default, and preferred method, is to use *rsh* to make the connection to target hosts. This allows *rdist* to be run without being *setuid* to *root.*

On each target host *rdist* will attempt to run the command

rdistd -S

or

rdistd path -S

if the *-p* option was specified. If no *-p* option is included, or the *<rdistd path>* is a simple filename, *rdistd* or *<rdistd path>* must be somewhere in the $PATH of the user running *rdist* on the remote (target) host.

Files

/usr/bin/rdist	Executable file
*/tmp/rdist**	Temporary file for update lists

Running uucico

The *uucico* daemon is the program that actually calls the remote system and transfers files and requests. *uucico* is normally started automatically by *uucp*. Most systems will also start it periodically to make sure that all work requests are handled. *uucico* checks the queue to see what work needs to be done and then calls the appropriate systems. If the call fails, perhaps because the phone line is busy, *uucico* leaves the requests in the queue and goes on to the next system to call. It is also possible to force *uucico* to call a remote system even if there is no work to be done for it, so that it can pick up any work that may be queued up remotely.

Utilities

uustat: The *uustat* program does many things. By default it will simply list all the jobs you have queued with *uucp* or *uux* that have not yet been processed. You can use *uustat* to remove any of your jobs from the queue. You can also use it to show the status of the *uucp* system in various ways, such as showing the connection status of all the remote systems your system knows about. The system administrator can use *uustat* to automatically discard old jobs while sending mail to the user who requested them.

uuname: The *uuname* program by default lists all the remote systems your system knows about. You can also use it to get the name of your local system. It is mostly useful for shell scripts.

uulog: The *uulog* program can be used to display entries in the *uucp* log file. It can select the entries for a particular system or a particular user. You can use it to see what has happened to your queued jobs in the past.

cu: The *cu* program can be used to call up another system and communicate with it as though you were directly connected. It can also do simple file transfers, though it does not provide any error checking.

REMOTE COMMAND EXECUTION (UUX)

The *uux* program is used to request the execution of a program on a remote system. This is how mail and news are transferred over *uucp*. As with *uucp*, programs and files on remote systems may be named by using *system!*. For example, to run the *rnews program on 'airs'* passing it standard input, you would say *uux -airs!rnews*. The '-' means to read standard input and set things up such that when rnews runs on *'airs'* it will receive the same standard input.

uux actually does not do any work immediately. Instead, it queues up requests for later processing. It then starts a daemon process which processes the requests and calls up the appropriate systems. Normally, the system will also start the daemon periodically to check if there is any work to be done. The advantage of this approach is that it all happens automatically. You don't have to sit around waiting for the files to be transferred. The disadvantage is that if anything goes wrong it might be a while before anybody notices.

uux gathers 0 or more files from various systems, executes a command on a specified system, and sends the standard output to a file on a specified system.

For security reasons, most installations limit the list of commands executable on behalf of an incoming request from *uux*, permitting only the receipt of mail *mail(1)*. Remote execution permissions are defined in */etc/uucp/Permissions*.

The command string is made up of one or more arguments that look like a shell command line, except that the command and filenames may be prefixed by *system-name!*. A null system-name is interpreted as the local system.

uux will attempt to get all files to the execution system. For files that are output files, the filename must be escaped using parentheses. For example, the command

uux a!cut -f1 b!/usr/file \(c!/usr/file\)

gets */usr/file* from system b and sends it to system a, performs a cut command on that file, and sends the result of the cut command to system c.

uux will notify you if the requested command on the remote system was disallowed or if the command fails (that is, returns a nonzero exit status). This notification can be turned off by the *-n* option. The response comes by remote mail from the remote machine.

Format

uux [-] [-bcCjnprz] [-a name] [-g grade] [-x debug_level] command-string

Arguments

-b	Returns whatever standard input was provided to the *uux* command if the job fails (that is, returns a nonzero exit status).
-c	Does not copy local file to the spool directory for transfer to the remote machine. This is the default.
-C	Forces the copy of local files to the spool directory for transfer.
-j	Outputs the *jobid* ASCII string on the standard output which is the job identification. This job identification can be used by *uustat* (1C) to obtain the status or terminate a job.
-n	Does not return any indication by *mail(1)* of success or failure of the job.
-p	Same as '-': the standard input to *uux* is made the standard input to the command string.
-r	Does not start *uucico(8C)*; just queues the job.
-z	Returns an indication by mail even if the job succeeds (that is, returns a zero exit status).
-a (name)	Uses name as the user identification replacing the initiator user ID. Notification will be returned to the user.
-g (grade)	A single letter or number, from 0 to 9, A to Z, or a to z; 0 is the highest grade, and z is the lowest grade. Lower grades will transmit the job earlier during a particular conversation. The default grade is A.

-x debug_level Produces debugging output on the standard output. debug_level is a number between 0 and 9; higher numbers give more detailed information. 5, 7, and 9 are good numbers to try; they give increasing amounts of detail.

Examples

uux "!diff osc!/usr/dorsey/file1 hdsa!/a4/dan/file2 > !~/dorsey/file.diff"

will get the *file1* and *file2* files from the *osc* and *hdsa* machines, execute a *diff* command, and put the results in *file.diff* in the local PUBDIR/dorsey directory.

The execution of commands on remote systems takes place in an execution directory known to the *uucp* system. All files required for the execution will be put into this directory unless they already reside on that machine. Therefore, the simple filename (without path or machine reference) must be unique within the *uux* request.

Files

/usr/bin/uux	Executable file
/usr/spool/uucp	Directory of queued *uucp* jobs
/usr/lib/uucp	Directory of *uucp* commands

BATCH COMMUNICATIONS

Putting a program into an unattended state where it continues to execute is referred to as putting it (the process or job) into the background. (Running a program on one machine and displaying its output on another via a windowing system like X is not considered backgrounding the job.) If a job is going to take an extended period of time to execute or if a large amount of output is to be printed, it is more convenient to execute in the background, independent of the terminal.

In MVS/TSO, the SUBMIT command is used to submit batch jobs. TSO/E allows the user to execute a CLIST or a series of commands in the background. However, the output produced by a background job differs from output in the foreground. The IBM Network Queuing System/MVS (NQS/MVS) provides users connected to MVS though TCP/IP a way to submit batch requests to another MVS platform. NQS protocol is also a popular method for submitting batch requests to remote UNIX machines. A workstation user that has TCP/IP and a connection to OpenEdition MVS (OS/390) through 3270 emulation can also utilize this feature.

Adding an **&** (ampersand) at the end of the command line instructs UNIX to run the job in the background in shells other than the Bourne shell.

jobname &

The response you receive will be something like this:

[1] 5432

This particular response means that you have one job running in the background (and its job number is 1), and its process identification number (PID) is 5432. You will need to know the PID if you want to stop the job. This is known as killing a job. To kill the job in the above example, you would type

kill 5432

The job number is used when switching a job that is processing in the foreground to the background, and one that is processing in the background to the foreground. To do the former, first press **Ctrl-z** to suspend the job. Then type

bg % jobNumber

To switch the job to the foreground, simply type

fg % jobNumber

If you have forgotten the job number, type the command *jobs* to see a list of the jobs that are running in the background at the moment.

Note: The rules imposed by system administrators about where and how to run background jobs varies from network to network and changes over time. It is important to stay current with the background job policy of your network.

The *nice* command is used to set the processing priority of a command. The priority of a process determines how much attention the system will devote to completing that job. The higher the priority, the more attention a job gets, which implies that it will take less time to complete than the same job run at a lower priority. There are two versions of nice. In the C shell, the syntax is

nice - priorityNumber command argument

In the Bourne shell, the syntax is

nice + priorityNumber command argument

The available priority numbers for users ranges from 1 to 19, with 19 being the lowest priority. In other words, the higher the nice value, the lower the processing priority. (Note: It is important to check the network policy for the required nice value for background jobs on your system; they are usually required to be niced and your job may be downgraded in priority if it was niced at the wrong value.) Set your command at the required *nice* value or higher. If you do not include a number argument, the value will default to 4 for the C shell and 10 for the Bourne shell.

For example, if you wanted to run a long noninteractive job, and you didn't have to have the results of this job right away, you should run it in the background and set a high *nice* value. Using the C shell, you would type

nice -19 jobname &

SUMMARY

UNIX provides a rich set of integrated facilities and commands for interprocess communication. MVS has a number of such facilities, such as remote job entry, but they are not integrated in the TSO set of facilities.

In addition, a number of vendor-dependent solutions permit communications between MVS and UNIX hosts.

16

Conclusions

Those of you who had prior knowledge of UNIX probably sailed through this text. Those of you who are completely unfamiliar with the UNIX environment were probably awed at the number of complex command constructs that can be generated from simple UNIX commands.

If you have a UNIX system installed, sat at the terminal, and experimented with the commands presented in the book, then you have a fairly good idea of the UNIX command structures. It is also possible that all the commands presented in this text are not available at your installation.

Neither the UNIX commands presented are comprehensive in nature, nor the book is intended to make you an expert in UNIX programming. However, I do hope that this book will serve you as a useful reference whether you are downsizing or rightsizing from MVS environments. In fact, you will find this book extremely useful even if you were using OpenEdition MVS (OS/390) or AIX on the mainframe.

Appendix 1

Command Summaries

There are thousands of commands and their variations in UNIX. Some of the commands are specific only to devices, while others are specific to a particular "shell" being invoked. Relatively, there are fewer commands in MVS, but they can be used in different contexts modified by JCL (job control language) statements.

In this appendix, only a most commonly used subset of those commands are listed with their MVS/TSO/ISPF equivalents.

UNIX Commands with MVS Equivalents

CATEGORY	UNIX FUNCTION	UNIX COMMAND	MVS EQUIVALENT	REFERENCE
Basic Commands				
	The current directory.	.		Ch. 7
	The parent directory.	..		Ch. 7
	Outputs the contents of file, filename to the screen.	***cat*** *filename*	**allocate, list**	Ch. 4, 5, 6
	Shows the number of lines, words, and characters in file.	***wc*** *filename*		Ch. 7
	Changes to the user's home directory.	***cd***	**free, allocate**	Ch. 4
	Changes working directory to *dir_name*.	***cd*** *dir_name*	**free, allocate**	Ch. 4, 6, 7
	Changes the permissions on a file or directory permission(s) filename(s).	***chmod*** *class(es) {+, -, =}*	**allocate, protect**	Ch. 6
	Changes the owner of a file.	***chown***	**allocate, protect**	Ch. 6, 7
	Compares two files.	***cmp***	**compare**	Ch. 7
	Compresses files and directories and reduces the size.	***compress***	**copy**	Ch. 7
	Expands compressed files.	***uncompress***	**copy**	Ch. 7
	Makes a copy of source and names it *dest*.	***cp*** *source dest*	**copy**	Ch. 6

UNIX Commands with MVS Equivalents *(cont.)*

CATEGORY	UNIX FUNCTION	UNIX COMMAND	MVS EQUIVALENT	REFERENCE
	Prints date and time.	***date***	**&SYSDATE, &SYSSDATE, &SYSTIME, &SYSSTIME**	Ch. 4, 11
	Echoes what follows.	***echo***		Ch. 11
	Tells what kind of file *filename* is.	***file*** *filename*	**listds**	Ch. 7
	Tells who is logged on to the local machine.	***finger***		Ch. 4
	Gives some information about user userid.	***finger*** *-m userid*		Ch. 4
	Checks for newly received mail.	***from***	**receive**	Ch. 14
	Is used to view the first few lines of a file.	***head***	**edit**	Ch. 7
	Command sends interactive messages between users. Identifies a user from the list printed by the previous *who* command. When users receive a message, they should respond. The interactive exchange is canceled by using the *Ctrl-d* keys. When this occurs, the message *end of message* appears on the other terminal, and control is returned to the shell.	***hello***	**send**	Ch. 4, 14
		login	**logon**	Ch. 4
		logout	**logoff**	Ch. 4
	Looks for words in the system dictionary.	***look***	**edit**	Ch. 6, 7
	Prints words matching *word* in the system dictionary.	***look*** *word*	**edit**	Ch. 6, 7
	Lists contents of the current directory.	***ls***	**listcat, listds, listalc**	Ch. 4, 5
	Identifies files, directories, and programs in the current directory.	***ls*** *-F*	**listcat, listds**	Ch. 4, 6
	Lists the contents of directory *dir_name.*	***ls*** *dir_name*	**listalc, listcat**	Ch. 5, 6
	Reads mail that was sent to you.	***mail***	**receive**	Ch. 14
	Sends electronic mail to *userid.*	***mail*** *userid*	**transmit**	Ch. 14
	Locates and prints the reference page for a specified item.	***man*** *(manual)*	**help**	Ch. 4

UNIX Commands with MVS Equivalents *(cont.)*

CATEGORY	UNIX FUNCTION	UNIX COMMAND	MVS EQUIVALENT	REFERENCE
	Permits or denies messages invoked using write.	***mesg*** *(message)*		Ch. 4
	Makes directory: makes a subdirectory under the current directory.	***mkdir***	**allocate**	Ch. 6
	Makes a new directory called *dir_name*.	***mkdir*** *dir_name*	**allocate**	Ch. 6
	Is like *cat* with a pause to read screenfuls of text. (Uses RETURN for next line and SPACE for next screenful.)	***more***	**<enter> key**	Ch. 6
	Moves (renames) source to *dest*.	***mv*** *source dest*	**rename**	Ch. 6
	Keeps user informed of current events.	***news***	**listbc**	Ch. 4
	Changes your password.	***passwd***	**logon**	Ch. 4
	Prints the file.	***pr***	**dsprint, dsprint**	Ch. 6, 7
	Processes status: reports on the active processes being run.	***ps***	**status**	Ch. 4
	Prints working directory.	***pwd***	**printds, output**	Ch. 5, 6
	Removes (erases) the file.	***rm***	**delete, free**	Ch. 6
	Removes directory: removes (deletes) a subdirectory under the current directory.	***rmdir***	**free, delete**	Ch. 6
	Removes the directory *dir_name*.	***rmdir*** *dir_name*	**delete, free**	Ch. 6, 7
	Prints out a list of all the current shell environments.	***set***		Ch. 4, 9, 10
	Suspends execution for a specified time interval, expressed in seconds.	***sleep***		Ch. 12
	Is used to view the last few lines of a file.	***tail***	**edit**	Ch. 7
	Archive files.	***tar***	**IEBCOPY/ IEHMOVE**	Ch. 7
	Times how long it takes to execute a given command.	***time***	**time**	Ch. 4, 11
	Shows the number of lines, words, and characters in file.	***wc*** *filename*		Ch. 7
	Displays a list of the users of the system.	***who***		Ch. 4, 5, 8, 11
	Gives your userid.	***whoami***	**&SYSUID**	Ch. 5

UNIX Commands with MVS Equivalents *(cont.)*

CATEGORY	UNIX FUNCTION	UNIX COMMAND	MVS EQUIVALENT	REFERENCE
Control Keys				
	This key is sometimes used as the rubout key instead of the DELETE key. Otherwise, it is mapped as a backspace key, which generates a *Ctrl-h* on the display.	*BACKSPACE*	**BACKSPACE**	Ch. 9
	Terminates with extreme prejudice (stronger than *Ctrl-c*); *Ctrl-* quits a program and saves an image of the program in a file called core for later debugging.	***Ctrl-***		Ch. 9
	Abort command; *Ctrl-c* interrupts a command or process in progress and returns to the command line. This will usually work; if it doesn't, try typing several *Ctrl-c's* in a row. If it still doesn't work, try typing *Ctrl-*, *q* (for quit), exit, *Ctrl-d*, or *Ctrl-z*.	***Ctrl-c***	**PF12**	Ch. 9
	End-of-text character. Can be used to terminate input to a program or to end a session with a shell.	***Ctrl-d***		Ch. 9
	Restarts output.	***Ctrl-q***		Ch. 9
	Pauses output.	***Ctrl-s***		Ch. 9
	Erases characters typed on entire current line.	***Ctrl-u***	**ERASE EOF**	Ch. 9
	Ctrl-w erases the last word on the command line.	***Ctrl-w***		Ch. 9
	Ctrl-z suspends a command or process in progress.	***Ctrl-z***	**PF3**	Ch. 9
	Acts as a rubout or erase key. Pressing DELETE once will backup and erase one character, allowing you to correct and retype mistakes.	***DELETE***	**DEL**	Ch. 9
Setup and Status Commands				
	Define command abbreviations.	***alias***		Ch. 4
	Displays or sets the date.	***date***	**&SYSDATE, &SYSSDATE, &SYSTIME, &SYSSTIME**	Ch. 4

UNIX Commands with MVS Equivalents *(cont.)*

CATEGORY	UNIX FUNCTION	UNIX COMMAND	MVS EQUIVALENT	REFERENCE
	Displays or change current environment.	***env***		Ch. 4
	Displays information about users.	***finger***		Ch. 4
	C shell command to display recent commands.	***history***		Ch. 4, 5
	Ends your session.	***logout***	**logoff**	Ch. 4
	Changes password by prompting for old and new passwords.	***passwd***	**new password**	Ch. 4
	Displays information about processes.	***ps***	**status**	Ch. 5, 6
	C shell command to set shell variables.	***set***		Ch. 4, 9, 10
	Sets terminal options.	***stty***	**PROFILE**	Ch. 4
Some Useful Filter Commands				
	Specifies all files, and using the switch *-n* will display on which line the text string is found.	* *wildcard*	**wildcards**	Ch. 4, 5
	Searches a file for a pattern.	***grep***	**edit**	Ch. 7
	Extracts lines containing **word**.	***grep*** *word*	**edit**	Ch. 7
	Displays only the first 10 lines.	***head***	**edit**	Ch. 7
	Breaks up output into screen-sized pieces for easier reading.	***more***	**<enter> key**	Ch. 4, 5, 6
	Converts data into displayable format.	***od***	**hex**	Ch. 7
	Sets file-creation masks.	***unmask***		Ch. 11
	Edits a stream of data.	***sed***		Ch. 7
	Sorts lines into alphabetical order.	***sort***	**TSOSORT**	Ch. 7, 11
	Archiving utility.	***tar***	**IEBCOPY, IEHMOVE**	Ch. 7
	Displays only the last 10 lines.	***tail***	**edit**	Ch. 7
	Responds with the elapsed time during the command, the time spent in the system, and the time spent in execution of the command.	***time***		Ch. 4
	Shows the number of lines, words, and characters in the input.	***wc***		Ch. 7

UNIX Commands with MVS Equivalents *(cont.)*

CATEGORY	UNIX FUNCTION	UNIX COMMAND	MVS EQUIVALENT	REFERENCE
Printing Commands				
	Checks print queue.	***lpq***		Ch. 6, 11
	Prints a file.	***lpr*** *filename*	**dsprint, printds**	Ch. 6, 11
	Removes a job from the print queue.	***lprm*** *job_number*	**dsprint, printds**	Ch. 6, 11
	Prints utility.	***pr*** *(print)*	**dsprint, printds**	Ch. 6
Input/Output Redirection C Shell Features				
	Places a stopped job in the background.	***bg***		Ch. 15
	Brings a background job into foreground or continues a stopped job.	***fg***		Ch. 15
	Shows jobs that are stopped or running in the background.	***jobs***	**status**	Ch. 4, 15
	Terminates a job.	***kill*** *job_number*	**cancel**	Ch. 15
	Terminates a process.	***kill*** *ps_number*		Ch. 15
	Is used to obtain a hard-copy printout of a file.	***lp*** *(line printer)*	**printds, dsprint**	Ch. 6, 7
	Shows process status.	***ps***	**status**	Ch. 4, 15
Other Nice C Shell Features				
	Repeats previous command.	***!!***		Ch. 5
	Repeats a command from the history list.	*!command_number*		Ch. 5
	Assigns a name of your choice to an existing command.	***alias***		Ch. 4
	Shows a list of recently used commands.	***history***		Ch. 4
Miscellaneous Simple Commands				
	Prints date and time.	***date***	**&SYSDATE**	Ch. 4
	Tells what kind of file filename is.	***file*** *filename*	**listds**	Ch. 7
	Tells who is logged on to the local machine.	***finger***		Ch. 4
	Gives some information about user userid.	***finger*** *-m userid*		Ch. 4

UNIX Commands with MVS Equivalents *(cont.)*

CATEGORY	UNIX FUNCTION	UNIX COMMAND	MVS EQUIVALENT	REFERENCE
	Gives information about programs running on the local machine.	***w***	**edit**	Ch. 9
	Gives your userid.	***whoami***		Ch. 4
Directory Management Commands				
	Changes directory.	***cd***	**free, allocate**	Ch. 4, 5
	Makes a subdirectory.	***mkdir***	**allocate**	Ch. 4, 5
	Prints current working directory.	***pwd***		
	Removes a subdirectory.	***rmdir***	**delete, free**	Ch. 4, 5
	Topmost directory in UNIX.	***root***		Ch. 4, 5
General Terms				
	System binary executables.	***bin***		Ch. 4, 5
	File for UNIX boot code.	***boot***		Ch. 4, 5
	Filenames for system devices, terminals, disks, etc.	***dev***		Ch. 4, 5
	System administration files and tools, system scripts (also TCP/IP information files).	***etc***		Ch. 4, 5
	Library routines.	***lib***		Ch. 4, 5
	Unreferenced files are placed here by *fsck*.	***lost+found***		Ch. 4, 5
	Empty directory used for mounting temporary file systems.	***mnt***		Ch. 4, 5
	Shared libraries.	***shlib***		Ch. 4, 5
	Scratch pad directory for temporary files. users must have read/write access.	***tmp***		Ch. 4, 5
	User files if a u filesystem is requested during installation.	***u***		Ch. 4, 5
	UNIX kernel.	***UNIX***		Ch. 2
	Application and system specific information.	***usr***		Ch. 2
	Prints calendar.	***cal***		Ch. 4
Getting Help				
	Online help facility.	***man***	**help**	Ch. 4

UNIX Commands with MVS Equivalents *(cont.)*

CATEGORY	UNIX FUNCTION	UNIX COMMAND	MVS EQUIVALENT	REFERENCE
Starting the Session				
	Logging on.	***login: omar***	**logon**	Ch. 4
	Reassigns the default special key functions to different keys.	***stty***	**profile**	Ch. 4

Appendix 2

Editing Command Summaries

SUMMARY OF COMMON EDITING AND ex COMMANDS

ex FUNCTION	*ex* COMMAND	*ISPF* TEXT EDITOR	*TSO* TEXT EDITOR
Appends text after the current line.	**a** (append)	**I** (insert)	**IN** (insert)
Changes specified lines or string or deletes current line and insert.	**c** (change)	**just type over existing text**	**C** (change)
Deletes current line.	**d** (delete)	**d** or **dd**	**DEL** (delete)
Deletes specified lines.	**x,yd** (delete)	**d** or **dd**	**DEL** (delete)
Sets edit buffer to contain a specified file and overwrites original contents.	**e** (edit)	**ispf** 2 (ISPF Editor)	**E** (edit)
Applies command to whole file.	**g** (global)		
Inserts text before the current line.	**i** (insert)	**up arrow, I** (insert)	**UP, IN** (insert)
Joins two lines to make one.	**j** (join)		**M** (merge)
Moves lines to a new place (cut and paste).	**m** (move)	**m** or **mm**	**MO** (move)
Includes line numbers.	**n** (number)	**number** or **renum**	**REN** (number)
Displays a specified file.	**f** (filename)	**view** (display data set)	**LISTD** dsname
Displays line 1 to current line.	**1,.**		**TOP + L**
Displays whole line.	**1,$**		**L** (display)
Displays current line to end of file.	**., $**		**L** * nnn (display)
Displays specified lines.	**p** (pointer)	**F** n (find & display)	**L** line1, line2
Displays line *x*.	**x**		**L** line**x**
Displays lines *x* through *y*.	**x,y**		**L** line**x**, line**y**
Leaves editor without saving changes.	**q!** (quit)	**F3** / **CANCEL** (quit)	**END** nosave
Leaves editor and saves changes.	**q** (quit)	**F4** / **END** (saves & quit)	**END** save
Reads a file into the editing buffer.	**r** (read)	**edit** dataset	**EDIT** dsname
Substitutes new character string for old.	**s** (substitute)	**CHANGE** str1 str2	**C** (change string)
Copies lines to a new location.	**t** (transfer)	**c** or **cc**	**CO** (copy lines)
Writes contents of edit buffer to file.	**w** (write)	**F4** or **SAVE**	**S** (save)
Appends buffer contents to alternate existing file.	**W** (write)		**S** dsname (save)

QUICK REFERENCE COMMAND SUMMARY
(*vi*, ISPF, and TSO Text Editors)

Below is a comparison of commonly used command functions. Note that almost all *vi* commands may be preceded by a positive repeat factor (e.g., typing *20w* is just like typing "**w**" 20 times). Arrow keys *move* the cursor *left*, *down*, *up*, and *right*.

CATEGORY	*vi* FUNCTION	*vi* EDITOR	*ISPF* TEXT EDITOR	*TSO* TEXT EDITOR
Cursor Movement	Moves the cursor right, left, up, or down.	arrow keys	arrow keys	arrow keys
	Moves the cursor left, down, up, and right, respectively. Is used when arrow keys are not available.	**h j k l**		**shiftl, DOWN shiftr, UP**
	Moves forward one word.	**w**	**right arrow**	**right arrow**
	Moves forward to next word, skipping punctuation.	**W**	**right arrow**	**right arrow**
	Moves backward one word.	**b**	**left arrow**	**left arrow**
	Moves backward to start of previous word.	**B**	**left arrow**	**left arrow**
	Moves forward to the last character of current word.	**e**	**right arrow**	**right arrow**
	Moves forward to the end of next word, counting punctuation strings.	**E**	**right arrow**	**right arrow**
	Moves to the beginning of current line.	**^**	**left arrow**	**left arrow**
	Moves to the beginning of current line.	**0**	**left arrow**	**left arrow**
	Moves to the end of current line.	**$**	**right arrow**	**right arrow**
	Moves forward one sentence.	**)**	**m, mm**	**DOWN** n
	Moves backward one sentence.	**(**	**m, mm**	**UP** n
	Moves forward to next blank line.	**}**	**F** n (**find**)	**DOWN** n
	Moves backward to a blank line.	**{**	**up arrow**	**UP** n
	Moves to top (home) line on screen.	**H**	**UP** data	**UP** n
	Moves to the middle line on screen.	**M**	**right arrow**	**DOWN** n
	Moves to the bottom line on screen.	**L**	**DOWN** data	**DOWN** n
	Moves cursor to last line in file.	**G**	**F8**	**B** (bottom)
	Moves cursor to first line in file.	**1G**	**F7**	**TOP**
	Moves cursor to nth line in file.	**nG**	**down arrow**	**DOWN** n
	Identifies the line number where the cursor is located.	**Ctrl-g**	**LOCATE** n	**V** (verify) **on**
	Moves forward half a screen page.	**Ctrl-d**	**DOWN** half	**DOWN** n
	Moves backward half a screen page.	**Ctrl-u**	**UP** half	**UP** n
	Moves forward one screen page.	**Ctrl-f**	**DOWN** page	**DOWN** n

CATEGORY	*vi* FUNCTION	*vi* EDITOR	*ISPF* TEXT EDITOR	*TSO* TEXT EDITOR
	Moves backward one screen page.	**Ctrl-b**	**UP** *page*	**UP** n
	Moves forward to next character *x*.	**fx**	**right arrow**	**F** (find) **'x'**
	Moves backward to next character *x*.	**Fx**	**up arrow**	
	Marks current cursor location with *x*.	**mx**		
	Moves to cursor location marked by *x*.	**`x**		**F** (find) **'x'**
	Moves to beginning of line of location marked by *x*.	**'x**		**F** (find) **'x'**
	Moves forward to the pattern.	**./pattern**	**F** *pattern*	**F** (find) *'patn'*
	Moves backward to the pattern:	**?pattern**	**F** *pattern* **PREV**	
	• *n* Repeats search in same direction.		**RFIND**	
	• *N* Repeats search in opposite direction.			
	• % Moves to parenthesis, brace or bracket matching the current cursor location.			
Screen Paging and Scrolling	Next line down (same column).	**j**	**down arrow**	**DOWN**
	Start of next line down.	**+**	**down arrow**	**DOWN**
	Previous line (same column).	**k**	**up arrow**	**UP**
	Start of previous line.	**-**	**up arrow**	**UP**
	Forward one screen.	**^F, Ctrl-f**	**down arrow**	**DOWN**
	Backward one screen.	**^B, Ctrl-b**	**up arrow**	**UP**
	Forward half screen (down).	**^D**	**down arrow**	**DOWN**
	Backward half screen (up).	**^U**	**up arrow**	**UP**
Entering Text	Inserts text before the cursor:	**i**	**I** (insert)	**I** (input)
	• Inserts beginning of the current line.	**I**	**I** (insert)	**Left arrow**
	• Opens a new line below cursor.	**o**	**I** (insert)	**IN** (insert)
	• Opens a new line above cursor.	**O**	**up arrow, I**	**UP + IN**
	• Inserts text after the cursor.	**a**	**type**	**IN** (insert)
	• Inserts text at the end of the line.	**A**	**F11, type**	**Right arrow**
	• Includes an external file.	**:r** *file*	**MOVE** *dsname*	**M** (merge) dsname
	• Writes to an external file.	**:w** *file*	**SAVE** *dsname*	**S** (save) *dsname*
	Terminates input mode.	**<ESC>**		**<RETURN>**
Command operators	Searches forward.	**/**	**F** *xxx*	**F** (find)
	Searches backward.	**?**	**F** *xxx* **PREV**	
	Uses after **/** or **?** to advance to next occurrence of the search pattern.	**n**		

CATEGORY	*vi* FUNCTION	*vi* EDITOR	*ISPF* TEXT EDITOR	*TSO* TEXT EDITOR
Moving Text	Moves text starting at the cursor:			
	• # of words.	**#w**		
	• To the end of the current word.	**e**		
	• To the beginning of the next word.	**w**		
	• From the letter before the cursor backward to the beginning of the word.	**b**		
	• From the cursor to the end of the line.	**$**		
	• From just before the cursor to the beginning of the line.	**0**		
	• From the cursor to the beginning of the next sentence.	**)**		
	• From just before the cursor backward to the beginning of the sentence.	**(**		
	• From the cursor to the end of the paragraph.	**}**		
	• From just before the cursor backward to the beginning of the paragraph.	**{**		
Deleting Text	Deletes text starting at the cursor:	**d**		
	• Deletes a word.	**dw**	**CHANGE**	**C** *'xxx' ''*
	• Deletes to the end of line.	**d$**	**CHANGE**	**carriage** *fwd*
	• Deletes a line.	**dd**	**d**	**DEL** (delete)
	• Deletes three lines.	**3dd**	**d, dd**	**DEL** (delete)
	• Deletes current line and the following *n* - 1 lines.	**ndd**	**d, dd**	
	• Deletes from the current character to the beginning of the current word.	**db**	**CHANGE**	**DEL** (delete)
	• Deletes to the end of the current word.	**de**	**CHANGE**	**DEL** * *count*
	• Deletes back to the beginning of the line.	**d0**	**CHANGE**	
	• Deletes to the bottom of the screen.	**dL**	**d, dd**	**DEL** (delete)
	• Deletes all characters from the current cursor location to the next blank line.	**d}**	**d, dd**	
	• Deletes all characters from the current cursor location to the end of the line.	**D**	**CHANGE**	**Carriage forward**

CATEGORY	*vi* FUNCTION	*vi* EDITOR	*ISPF* TEXT EDITOR	*TSO* TEXT EDITOR
	• Deletes a single character.	**x**	**CHANGE forward**	**Carriage**
	• Deletes character before the cursor.	**X**	**CHANGE**	**Backspace**
	• Deletes character before the cursor.	**Ctrl-h**	**CHANGE**	**Backspace**
Delete and Insert	• Deletes indicated text starting at the cursor and insert.	**c**	**CHANGE, I**	**MO** (move)
	• Same as *dd* and inserts at beginning of line.	**cc**	**DEL, I**	
	• Deletes from cursor to beginning of next word and inserts.	**cw**	**CHANGE PREFIX, I**	
	• Deletes from the cursor to the end of the word.	**ce**	**CHANGE SUFFIX, I**	
	• Deletes from the cursor to the end of line and inserts.	**c$**	**CHANGE, I**	
	• Overwrites to the end of the line.	**C**	**CHANGE**	
Yank and Put Operators	Yanks a copy of text into a temporary buffer. The copy is then pasted using the *put* command.	**y**	**edit COPY**	**EDIT COPY**
	• Yanks current line into temporary buffer; unlike *d*, line is not deleted.	**Y**	**c**	**CO** (copy)
	• Yanks a word.	**yw**		
	• Yanks a line.	**yy**	**c**	**CO** (copy)
	• Yanks to the end of the line.	**y$**		
	• Yanks current line and the following *n* - 1 lines into temporary buffer. Unlike *d*, lines are not deleted.	**nY**	**c** n **cc**	**CO** (copy)
	• Yanks current line and the following *n* - 1 lines into buffer named *x* (any letter can be a valid buffer name).	**n"xY**		
	Puts contents of temporary buffer after current cursor location:	**p**		**MO** (move) *dsname*
	• Puts contents of buffer *x* after current cursor location.	**"xp**		**MO** (move) *dsname*
	• Puts whatever last deleted or yanked, after or below the cursor.	**P**		**CO** (copy)
	• Puts contents of buffer *x* before current cursor location.	**"xP**		**UP, MO** (move) *dsname*
	Joins next line to the end of current line.	**J**		
Changing Text	Replaces a single character.	**r**	**CHANGE** *x y*	**C** *'c' 'n'*
	Replaces until terminated by <ESC>.	**R**		

CATEGORY	*vi* FUNCTION	*vi* EDITOR	*ISPF* TEXT EDITOR	*TSO* TEXT EDITOR
	Substitutes one or more characters for a single character.	**s**	**CHANGE** *x yyy*	**C** (change) *str1 str2*
	Substitutes the current line with a new one.	**S**	**CHANGE**	**C** (change) *str1 str2*
	Switches case of character at current cursor location, ignoring punctuation.	**~**	**CAPS**	
	Replaces character at the current cursor location with new character *x*.	**rx**	**CHANGE** *x y*	**C** (change) *str1 'x'*
	Clears current line and replaces with newtext.	**S*newtext*** **<ESC>**	**d, i**	**C** (change) *str1 str2*
	Clears *n* lines, starting at current line, and replaces with newtext.	**nS*newtext*ESC**	**d**n, **i**	**C** (change) *str1 str2*
	Replaces characters from current cursor location to end of line with newtext.	**C*newtext*** **<ESC>**	**CHANGE** *xxx yyy*	**C** (change) *str1 str2*
	Replaces characters from current cursor location to end of word with newtext. Text is entered in insert mode.	**cw*newtext*ESC**	**CHANGE** *xxx '', **i***	**C** (change)
Undo	Undoes last change. Only one level of undo is provided	**u**	**UNDO**	
	Restores current line to its original state.	**U**	**UNDO**	
	Most recently deleted text. Deleted text is inserted after current cursor location.	**h**	**UNDO**	
	Repeats most recent modification command (including inserts, but excluding plain movement commands).	**. (dot)**		
Pattern Searching	Seaarch for a pattern: • Forwards for a pattern.	**/pattern** <RETURN>	**F** *c'patrn'*	**F** (find)
	• Backward for a pattern.	**?pattern** <RETURN>	**F** *c'patrn'* **PREV**	**TOP, F**
	• Repeats previous search.	**n**	**RFIND**	
	• Repeats previous search in reverse direction.	**N**	**RFIND**	
Searching with Special Characters	Matches any of the characters cccc: • Matches all characters except cccc.	**[cccc]** **[^cccc]**	**F** c *'patrn'*	**F** (find)
	• Matches any characters between c1 and c2.	**[c1-c2]**	**F** *xxx* **range**	

CATEGORY	*vi* FUNCTION	*vi* EDITOR	*ISPF* TEXT EDITOR	*TSO* TEXT EDITOR
	• Matches words beginning with cccc.	**\<cccc**	**F** 'cccc' **ALL**	
	• Matches words ending with cccc.	**cccc\>**		
	• Matches lines beginning with cccc.	**^cccc**	**F** 'cccc' **ALL**	
	• Matches lines ending with cccc.	**cccc$**	**F** 'cccc' **ALL**	
	• Matches any single character.	**.**	**F** 'cccc' **ALL**	
	• Matches the character c zero or more times.	**c***		
	• Matches any characters.	**.***	**F** *x* F *xxx*	
Leaving the Editor	Writes and saves the current file.	**:w**	**SAVE**	**END** *save*
	Quits editor without saving.	**:q**	**CANCEL**	**END** *nosave*
	Writes and quits.	**:wq**	**END**	**END** *save*
	Writes and quits. Same as *:wq*.	**ZZ**	**END**	**END** *save*
	Quits without saving changes.	**:q!**	**CANCEL**	**END** *nosave*
	Quits *vi* without saving and begins an *ex* session.	**Q**		
	Prompts for an *ex* command.	**:**		
	Enters a *shell* command.	**!**		
Edit Examples	Edits file placing the cursor at the beginning of file:	**vi** *file*	**edit** *dsname*	**EDIT** *dsname*
	• Edits file placing the cursor at line *n* of the file.	**vi +n** *file*	**down arrow**	**DOWN** *n*
	• Edits file placing the cursor at the last line of the file.	**vi +$** *file*	**F8**	**B** (bottom)
	• Edits file placing the cursor at the first occurrence of the string matched by pattern.	**vi +/*pattern*** file	**F** *'pattern'*	**F** *'pattern'*
	• Edits file for purposes of reading and not modifying the file.	**vi -R** *file*		
	• Edits file but stores file in encrypted form. Encryption key must be supplied.	**vi -x** *file*		
	• Recover screen-editing session invokes editor on last version of file that might have been saved when the system crashed during editing session.	**vi -r** *file*		
	• Edits all files in the current directory.	**vi ***		

USEFUL vi OPTIONS

COMMAND OPTION	DEFAULT	ACTION
autoindent	*noai*	Automatically indents each line of text.
number	*nonu*	Prefixes lines with line number.
term	*$TERM*	Sets type of terminal to use.
scroll	*scroll=11*	Sets number of lines scrolled with Ctrl-d and Ctrl-z.
shell	*sh=/bin/sh*	Defines the shell used for UNIX commands. This value is taken from the SHELL environment variable.
shiftwidth	*sw=8*	Sets the number of spaces for use with auto-indent.
wrapmargin (wm)	*wm=0*	Specifies number of spaces lines are broken before right edge of the screen.

Appendix 3

File Management Commands

File Management Command Summary

CATEGORY	UNIX FUNCTION	UNIX FILES	MVS FILES	MVS COMMENTS
Manipulation Commands: Files	Outputs the contents of file and filename to the screen.	***cat*** *filename*	**ALLOCATE** **LIST**	Creates data sets. Displays the contents of data sets.
	Displays contents of a file. Pipes the output of the *cat* command to use as input to *more* command. Displays a file one page at a time.	***cat*** *[option(s)] file(s)* ***cat*** *[file(s)]* | ***more***	**LIST** *data-set-name* [member] [/password]	Displays contents of a sequential or a member of a partitioned data set, with \ or without a password, either to a data set or a printer.} Carriage return advances to next page.
	Change directory: is used to change the current directory.	***cd***	**FREE** **ALLOCATE**	Unallocates old data set(s). Allocates new data set(s).
	Changes to the user's home directory.	***cd***	**FREE** **ALLOCATE**	Unallocates old data set(s). Allocates new data set(s).
	Changes working directory to *dir_name*	***cd*** *dir_name*		
	Changes the permissions on a file or directory permission(s) filename(s).	***chmod*** *class(es) {+, -, =}*	**ALLOCATE** **PROTECT** **DSLIST**	Creates and provides access to data sets grants and/or revokes access to data sets. Displays security protection information.
	Changes the owner of a file.	***chown***	**same as ALLOCATE / PROTECT**	Establishes or changes permissions that must be specified to gain or grant access to your data sets.

File Management Command Summary *(cont.)*

CATEGORY	UNIX FUNCTION	UNIX FILES	MVS FILES	MVS COMMENTS
	Copies file(s). Makes a copy of source and names it *dest.*	***cp*** ***cp*** *source dest*	**COPY**	Copies data sets and data set members.
	Changes group ownership of a file.	***chgrp***		RACF can provide similar functions.
	Compares two files.	***cmp***	**COMPARE**	Compares the contents of two data sets and lists any differences.
	Compresses files and directories and reduces the size.	***compress***	**COPY** **COMPRESS**	Copies and condenses partitioned data set to increase the amount of unused area.
	Expands compressed files.	***un compress***	**COPY** **EXPAND**	Copies and expands a sequential data set to a sequential or a member of a partitioned data set.
	Compares two files or directories for any differences.	***diff***	**COMPARE**	Compares the contents of two data sets and lists any differences.
	Summarizes disk usage.	***du***	**LISTDS**	Lists data set characteristics.
	Tells what kind of file *filename* is.	***file*** *filename*	**LISTDS**	Lists data set characteristics.
	Finds files.	***find***	**LISTALC** **LISTDS** **LISTCAT**	Lists the allocated data set(s). Lists members of a partitioned data set(s). Lists the names of data sets in a catalog.
	Searches a file for a specific pattern.	***grep***	**FIND**	Locates one or more occurrences of a search string.
	Displays group memberships.	***groups***		Chapter 7.
	Is used to view the first few lines of a file.	***head***	**TOP** **F** [n]	Shows first line 9s) of file under ISPF Edit control.
	Makes links.	***ln***	**LINK**	Links object modules only.

File Management Command Summary *(cont.)*

CATEGORY	UNIX FUNCTION	UNIX FILES	MVS FILES	MVS COMMENTS
	Lists contents of the current directory.	***ls***	**LISTCAT**	Lists the data sets in a catalog.
			LISTDS	Lists the members in a partitioned data set.
			LISTALC	Lists user and temporary data sets.
			LISTB	Lists broadcasts from system operator.
	Permits or denies messages invoked using *write*.	***mesg*** *(message)*		
	Make directory: makes a subdirectory under the current directory.	***mkdir***		
	Make (creates) a new directory called *dir_name*.	***mkdir dir_name***	**ALLOCATE**	Creates and provides access to data set(s).
	Displays information one page at a time like *cat* with a pause to read screenfuls of text. (Uses RETURN for next line and SPACE for next screenful.)	***more***	**RETURN**	Carriage return advances to next page.
	Renames or moves a directory. Moves (renames) source to *dest*.	***mv*** ***mv*** *source dest*	**RENAME**	Renames data sets and data set members.
	Converts data into displayable format in octal, decimal, hexadecimal, or ASCII.	***od***	**HEX**	Displays the hexadecimal representation of the data.
	Prints the file.	***pr***	**DSPRINT**	Prints data set to a destination printer.
			PRINTDS	Prints contents of data sets and data set members.
	Removes (erases) or deletes files.	***rm***	**DELETE**	Deletes data sets and data set members.
			FREE	Unallocates old data set (s).

File Management Command Summary *(cont.)*

CATEGORY	UNIX FUNCTION	UNIX FILES	MVS FILES	MVS COMMENTS
	Remove directory: removes (deletes) a subdirectory under the current directory.	***rmdir***	**DELETE** **FREE**	Deletes data sets and data set members. Frees an allocated data set with or without DELETE option to delete the data set or its member.
	Sorts or merges files.	***sort***	**TSOSORT**	Sorts a data set from TSO.
	Copies fields to or from a *tar* archive.	***tar***	**IEBCOPY or IEHMOVE utility**	Selectively merges, moves, copies sequential data sets and/or members of partitioned data sets.
	Is used to view the last few lines of a file.	***tail***	**BOTTOM** **L** [n]	Shows last line (s) of file under ISPF Edit control.
	Archives files.	***tar***	**IEHMOVE, IEBCOPY**	Archives to tape or disk.
	Updates access and modification times of a file.	***touch***		Consult RACF documentation from IBM.
	Translates characters in a file.	***tr***		Copies the standard input to standard output with substitution or deletion of selected characters.
	Sets default file protection.	***umask***	**PROTECT**	Creates and provides access to data sets. Grants and/or revokes access to data sets.
	Counts the number of lines, words, and characters in a file.	***wc*** *filename*		
Display Commands: Directories	Lists contents of current directory.	***ls*** *-[options] [arguments]*	**LIST** *data set name* **LISTCAT** [operand] (data set name) **LISTDS** *data set name* [member] **LISTALC** [data set{(member)} [history] [status]	Lists contents of a data set. Lists data set names in the catalog. Lists data set or member characteristics. Displays names of all user allocated and temporary data sets or displays history and status of members.

File Management Command Summary *(cont.)*

CATEGORY	UNIX FUNCTION	UNIX FILES	MVS FILES	MVS COMMENTS
			LISTB [notices/ nonotices] [mail/nomail]	Lists broadcast messages or notices.
	Identifies files, directories, and programs in the current directory.	***ls*** *-F*	**LISTCAT**	Lists data set names in the catalog.
	Lists the contents of directory *dir_name.*	***ls*** *dir_name*	**LISTCAT**	Lists data set names in the catalog.
	Looks for words in the system dictionary.	***look***		
	Prints words matching *word* in the system dictionary.	***look*** *word*		
	Prints files to a line printer. Titles and paginates files.	***lpr***	**DSPRINT**	Prints data set to a destination printer.
	Formats text for a print device.	***pr***	**PRINTDS**	Prints contents of data sets and data set members.
	Outputs name of the current directory.	***pwd***	**LISTCAT**	Lists the data sets in a catalog.
	Displays a listing of disk storage use and limits.	***quota***	QUERY DISK **in VM**	Displays information about spaces allocated and used on all minidisks accessible to a user.
Manipulation Commands: Directories	Changes directory.	***cd***	**FREE** **ALLOCATE**	Unallocates old data set(s). Allocates new data set(s).
	Makes a subdirectory.	***mkdir***	**ALLOCATE**	Creates and provides access to data sets.
	Removes a subdirectory.	***rmdir***	**DELETE** **FREE**	Deletes data sets and data set members. Frees an allocated data set with or without DELETE option to delete the data set or its member.
	Topmost directory in UNIX.	***root***		System catalog.

Appendix 4

Commonly Used UNIX Files and Directories

INTRODUCTION

There are thousands of files and their variations in UNIX. Some of the files are specific only to devices, while others are specific to a particular version of UNIX or "shell" being invoked. Relatively, there are fewer system files in MVS, but they can be used in different contexts modified by JCL (job control language) statements. In this section, only most commonly used subsets of UNIX files are listed.

UNIX FILES

FUNCTION	UNIX FILE
This is the root directory. It is always at the top of the hierarchical file system. The **/root** directory contains files related directly by to the kernel.	/
System libraries.	***/lib***
The **/usr** directory is the primary directory for commands, program files, and user data. Typically, a file system, for example /users, is mounted under the /usr directory. Users can create further levels of directories under it to logically catalog their own groups of files, by project, username, or type of file (e.g., executable, data, source, etc.).	***/usr***
This is a general-purpose directory that contains a number of subdirectories which are for general use: **/usr/bin** Utility programs **/usr/tmp** Temporary files **/usr/dict** Word lists **/usr/games** Games **/usr/include** C include files **/usr/mail** Mailboxes **/usr/lib** Object libraries **/usr/man** Programmers manual	
Originally, all the home directories for users were kept under this directory, but on many present-day systems, these home directories may be kept on a different disk which is normally defined directly under the root directory.	

UNIX FILES (cont.)

FUNCTION	UNIX FILE
Directory with user system libraries/files.	***/usr/lib***
Schedule of programs to be run by ***/etc/cron*** at certain intervals.	***/usr/lib/crontab***
System mail environment.	***/usr/lib/Mail.rc***
uucp utility directories.	***/usr/lib/uucp***
System routines.	***/usr/sys/...***
Maintains history list for the terminal session.	***~user/.history***
Defines remote hosts.	***~user/.rhosts***
User's mail file	***~user/mbox***
Defines environment for the entire terminal session.	***~user/.login***
Contains commands executed at logout time.	***~user/.logout***
Defines environment for the Bourne shell.	***~user/.profile***
C shell environment.	***~user/.cshrc***
This contains the most commonly used utility programs or commands. Other commands are normally located in ***/usr/bin*** and ***/etc***, although any directory can contain commands.	***/bin***
Login program.	***/bin/login***
This is the devices directory and contains information about the special files that are used to interface to hardware devices, such as terminals, printers, disks.	***/dev***
Null device used to discard output or input an EOF (end-of-file).	***/dev/null***
File connected with a terminal connection.	***/dev/tty...***
The ***/etc*** directory contains any files, programs, and tables required for booting and halting the system, as well as the password table, which is used to record data on users. This directory also may include "the message of the day," system start-up procedures, and the file containing terminal characteristics. This directory is under exclusive control of the systems administrator and no user data should be allowed in the */etc* directory. In fact, no files in this directory should have write permission for anyone but the systems administrator.	***/etc***
Program to perform tasks at preset intervals.	***/etc/cron***
Program to determine terminal characteristics.	***/etc/getty***
Name of a group and login members.	***/etc/group***
All hosts connected via a network.	***/etc/hosts***
Program to initiate a terminal session.	***/etc/init***
Identifies each user of the system.	***/etc/passwd***
Site specific information.	***/etc/rc.local***
Terminal initialization information.	***/etc/ttys***
This directory contains temporary files which will be automatically deleted at a later stage.	***/tmp***
This is the file containing the heart of the UNIX operating system, called the kernel.	***/unix***
Defines environment to the **C** shell.	***.cshrc***
Defines editing environment to the *ex* editor.	***.exrc***
Defines a forwarding address for electronic mail.	***.forward***

UNIX FILES (cont.)

FUNCTION	UNIX FILE
Saves history list.	***.history***
Disable *login* messages.	***.hushlogin***
Defines environment at login time, regardless of shell.	***.login***
Defines environment at logout time.	***.logout***
Defines environment for the *mail* program.	***.mailrc***
Defines parameters to *ftp* (file transfer program).	***.netrc***
Defines environment to the Bourne shell.	***.profile***
Defines private remote hosts.	***.rhosts***

Bibliography

ANDERSON, B., B. COSTALES, AND H. HENDERSON. *UNIX Communications*, Howard W. Sams, Indianapolis, Ind., 1987.

ANDERSON, GAIL AND PAUL ANDERSON. *The UNIX C Shell Field Guide*, Prentice Hall, Englewood Cliffs, N.J., 1986.

ANDLEIGH, P. *UNIX System Architecture*, Prentice Hall, Englewood Cliffs, N.J., 1990.

ARICK, MARTIN. *UNIX C Shell: Desk Reference*, QED Technical Publishing, Boston, 1992.

AT&T. *UNIX System V Release 4 BSD/XENIX Compatibility Guide*, Prentice Hall, Englewood Cliffs, N.J., 1990.

BACH, MAURICE J. *The Design of the UNIX Operating System*, Prentice Hall, Englewood Cliffs, N.J., 1986.

BATES, BUD. *Introduction to T1/T3 Networking*, Artech House, Boston, 1992.

BECKER, GEORGE. *Solaris Implementation: A Guide for System Administrators*, Sun Microsystems, Calif., 1991.

BOSLER, KURT. *MVS TSO ISPF: A Guide for Users and Developers*, McGraw-Hill, New York, 1993.

BOURNE, PHILIP E. *Unix for VMS Users*, Digital Press, Burlington, Mass., 1990.

BOURNE, S. R. *The UNIX System*, Addison-Wesley, Reading, Mass., 1983.

BUREAU OF NAVAL PERSONNEL. *Basic Data Processing*, Dover Publications, New York, 1971.

CHRISTIAN, KAARE AND RICHTER SUSAN. *The UNIX Operating System*, John Wiley & Sons, New York, 1994.

CLAUDE, J. P. *Advanced Information Processing Techniques for LAN and MAN Management*, Van Nostrand, North-Holland, New York, 1994.

COFFIN, STEPHEN. *UNIX: The Complete Reference*, McGraw-Hill, New York, 1988.

DATAPRO SERIES. *Datapro Reports on UNIX Systems and Software*, McGraw-Hill, New York, 1991.

DUCHARME, BOB. *The Operating Systems Handbook*, McGraw-Hill, New York, 1994.

DUNPHY, E. *The UNIX Industry*, QED Technical Publishing, Boston, Mass., 1991.

ENCK, J. A *Manager's Guide to Multivendor Networks*, Professional Press Books, Horsham, Pa., 1991.

FENG, LYNDA. *System Files and Devices Reference: UNIX SVR4.2*, Prentice Hall, Englewood Cliffs, N.J., 1992.

FIEDLER, DAVID, AND BRUCE H. HUNTER. *UNIX System Administration*, Hayden Books, Carmel, Ind., 1986.

FOSDICK, HOWARD. *Using IBM's ISPF Dialog Manager Under MVS, VM, and VSE*, Van Nostrand, New York, 1987.

FRISCH, AELEEN. *Essential System Administration*, O'Reilly & Associates, Sebastopol, Calif., 1990.

GARDNER, JAMES. *Learning UNIX*, Howard W. Sams, Indianapolis, Ind., 1991.

GARGIULO, GABRIEL F. *MVS/TSO: Mastering Native Mode and ISPF*, QED Technical Publishing, Boston, 1990.

GLINES, STEVEN C. *Downsizing to UNIX*, New Riders, Carmel, Ind., 1992.

GOSCINSKI, A. *Distributed Operating Systems: The Logical Design*, Addison-Wesley, Reading, Mass., 1991.

GRACE TODINO, JOHN STRANG, AND JERRY PEEK. "Learning the Unix Operating System," O'Reilly and Associates, Inc., Sebastopol, Calif., 1991.

GRAMPP, F. T. AND R. H. MORRIS. "UNIX Operating System Security," *AT&T Bell Laboratories Technical Journal*, 1984.

GRAY, PAMELA A. *Open Systems: A Business Strategy for the 1990s*, McGraw-Hill, London, 1991.

GROFF, W. *Conceptual Understanding of UNIX*, Que, Carmel, Ind., 1989.

HANDEL, RAINER AND MANFRED N. HUBER. *Integrated Broadband Networks: An Introduction to ATM-Based Networks*, Addison-Wesley, New York, 1991.

HEDRICK, CHUCK. *Introduction to Administration of an Internet-based Local Network*, Rutgers University, Brunswick, N.J., 1987.

HELGERT, H. *Integrated Services Digital Networks: Architectures, Protocols, Standards*, Addison - Wesley, Reading, Mass., 1991.

HELMERS, S. *Data Communications: A Beginner's Guide to Concepts and Technology*, Prentice Hall, Englewood Cliffs, N.J., 1989.

HOLLIKER, WILLIAM. *UNIX Shell Commands: Quick Reference*, Que, Carmel, Ind., 1994.

HORNBERGER, REED. *Rightsizing for Corporate Survival: An IS Manager's Guide*, Prentice Hall, Englewood Cliffs, N.J., 1994.

HOULDSWORTH, J., M. TAYLOR, K. CAVES, A. FLATMAN, AND K. CROOK. *Open System LANs*, Butterworth Heinemann, Newton, Mass., 1991.

HUNTER, BRUCE H. AND KAREN BRADFORD HUNTER. *UNIX Systems: Advanced Administration and Management Handbook*, Macmillan, New York, 1991.

INTERNATIONAL BUSINESS MACHINES CORP. *Vocabulary for Data Processing, Telecommunications, and Office Systems*, IBM, 1981, Poughkeepsie, N.Y.

INTERNATIONAL BUSINESS MACHINES CORP. *MVS to AIX Application Migration Cookbook*, IBM, 1994. GG24-4375, Poughkeepsie, N.Y.

INTERNATIONAL BUSINESS MACHINES CORP. *Introducing OpenEdition MVS*, IBM, 1993. GC23-3010, Poughkeepsie, N.Y.

INTERNATIONAL BUSINESS MACHINES CORP. *AIX/ESA Command Reference*, IBM, 1992. SC23-3075, Poughkeepsie, N.Y.

INTERNATIONAL BUSINESS MACHINES CORP. *OS/VS2 TSO Command Language Reference VS2 Release 3.7*, IBM, 1994. GC28-0646, Poughkeepsie, N.Y.

INTERNATIONAL BUSINESS MACHINES CORP. *Interactive System Productivity Facility (ISPF) Getting Started*, IBM, 1994. SC34-4440, Poughkeepsie, N.Y.

INTERNATIONAL BUSINESS MACHINES CORP. *Interactive System Productivity Facility (ISPF) Edit and Edit Macros*, IBM, 1994. SC34-4446, Poughkeepsie, N.Y.

INTERNATIONAL BUSINESS MACHINES CORP. *TSO Extensions (TSO/E): IDTF User's Guide*, IBM, 1983. GC28-1104, Poughkeepsie, N.Y.

INTERNATIONAL BUSINESS MACHINES CORP. *TSO Extensions Version 2, Command Reference*, IBM, 1993. GC28-1881, Poughkeepsie, N.Y.

INTERNATIONAL BUSINESS MACHINES CORP. *TSO Extensions User's Guide*, IBM, 1987. SC28-1333, Poughkeepsie, N.Y.

INTERNATIONAL BUSINESS MACHINES CORP. *MVS/ESA OpenEdition MVS Command Reference*, IBM, 1994. SC23-3014, Poughkeepsie, N.Y.

INTERNATIONAL BUSINESS MACHINES CORP. *MVS/ESA Operations: System Commands*, IBM, 1993. GC28-1826, Poughkeepsie, N.Y.

INTERNATIONAL BUSINESS MACHINES CORP. *IBM Publishing Systems SGML Translator: Programming Guide and Reference*, IBM, 1992. SC34-5072, Poughkeepsie, N.Y.

INTERNATIONAL BUSINESS MACHINES CORP. *IBM Publishing Systems SGML Translator: General Information*, IBM, 1992. GC34-5071, Poughkeepsie, N.Y.

INTERNATIONAL BUSINESS MACHINES CORP. *Document Composition Facility, SCRIPT/VS Text Programmer's Guide*, IBM, 1992. SH35-0069, Poughkeepsie, N.Y.

INTERNATIONAL BUSINESS MACHINES CORP. *Document Content Architecture: Revisable Form—Text Reference*, IBM, 1986. SC23-0758, Poughkeepsie, N.Y.

INTERNATIONAL BUSINESS MACHINES CORP. *AIX/370 LAN Performance*, IBM, 1990. GG66-3180, Poughkeepsie, N.Y.

INTERNATIONAL BUSINESS MACHINES CORP. *AIX Distributed Environments*, IBM, 1990. GG24-3489, Poughkeepsie, N.Y.

INTERNATIONAL BUSINESS MACHINES CORP. *Rightsizing the Database Environment: DB2 for MVS to DB2/6000*, IBM, 1994. GG24-4431, Poughkeepsie, N.Y.

INTERNATIONAL BUSINESS MACHINES CORP. *AIX CICS/6000 and RDBMSs Integration: Experiences with the XA Interface*, IBM, 1994. GG24-4214, Poughkeepsie, N.Y.

INSTITUTE OF ELECTRICAL AND ELECTRONIC ENGINEERS. *IEEE Standard: Portable Operating System Interface for Computer Environments (POSIX)*, IEEE, New York, 1988.

KERNIGHAN, BRIAN W. AND ROB PIKE. *The UNIX Programming Environment*, Prentice Hall, Englewood Cliffs, N.J., 1984.

KERNIGHAN, BRIAN W., AND DENNIS M. RITCHIE. *The C Programming Language*, Prentice Hall, Englewood Cliffs, N.J., 1988.

LEFFLER, S. J. MCKUSICK, M. K. KARELS, M. J. AND QUARTERMAN, J. S. *The Design and Implementation of the 4.3 BSD UNIX Operating System*, Addison-Wesley, Reading, Mass., 1989.

LETWIN, GORDON. *Inside OS/2*, Microsoft Press, Redmond, Mass., 1988.

LEVINE, DONALD. *POSIX Programmer's Guide*, O'Reilly & Associates, Sebastopol, Calif., 1991.

LEVINE, JOHN R. AND MARGARET LEVINE YOUNG. *UNIX for Dummies*, IDG Books, San Mateo, Calif., 1993.

LIBES, DON AND SANDY RESSLER. *Life with UNIX*, Prentice Hall, Englewood Cliffs, N.J, 1989.

LOWE, DOUG. *MVS/TSO Concepts, Commands, JCL, and CLISTS*, IBM, 1984, Poughkeepsie, N.Y.

MASSOUDI, ROBERT A. *Rightsizing for Corporate Survival: An IS Manager's Guide*, Prentice Hall, Englewood Cliffs, N.J., 1994.

MERUSI, DONALD E. *OSF/1 Operating System*, OSF, Boston, 1994.

MERUSI, DONALD E. *UNIX System Administration Handbook*, Prentice Hall, Englewood Cliffs, N.J., 1994.

MERUSI, DONALD E. *LAN Primer*, M&T Books, New York, 1992.

MERUSI, DONALD E. *Open Systems*, Prentice Hall, Englewood Cliffs, N.J., 1992.

MERUSI, DONALD E. *Software Implementation Techniques*, Digital Press, Burlington, Mass., 1992.

MERUSI, DONALD E. *Guide to OSF/1: A Technical Synopsis*, O'Reilly & Associates, Sebastopol, Calif., 1991.

MERUSI, DONALD E. *MVS/TSO: Mastering CLISTs*, QED Technical Publishing, Boston, 1990.

MERUSI, DONALD E. *OSF Distributed Computing Environment (DCE)*, OSF, Boston, 1989.

QUARTERMAN, JOHN S. AND SUSANNE WILHELM. *UNIX, POSIX, and Open Systems: The Open Standards Puzzle*, Addison-Wesley, New York, 1993.

RANADE, J. AND GEORGE C. SACKETT. *Introduction to SNA Networking*, McGraw-Hill, New York, 1989.

ROCHKIND, MARC J. *Advanced UNIX Programming*, Prentice Hall, Englewood Cliffs, N.J., 1985.

ROSE, M. *The Open Book: A Practical Perspective on OSI*, Prentice Hall, Englewood Cliffs, N.J., 1990.

SALUS, PETER H. *A Quarter Century of UNIX*, Addison-Wesley, Reading, Mass., 1994.

SANTA CRUZ OPERATION (SCO). *SCO Open Server: System Administrator's Guide*, Prentice Hall, Englewood Cliffs, N.J., 1994.

SILVESTER, PETER P. *The UNIX System Guidebook*, Springer-Verlag, New York, 1988.

SIMON, ALAN R. *Implementing the Enterprise*, Bantam Books, New York, 1993.

SOUTHERTON, ALAN. *Modern UNIX*, 1993.

SPENCER, DONALD D. *Introduction to Information Processing*, Charles E. Merrill, Columbus, Ohio, 1977.

STALLINGS, W. *Handbook of Computer Communications*, Volume 3, *Standards*, Macmillan, New York, 1988.

STANLEY, TIMOTHY, S. *Windows 3: Quick Reference*, Que, Carmel, Ind., 1990.

STEVENS, W. RICHARD. *UNIX Network Programming*, Prentice Hall, Englewood Cliffs, N.J., 1990.

STEWART, MARTY C. *INTERACTIVE UNIX Operating System: A Guide for System Administrators.*

TANENBAUM, A. *Modern Operating Systems*, Prentice Hall, Englewood Cliffs, N.J., 1992.

TANENBAUM, ANDREW S. *Computer Networks*, Prentice Hall, Englewood Cliffs, N.J., 1988.

TOPHAM, DOUGLAS W. *Portable UNIX*, Springer-Verlag, New York, 1992.

TOPHAM, DOUGLAS W. *A System V Guide to UNIX and XENIX*, Springer-Verlag, New York, 1992.

TROMBETTA, MICHAEL, SUE CAROLYN FINKELSTEIN, AND MICHAEL TROMBETTA. *MVS JCL & Utilities: A Comprehensive Treatment*, Prentice Hall, Englewood Cliffs, N.J., 1989.

WELCH, FRANK. *Integrated Computer Network Systems*, Marcel Dekker, New York, 1992.

WHEELER, TOM. *Open Systems Handbook*, Bantam Books, New York, 1992.

WILSON, J. *Berkeley UNIX: A Simple and Comprehensive Guide*, John Wiley & Sons, New York, 1991.

WOODCOCK, JOANNE, HALVORSON, MICHAEL, AND ROBERT ACKERMAN. *Running UNIX: An Introduction to SCO UNIX System V/386 and XENIX Operating Systems*, Microsoft Press, Redmond, Wash., 1990.

ZLOTNICK, FRED. *The POSIX Standard: A Programmer's Guide*, Benjamin/Cummings, Menlo Park, Calif., 1992.

Index